Thanks for all your
contributions to La Leche League,
Pam. My very best wishes to
you and your family.
LLLove,
Mary Ann Kerwin

Learning a
Loving Way of
Life

To Pam
with best wishes,
Marean Tompson

With love,
Ki Lennon

Learning a Loving Way of Life

Compiled and edited by
Virginia Sutton Halonen
and Nancy Mohrbacher

La Leche League International
Franklin Park, Illinois

July 1987

© 1987 La Leche League International, Inc.

All Rights Reserved

Printed in the USA

Cover photos: top, © Richard Ebbitt; others, Darrell
   Rideout

Photo credits: Page 3, Darrell Rideout; pages 52, 93, 101,
   268, 313, © Richard Ebbitt; page 63, The Petitclerc
   family from l'art de l'allaitement maternel, 1983; page
   82, The Ghiringhelli family; page 161, Lynda and
   Bonny Taylor; page 196, Kathleen and Timothy Covi;
   page 231, Marilyn and Leanne Froehlich; page 309,
   Jim Prisching, Pulitzer-Lerner Community
   Newspapers; page 311, Hammill Studios.

Executive Editor and Design: Judy Torgus

ISBN: 0-912500-35-2

Library of Congress Card No: 87-081824

La Leche League International
P O Box 1209
Franklin Park IL USA 60131-8209

Dedication

*For my mother, Patricia Scott Black, who didn't
breastfeed her babies, but nurtured us in the value of
people before things.*   *N.M.*

*For my daughters, Constance and Rebecca, without
whom I would never have known the joys of
breastfeeding and the happiness of family life.*   *V.S.H.*

Contents

Part Two   Being a Father
Tenderness and Love

"Loving Memories"

Part Three   The Family Grows
Sharing the Miracle of Life

"Moments"

Part Seven

Working Together
The Family and the Medical Community

Foreword

If you've been part of La Leche League for any length of time, LEARNING A LOVING WAY OF LIFE will be like a trip down memory lane. Certainly, it unleashed a flood of memories for me, coming upon familiar names and favorite stories from the past and recalling the circumstances through which they first touched my life.

Yet make no mistake, this isn't just a book of recollections. In fact it might even more accurately be described as an Owner's Manual for the parents of today. For the dialogues, the humor, the challenges, and even the heartaches described herein are timeless. They speak to us with the wisdom of parents who started with a common decision to breastfeed their babies and found that through the experience of breastfeeding their perspective and priorities were forever changed.

This is the kind of book we need in our schools when young people study society and family life. These short autobiographical pieces, honestly expressed, explain better than any study guide ever could what it feels like to be a parent.

Nancy Mohrbacher and Virginia Halonen have done a masterful job in sifting through 26 years and 156 issues of LLL NEWS to bring us a book that we all can use. It provides inspiration and advice, leavened with humor for those in the midst of raising their children. It illustrates in practical detail how commitment and fidelity are expressed in family life for those whose parenting days lie ahead. And for those whose childbearing days are past, it gives us hope for the future. For accepting that the family is the seedbed of society, these accounts give us tangible hope for a better world.

Marian Tompson
LLL Founder
1987

Preface

About LA LECHE LEAGUE NEWS

LA LECHE LEAGUE NEWS—like La Leche League itself—had humble beginnings. La Leche League was founded late in 1956, but it was more than eighteen months before the first issue of LLL NEWS appeared. The May-June issue of 1958 was all of five mimeographed pages and ran under the original title, LA LECHE LEAGUE NEWSLETTER.

Packed full of various bits of information, the very first bimonthly issue was compiled and edited by one of the League's founders, Marian Tompson. That first year, in true cottage industry style, the editing, assembling, and preparation for mailing took place on her dining room table. Sent originally to 100 names on a mailing list, a yearly subscription cost one dollar.

That first issue explained the hows and whys of the founding of La Leche League, named the founders, and contained a book review, a poem, and a listing of when and where various League meetings were held. A column on nutritious "know-hows" featured helpful hints on preparing beef heart.

A "New and Nursing" column introduced readers to new babies, while relating details about prepared childbirth, home births, and breastfeeding joys and challenges. Bits of correspondence appeared, too, reflecting the concerns of mothers who were in contact with the League.

Also mentioned in the first issue was the plan for a course-by-mail on breastfeeding that eventually evolved into La Leche League's manual, THE WOMANLY ART OF BREASTFEEDING.

By the early sixties, LLL NEWS was printed instead of mimeographed, averaged twelve pages in length, and had almost 5,000 subscribers. To meet the needs of League Groups, which had blossomed all over the country and the world, an insert sheet was added to LLL NEWS to provide local information about meetings and new babies. These inserts later expanded their focus to include personal stories from parents in each local area.

During these early years the views expressed by La Leche League and LLL NEWS often differed from the conventional thinking of the time. The average mother of the fifties and sixties chose to bottle feed her babies and was typically drugged and unconscious during their births. For the few who felt strongly that breastfeeding and prepared childbirth were a better way, La Leche League—through its Group meetings and LLL NEWS—provided hard-to-find information and the support of like-minded families.

LLL NEWS offered first-hand stories from women who experienced awake and aware childbirth, from families who worked to change hospital policy to allow fathers in the delivery room, and—as always—LLL NEWS featured the latest information on breastfeeding.

Many breastfeeding mothers felt strong social pressures against nursing in public. So when readers complained in the sixties that nursing fashions were hard to find, LLL NEWS obliged by printing sewing tips. This made it easier to dress stylishly and still nurse discreetly while out and about.

Articles on weaning, starting solids, and other topics that originally appeared in LLL NEWS were developed into Information Sheets printed and distributed by La Leche League International and handed out at local Group meetings. From the pages of LLL NEWS, readers became aware of new LLL publications, including THE WOMANLY ART OF BREASTFEEDING, a cookbook, new Information Sheets as they appeared, and a variety of books.

Regular features developed a following among readers. "Memos from Marian," a column written by LLL's president, Marian Tompson, first appeared in LLL NEWS in 1960 and continued on the back cover until 1980. In her warm and personal style, Marian's columns touched on a variety of subjects including her own family, the state of La Leche League, and breastfeeding around the world.

Other columns written by LLL founders became popular, including Betty Wagner's "Notes from Grandma"—a collection of remembrances and commonsense suggestions—and Mary White's reports on breastfeeding research and health trends in "Information, Please."

In the seventies, the layouts became more sophisticated and more pages were added to LLL NEWS, allowing for more first-person stories covering a wider range of issues relating to childrearing, discipline, and family life.

Statistics were offered, too. A small box featured in each issue listed the number of League Leaders, League Groups, and the number of countries in which La Leche League was represented.

As LLL NEWS grew and changed, certain issues became devoted to special themes. The January-February issue featured the best stories from the Area LLL NEWS inserts, and fathers received special attention in the May-June "fathers' issue." Every two or three years, readers learned about La Leche League's International Conference in the "Conference issue," which included reports on the Conference, excerpts from the sessions, and comments from families who attended.

Subscriptions to LLL NEWS reached their peak at nearly 60,000 in 1980. During its twenty-six year history, LA LECHE LEAGUE NEWS consistently reflected the ideas and concerns of its readership by printing their personal stories. Within these pages a mother could tell *her* story—of birth, of the challenges of raising a family, of breastfeeding—to an interested audience. And she, in turn, could benefit from the insights of other families. All of the stories, poems, and quotes in this book appeared originally in the pages of LLL NEWS.

With the November-December issue of 1984, the twenty-six years of LA LECHE LEAGUE NEWS concluded. Reflecting the changes of nearly thirty years of LLL, a new publication was born, NEW BEGINNINGS. The graphics are different, the regular columns changed, but the first-person stories are still there. NEW BEGINNINGS is carrying on the tradition that was LLL NEWS.

Acknowledgement

We would like to acknowledge the dedication and hard work of the editors of LA LECHE LEAGUE NEWS.

Marian Tompson	1958
Mary Ann Cahill	1959-1962
Florence Carlson	1962-1963
Rose Mary Fahey	1964-1967
Nell Ryan	1967-1970
Melanie Tompson	1970
Mary Carson	1970-1978
Judy Torgus	1979-1984

In addition to the various editors, staff members in LLLI's Publications Department worked hard to get each issue of LLL NEWS out to subscribers. For many years all typesetting and layouts were done by LLLI staff members.

In preparing this manuscript, a special word of thanks goes to Elayne Shpak for her many hours at the word processor—days evenings, and weekends—as stories were typed, deleted, rearranged, edited, and re-edited before the final version met with everyone's approval. We could not have done it without her dedication and ability.

Introduction

"What La Leche League has to offer mothers is a new way of life, a way of living and giving whereby we all end up as winners along with our babies."

Mary White, LLL Founder, 1981

The stories compiled in this book share a common outlook on raising children, which may be surprising since they were written by many different individuals and published over a twenty-six year period from 1958 to 1984. The world of the fifties was undoubtedly a different place to be a parent (particularly for the nursing mother) than the world of the eighties. But the mothers and fathers who sent their stories to LA LECHE LEAGUE NEWS shared a common point of view that was as apparent in the first issue as it was in the last.

LLL's message has always been: "A baby's wants are the same as his needs. Respond to your individual baby without fear of spoiling. Lovingly and consistently give him appropriate limits as he grows. Take advantage of breastfeeding's natural benefits to bring you and your baby closer and build a foundation of lifetime trust and security." Although this approach contrasted with the rigid routines and schedules often recommended during the fifties, as time has passed more and more experts have recognized the value of giving unconditionally to a baby and respecting each child's uniqueness.

In this book, parents describe how this philosophy enriched their families' lives. Emphasizing the practical, day-to-day aspects of childrearing, they give their insights: some as first-time parents of a tiny baby, others adjusting to the newly discovered abilities of a toddler or older child, and finally as parents of grown children. Some of the parents whose stories are used in this book were ahead of their time, writing of feelings and expectations that were not being expressed by others at that point; they were also the ones who led the way for some of the experiences parents today take for granted. These mothers and fathers tell of their difficult moments, their rewards and successes, their times of fun and laughter, and of deepest sorrow. They share their experiences for the benefit of others also traveling the sometimes rocky path of learning to be a family and finding a loving way to live their lives.

Part One

Becoming a Mother

Learning about Love

Twenty Minutes

Karen Burdette
Virginia
1979

The man was here to clean the carpet
And he said good carpet maintenance
Means dusting and vacuuming once a day
Which isn't bad because all it takes is
Twenty minutes.

My mother-in-law says if I could just
Write a quick note
At least every week it would only take
Twenty minutes.

The article I read on physical fitness
Says there's no excuse for not
Keeping in shape
Because all it takes each day is
Twenty minutes

My husband said if I could only make
Those two calls today
It would only take
Twenty minutes.

And I make such good bread
I really should start making it again
Because all it takes to mix and knead it is
Twenty minutes.

And there's no excuse for having dirty
Dishes in the sink
Or dirty clothes in the hamper
Because all it would take to do them is
Twenty minutes.

And I probably could clean all the finger
Smudges in the
Whole house in about
Twenty minutes.

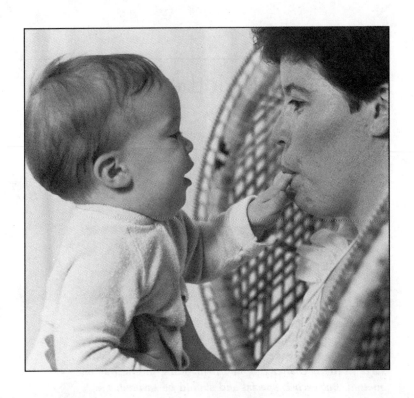

I really should read the newspaper every
Day and be an
Informed citizen because all it would take
Is about
Twenty minutes.

But I just got the baby to sleep
And I put on a Sesame Street record;
I went out to get the mail,
Stuffed the bills in a drawer,
Stashed the magazines on the end table,
Answered the phone and said no this is
Not Allstate Insurance
And just then
My twenty minutes
Were up.

1

Moments of Mothering

"It's true that we often look for that bluebird of happiness in the future. We are so busy thinking how much better the future is going to be that we miss the present. We don't take time to enjoy what we have. Each stage in life is challenging and demanding in one way or another. But each is special and should be savored, because when it is gone it will never return."

Betty Wagner, LLL Founder, 1981

Rainstorms

Jane Peddler
New Jersey
1978

Quietly, in the very early morning when the city is still asleep and all is dark, my four-month-old baby burrows against me. Drowsily I nurse him, both arms enclosing him in a protective grip of love. Then the rain that's been threatening all through the night begins. The water pours down from the sky in a sudden flood, furious and intense; the drops pouring on the metal awnings intensify the sound to an almost frightening degree.

My baby releases my breast and listens. It's the first time he's ever actually listened to the sounds of a storm. His brow wrinkles in concentration, he cocks his head. Will he cry? Certainly the storm sounds scary enough. But no—his eyes lock into mine, and in the dim light I see his tiny face bloom into a dimpled smile. Then he sighs and goes back to his drinking. Right now, my nursing baby can know no fear, as long as mother's arms enclose him. A precious time—a short time in the span of childraising, but one to be appreciated to the fullest. It's that perfect trust—perfect love that transcends all fear.

Gifts of Motherhood

Cheryl Wines
California
1971

I look down at my baby son at my breast and the beauty of motherhood is easy to see. The joy of motherhood is in sharing gifts: The gifts of life, of good and perfect nourishment, of warmth and closeness, of the world, and of love.

When you give the gift of life, there is ecstasy in the sound of that first lusty cry. As you nurse your baby, you can feel his appreciation in what he does. His small, soft hands hold your breast, treasuring every feeding. His sparkling eyes smile up at you, and finally he lets go just long enough for that satisfied smile. He shows you the need for your closeness and warmth by his cry; it ceases when you hold him. As he grows, and you show him the beauty of the world, he learns. For all your acts of love he returns them two-fold, saying, in his way, "Thank you for sharing so completely and unselfishly the gifts you have given me."

Three Essentials of Life

Pan Usticke
New York
1979

I've read that the three essentials of life are something to do, something to love, and something to hope for. How beautifully mothering fulfills these requirements.

Something to do. Mothers are always busy—nursing, rocking, singing, reading, playing, chaperoning, listening, not to mention changing, wiping, bathing, washing, buttoning, unzipping—the list can go on and on.

Something to love. It starts the moment we know there's a life growing inside us and never ends throughout our lives. We love our children whether they are babies, toddlers, preschoolers, school children, pre-adolescents, teens, young adults, parents, middle-agers, or grandparents. It's loving that lasts forever.

Something to hope for . . . ah, yes. What hopes we have when we first find we're pregnant. What hopes as our children start school, go out into the world, marry, become parents themselves. The present is always a time of hope for mothers, and we welcome the future with hope.

Mothering truly fulfills the three essentials of life.

What I Want

Victoria Peterson Cavalier
Virginia
1984

The other day I was feeling sorry for myself because I lacked the time to do many of the things I enjoy. Before the birth of my two children, I worked full-time as an artist and have always had many interests including crafts, sports, photography, and free-lance writing. But since Sierra was born last year, it's difficult to keep up with diaper changing, nursing, reading books, not to mention making dinner, washing closthes, and trying to keep some sort of order in the house. While three-year-old Ian was asking me to help him do the activities in his *Sesame Street Magazine,* Sierra was standing with her arms outstretched holding a book of her own, with the loud squeal I know means, "Read to me!" I looked from Ian to Sierra, to the pile of dirty dishes, and wondered "What about me?" How nice it would be to sit uninterrupted at a potter's wheel, go for a run, or even take a long bath. When do I get a chance to do something for me?

As I was pondering my situation, a realization occurred. I was doing something for myself, something I had always wanted to do . . . mothering.

I have chosen to stay home with my children during their early years, to answer the endless questions, kiss the bumps, and teach what I can. I enjoy the satisfaction and joy of meeting their needs

and seeing all their discoveries and accomplishments first-hand.
Now is such a precious time; Sierra is learning to walk, and Ian
is opening up to all he sees. This time will never come again. I
love to have Ian sit on my lap while I read to him. I love the sweet
soft noise Sierra makes when I climb into bed and she nuzzles
for my nipple. What could possibly smell better than the intox-
icating perfume of a baby's soft hair? Children are small for only
a few years.

My artwork is reserved for an occasional portrait of my babies,
my photographs are of them, and the rest can wait. I've found
I can exercise at night after they go to bed, and do the dishes then,
too. My husband helps when he can, and is wonderful with them;
he, too, realizes they are small for such a short time. I will go back
to my career when Sierra is in school. Until then, I'm going to
enjoy the life I chose. I'm doing exactly what I want.

2

I Wish I'd Known That Before

"Mothering instinct isn't something with which women are born or even something that happens when we give birth. Mothering instinct is something which grows when mothers and babies are together."

> *Sharon Duff*
> *Oregon*
> *1982*

My Obstacle Course

> *Toby Speed*
> *New York*
> *1984*

I went to my first La Leche League meeting three years ago rather reluctantly. What could there possibly be to say about breastfeeding for two full hours? As I explained to my local Leader when I called, all I wanted were some quick "how-to" tips on nursing the baby I was due to deliver several days hence. I already knew everything about cribs, feeding schedules, discipline, and the like. But she convinced me there was more to breastfeeding than I thought, and I was persuaded to go. The seeds were planted that night that led to a total re-evaluation of my lifestyle and self-image and a maturing of my basic feelings about family, society, and personal fulfillment—but those seeds took three years to fully germinate.

My daughter Vanessa was born after an arduous, medicated labor, and we were both drowsy and "untuned" to each other for the entire five-day hospital stay. She was lazy about nursing and slept through every feeding session, and every time I sent her back to the nursery I was in tears because I was so frustrated. To make things worse, the pediatrician seemed to be scolding me for what he called her "extreme" weight loss, and he warned that I might have to give up breastfeeding altogether because she was slightly jaundiced. In addition, I was tormented by feelings of remoteness from my daughter, inadequacy about my body, and anger about my birth experience.

When I got home, under the advice of the pediatrician I began supplementing Vanessa's feedings with formula. The result of this, as so many mothers have found, was even greater confusion and less confidence on my part and an almost constant worrying about how much milk the baby was actually getting. For two weeks, Vanessa remained a lazy nurser. During that time I developed extremely sore nipples and can remember sitting up in the nursery with the lights on for hours each night while she nursed on and off. I gritted my teeth as the minutes clicked by on the digital clock—to the tune of my husband snoring in our comfortable bed across the hall.

During those first two months, I had my ideas challenged about:

- **Cribs.** It was not fun putting Vanessa in her crib, enduring her furious screams, taking her out, putting her in again, only to start the cycle over. I also tired of constantly running from wherever I was in the house to check on her in her crib.

- **Feeding schedules.** The four-hour schedule didn't work; the three-hour schedule didn't work; the two-hour schedule didn't work.

- **Weaning.** She didn't want to wean at nine months, twelve months, or fifteen months.

- **Solid foods.** She spit out everything that entered her mouth, except my milk, until the age of seven months.

All these issues and many more I struggled with as though I were negotiating an obstacle course instead of caring for a unique child who had not read the same books I had. But eventually—as I learned to be more flexible and to trust myself—I resolved them all. Attendance through at least four series of LLL meetings was a major contributing factor in my growth as a mother. Happily

I can add that Vanessa and I survived all our nursing problems, and she recently weaned herself at twenty-seven months.

And today? Well, they say mothering is easier the second time around, and it is—once you eliminate all the old, preconceived ideas. Our little Kate was born not quite three weeks ago following a quick and easy labor during which I was totally relaxed, unmedicated, and very happy, and the two of us were nursing well from the first minute of her life. We went home within two days, and she hasn't even touched the crib yet. Kate goes where I go, either in my arms, on my lap, in her carrier against my chest, or napping in her roll-around-the-house bassinet. People tell me how serene she is, and they're right. She never has long to wait with her mother always nearby to attend to her needs.

"If I Knew Then What I Know Now"

Beth Leanza
New York
1977

We have just recently welcomed our third daughter, Rachel Marie, into the family. She is a placid easygoing baby, and she is no trouble. I've been thinking that part of the reason she isn't any "trouble" is my changed attitudes. They are quite different from what they were six years ago when our first baby was born.

Though I would never let a baby "cry it out," I had always felt that something must be wrong if she had to be held all the time. After all, I thought, a baby should be asleep in her crib. Nowadays, if Rachel can't get to sleep immediately after she nurses, I just hold her. Most of the time she falls asleep on my shoulder. I no longer have a hang-up about where a baby should be.

When my second baby fell asleep nursing, I remember taking great pains to keep her awake so she would nurse longer. After all, I thought, a baby should get a bigger feeding and not have to be fed too often. Now with Rachel, I no longer have a predetermined idea about the length of a baby's nursing. I find life much less frustrating with this attitude. If Rachel falls asleep after a short nursing I might put her down in her cradle. If she awakens shortly after, that's okay too—I just nurse her again. It helps not to think of nursing as "feeding." Nursing is also caring for and comforting.

With Rachel I am finding it a lot easier to accept help from visitors when they offer to cook, wash dishes, and do laundry, while

I enjoy just being available for Rachel (and my older children, too). I know that Rachel will get bigger and more independent and all too soon I'll be able to handle my housework.

Had I but known then what I know now about this easy way of mothering when my six-year-old Cherie and my four-year-old Karen were infants, life would have been much simpler and less frustrating.

Notes from Grandma

Betty Wagner, LLL Founder, 1978

No matter how much experience we've had taking care of baby brothers or sisters, sitting with other people's babies, watching others parent, taking classes on child care, or whatever, no matter how prepared we think we are, it still comes as a shock to most of us when we are presented with the total care of our own first baby.

To be totally responsible for the care and feeding of one so small is frightening. To know we will be held responsible for anything that happens to this new baby is awe-inspiring. All this newness, these feelings and responsibilities, take time to comprehend and accept. No wonder some mothers (and fathers, too, I bet) experience those postpartum blues.

The new mother can comfort herself with the thought that a mother is born at the same moment as a baby. She may be new at being a mother, but the baby doesn't realize that he is her first. He just knows that he has a mother who feeds him when he is hungry, keeps him warm and dry, looks into his eyes, talks to him, rocks him, and loves him. What more could any baby want?

A mother is the most important person in the world to her baby. Babies very quickly identify their mothers. When a mere nine days old, an infant prefers a human face to a head-shaped outline. By four weeks of age, he knows his mother's face and will respond to her. He soon recognizes her smell as well.

With time, mother finds that she is equal to the new demands that life has placed upon her and feels quite comfortable in this new role. As a matter of fact, it soon seems that the baby has been part of her family forever, and it's hard to remember how life was before he was born. What's more, she discovers that she is really enjoying this lovable, darling, interesting baby. And why shouldn't she?—it's the brightest, most gorgeous baby in the world. . . .

"Can I Help?"

Betty Doyle
Oklahoma
1982

When I had three little ones, all still in diapers, my mom used to come through the door rolling up her sleeves. She'd say, "I have an hour. What needs to be done?" You wouldn't believe what that lady could do in an hour, and she will never know just how often she lifted my spirits. But I was not always able to accept her help without feeling less of a person for not being able to do everything myself. I'd find myself apologizing because I always seemed to be behind. She would assure me that she didn't know how I could possibly get as much done as I did. I think her attitude of loving concern and her own need to help made accepting help from her as easy as receiving a reassuring hug. As I learned to accept and be thankful for the time she gave me, I realized just how valuable those few minutes were in helping me put things into their proper perspective. Her support made my role as mother and wife so much easier.

So many mothers today are having such good birth experiences. With no drugs and no episiotomy, they are home in just a couple of hours. Such beautiful beginnings leave Mom feeling fine and baby nursing well. In fact everything seems to be going so well that all help disappears the first week. Grandma goes home, and Daddy goes back to work. Sometimes I think the new mother is even eager to prove to a probably skeptical grandma that having a baby is a cinch. Maybe inside we all want to be super moms. So it fits the picture that we will be back in the kitchen, doing the laundry, and driving in the car pool in short order. What can happen, though, is that while we are scurrying to prove just how strong we are, we might just lose that precious, "newborn baby time" with our little one. It is a special time to feel protected by being cared for by others.

Not everyone's lucky enough to have a mother who lives close enough to drop in to help now and then. But almost all of us have had that genuine offer, "Is there anything I can do to help?" How many of us ever take advantage of such offers? And how many of us could use some help long after the "new baby" stage? We need to get past the "super mom" image enough to admit that we really could use some help and then feel okay about accepting help from someone who cares. Accepting this bit of support could go a long way in enriching our mothering experience.

The Need for Loving Ways

Ghazala Hussain
Texas
1984

I became a mother when I was finishing my residency in psychiatry. I thought I had it all together about myself and my relationships with my husband and my mother. I thought I knew a lot about child development, love, and affection.

However, the opposite was true. As I tried to respond to the needs of my baby, I realized that I had never truly loved anybody. I had no idea how much caring and sacrifice would be required of me as a mother. I also realized that I did not love myself too well, because I had a hard time accepting my child's resemblance to me.

I was hearing La Leche League suggest that I accept my child's need to be held and rocked and nursed frequently. I was hearing many other people imply that if my child was fed and dry that any other fussing or crying was needless and manipulative. Some even implied that she was "bad."

My instincts told me to follow what I had heard through La Leche League. One day it occurred to me that the warnings I heard about "spoiling" her with frequent holding and nursing were very similar to the warnings from my psychiatry professors. They had emphatically instructed me not to meet my patients' emotional needs for professional reasons.

The prevalent environment in psychiatry discourages touching or hugging a patient. Further, the psychiatrist never explicitly tells the patient about his own feelings of affection for the latter. He also does not answer any questions when the patient asks for guidance and advice, other than by reflecting them back to the patient. It is also uncommon for psychiatrists to share personal information about themselves, including their own life experiences.

I had come to believe and practice all the above methods of psychotherapy. Now that I held my child to my breast, it occurred to me that I believed them because that was what I had been taught, not because they made any sense! They certainly were not very effective in reaching the hearts of people.

I resolved to start sharing my own affection for my patients in words and in actions when appropriate. I found that many times I could break through impenetrable barriers by holding a hand or giving a hug.

Of course, I had to decide when to do what with whom, because what is reassuring to one person can be a threat to another. I also started sharing with them my own life experiences and what I had found to be helpful. This helped them to relax because they now knew that they were not alone in having problems. Many patients said to me, "This is the first time I feel comfortable in therapy. I don't feel that someone is looking down on me."

It took a lot of courage for me to continue to practice my "new methods" because most other psychiatrists were practicing so differently. But my belief in the importance of showing affection was so profound that I continued. Soon patients, their families, and some doctors in the area began reinforcing me with their strong appreciation and support.

I have been practicing these methods for two years. I have presented my methods and my approach to some audiences and have been very well received.

The biggest fear people have of my affectionate methods is: "What if the patient or somebody else sees this sexually?" I would have thought the same until I understood infantile sexuality as my own baby (later toddler) nursed at my breast. I realized that sexual attractions followed affectional relationships and that the really important need was the emotional need to be loved and to feel special. I share this perspective with my patients.

The other common fear is: "What if your patient gets too dependent on you?" I am sure that sounds familiar to La Leche League mothers, because the same objection is raised about nursing the toddler and about the family bed. I find it amazing how the acceptance of emotional needs helps to build internal security and eventually decreases dependency on others, whereas the child or patient who has had to "tough it out" is forever needy of outside support because he did not receive enough love to feel lovable.

Psychoanalytically oriented psychiatry and behavioral psychology both fail to appreciate and validate the important human need for love. Good luck to them! For me, there is no turning back to the aloofness and "neutrality" of traditional psychiatry.

Growth in Mothering

Pamela Duffy
Colorado
1978

When our first child was born I was the recipient of a deluge of well-meant advice that seemed to have no end. It began the day of departure from the hospital with my new baby. On that morning, my doctor wrote a "prescription" and told me to follow it to the letter if I wanted to become a well-adjusted and happy mother. His orders read as follows:

"Patient and husband get away (from baby) for a few hours by going out together, and repeat as often as necessary." He explained that time away is important in order to preserve one's identity and one's marriage and would help me to be a better mother. How understanding he is, I thought, and what a great idea! Much later I came to realize that for most mothers and babies during the first months this can be confusing and often detrimental advice.

My first few weeks at home were anything but joyful. I was nursing but didn't have much knowledge about breastfeeding; therefore I made the classic mistakes. When it seemed that the difficulties were over, friends and family kept telling me to "get out a little." "Mothers are people, too," they said. I fretted about the little time I now had "to myself." I mourned for my "carefree" days. (Were they really?) I began taking painting classes and involved myself in more outside activities, leaving my tiny one with Daddy, Grandma, or a babysitter. (It never occurred to me to take him with me!) My time out became increasingly more important to me because I was afraid of "losing my identity" and letting people think that now I was "only a mother."

In the process of all this advice I never learned how to really enjoy my baby. I had no doubts as to my love for him; I just didn't know how to live with him and to give and receive the enjoyment of day-to-day life with him. In my preoccupation with my own needs and my desire to preserve my own talents, I lost sight of the most important thing at this time—my baby's needs. I now believe that fulfilling these needs is the best way of helping baby develop to his own full and loving potential. I learned that parenting is sometimes inconvenient (like a baby crying at 3 AM), but most times joyous if approached with the right attitude.

With my second and third children, things were much different. My attitudes and outlook had matured. Each baby "roomedin" with me in the hospital and at home. My considerate husband (after a period of adjustment!) enjoyed our babies in bed with us at night, realizing their need to be close to us, as well as our need to be close to them.

When we wanted to go out, we took the baby along until each reached the point when he was happy to be left with a babysitter. Admittedly it was not always as exciting as going out alone, but it was nice to know that no one was left unhappily at home.

The enormous lesson I've learned is the importance of staying close to my baby. There is always time for me to grow in my own endeavors without letting them conflict with baby's needs. (Baby's naptimes are productive in this way for me.) I'm thankful to my children for teaching me the true meaning of "growth."

The Gift of Memory

Carole DeGroat
New Jersey
1983

Today I had a glimpse into the future—to the day when my older daughter Kira (five years old) will be a mother. I felt joy and pride at what I saw.

This morning one-year-old Abbe got another bump while attempting walking. Before I could reach her, Kira gathered Abbe (all twenty-five pounds of her) onto her lap and sat on the floor stroking Abbe's face. As she rocked, she whispered, "It's all right, Abbe. I remember what it was like when I was little. Don't cry, honey." Abbe looked up at Kira and stopped crying. She was probably surprised at such gentleness from her usually exuberant sister.

The thought struck me that if I could give my girls one legacy, it would be the gift of memory—of what it means to be small and helpless. Isn't that the essence of mothering? When I think back to the most empathetic mothers I have known, the key to mothering seems to be that their actions were guided by the knowledge of what it meant to be a baby. Somewhere in our subconscious, we all "remember." If we concentrate on putting ourselves in the baby's place, babies would never be left so Mom could have a "break" or put into a crib to cry it out. We would understand the anguish the baby feels at being separated from Mom. If we carry this one step further as we mother our toddlers or older children, we would never cut off a child in mid-sentence or refuse to drop everything because a child had a new accomplishment to show us right then. Our memories of how we felt as children would be too fresh.

Kira gave me something to think about today. As I continue to mother, I will try harder than ever to stop and "remember."

Natural Mothering

Trudy Darter
California
1984

Our culture doesn't really prepare women for motherhood: we are an adult-centered society. Most women having their first baby don't really understand how demanding motherhood can be. Many women expect to continue living their lives just as they did before they became mothers; that's why problems and frustrations often arise.

While I was pregnant with my daughter Amy, my cat Molly gave birth to seven kittens. She was truly an inspiration to me. Watching her in labor was a lesson all by itself. She was so relaxed and breathed perfectly without going to any classes! Twelve hours after her labor began, she gave birth to her seventh kitten while nursing the other six. After George—the runt of the litter—was cleaned up, she quickly made sure that he was nursing, too. Then she contentedly fell asleep.

In the first weeks, Molly's mothering was very intense and demanding. She was either nursing or cleaning her kittens. The only time she left was to eat or "dig in the sand box," and yet she didn't seem to mind. Since it was winter, Molly's box was in our bedroom. At night I had a hard time falling asleep because of the noise. It wasn't from the kittens, she quickly silenced them; it was Molly. She was purring very loudly because she was contented and relaxed.

In the early days, all the kittens would cuddle up next to their mama to sleep, and they would all be touching. As her kittens grew, Molly's mothering became more carefree. She would play with them and teach them. When they were ready, they began to eat solid food, but no one could force them to eat before they were ready!

We kept George, the runt, and he continued to nurse until he was seven months old. He gradually weaned himself. Molly would roam with George, teaching him things as they went, and finally, George began to come and go by himself.

During this time, I watched Molly's role as a mother change as she went from an intense period of almost twenty-four-hours-a-day caretaking to a gradual lessening of physical care, when she had time for more playfulness but continued emotional responsibility. Eventually, Molly's routine returned to what it had been before she became a mother.

We have four cats now, and Molly is somehow related to all of them. Even to this day—several years later—when the food is put out, Molly is the first to sniff the food to make sure it's all right. She steps back and let's her "children" eat all they want, then she finishes what is left. If danger is around, Molly is first out to defend everyone, even though George is a huge tom cat who outweighs her by four pounds. Molly will always be a loving mother. If she finds George quietly resting, she will give him a thorough wash job. Although her babies are all grown, Molly continues to feel emotional responsibility for her children.

Most new mothers are destined to go through this same period of intense, twenty-four-hours-a-day mothering that Molly went through. Like Molly, it is common among many human cultures for mother and baby to sleep together touching and to awaken during the night to nurse. And of course, we try to teach our children the ways of life they will need to know. As they grow and change, so does our family lifestyle. Gradually, the intensity of their demands lessens. As the years pass and our children make their own lives for themselves, we again will be free to do as we please, though we will always love and be concerned about our children.

It is an awesome responsibility to be the mother of an infant—definitely a full-time job. If we can understand this natural sequence of events while we are pregnant and when our children are infants, it will be easier to relax and enjoy motherhood. Since we know what to expect, we can keep in mind that "this too shall pass," and perhaps the common problems and frustrations will be easier to handle.

3

A Worthwhile Career

*"In order to continue to speak out for babies, we must
speak out loud and clear for mothering as an important
and worthwhile career. . . . I think we must show all
mothers how important full-time mothering is to their
babies, to themselves, and to their whole families...the
needs of their babies are not only for mother's milk, or
mother's breast, but for all of her."*

    Mary White, LLL Founder, 1981

Liberated as a Mother

    Carolyn Keiler Paul
    New York
    1977

Within weeks after the birth of our first child, Jacob, I began to
hear the question: "What are you doing with yourself?" and
"When do you plan to go back to work?" As if I didn't already
have a full-time job!

Perhaps in New York, where the large majority of women work,
the pressure is greater than elsewhere, but I imagine that even
in more family-oriented communities, mothers run away from
their babies each day to do something "meaningful." Nearly all

the women with small children I know are itching to get back to work or back to school or just OUT.

So what's wrong with me? I have a college degree, and I enjoyed working before Jacob was born. I liked taking full advantage of the cultural offerings of this great city. (At the ballet in my ninth month, I could have sworn unborn Jacob kicked every time Rudolf Nureyev did!) But now I am content—and sometimes ecstatically happy—to spend every waking moment (and many sleeping ones, too) with my children. (Our second child, Hannah, was born last December.) My husband, David, and I talk of calling a babysitter and going to a concert or a movie, but then we decide it would be best to wait until Hannah is older. We take our children wherever we go—including all of David's conferences scattered around the country. I love having them with me and miss them during brief separations, which are becoming more common now that Jacob, two and a half, is getting very independent.

Feminists may be right when they strive for "equal pay for equal work" and for better job opportunities for women. But as women gain self-esteem, they should take pride in the things only women can do instead of demeaning them. If a woman leaves a small child to return to work only because she thinks this is what a liberated woman should do, is she really liberated?

I think it's time we stop apologizing for being "just a mother." Childrearing is not a menial job. It calls for all of our talents and resources. My college education isn't going to waste, because it has enriched me so that I may in turn enrich the lives of my children. Besides, eventually my children will no longer need me full time, and I may want to find a new job.

Some of my relatives are more pleased with my efforts to learn to draw than they are with my efforts to raise my children. But my feeling is: what could be more creative than molding a human being? That I don't receive a salary gives my job something else in common with great artists! Like an artist, I am paid with the gratification of my work and its product.

David has helped me to feel proud of the job of raising our children, and our children reflect the joy I take in them. A woman's "place" may be in the home, or it may not, but let's not choose the latter just to make a point.

At Last

Terri Barile
New Jersey
1978

Signed up for a six-week tennis course
and only took three lessons.
Decided to paint a picture
and the canvas is still bare.
Wanted to read the latest best seller
and the book lies untouched.
Knew I should be more economical
and forgot the sale was yesterday.
Brought home a baby daughter
and put her to my breast.
Committed, at last.

And Then Came Aleksander

Merike Tamm
South Carolina
1982

Recently I came across an article about Charlotte Curtis, an associate editor of *The New York Times* and one of the subjects of Jane Adams' book, *Women on Top*. The reporter wrote that Curtis "has never yearned for, nor missed, children."

As I lay in bed at 5:45 this morning, with my four-month-old son sucking contentedly at my breast, those words kept going through my head. If I had not had Aleksander, I too would have felt that my life was full and complete—that acquiring a PhD, teaching, writing, discussing politics, traveling, having friends and a loving husband provided sufficient joy and excitement for any woman's life.

I am a feminist. I am proud that women are making their mark in the worlds of politics, journalism, business, science, and art. But I have often felt angry in recent months because feminists' concern for expanding women's opportunities and power outside the home has often led them to denigrate the joys and satisfaction of motherhood.

Although biological differences have been used by men to justify oppression of women, one should admit that biology *does* make a difference in our destiny. If we listen to our bodies, we can hear the instinctive, physical message. I have been in love twice in my life. Both times I knew because I wanted to bear that man's child. But I kept that feeling secret for a long time. When I finally told it to a feminist friend, she was disgusted.

Just a year ago I thought that mothers and fathers were equally qualified to take care of infants. I bristled with anger and disappointment when a scientist friend told me she would stay home for a few years after her baby was born. Why shouldn't her husband give up his job, I thought. Why does the woman always have to make more sacrifices when a couple decide they want children?

Only in a society in which men dominate obstetrics and pediatrics, in which women are commonly drugged for childbirth, and in which bottle feeding is accepted as equal or even superior to breastfeeding, could such a wild idea gain currency as men's equal capacity to nurture infants. Childcare has been primarily a feminist issue, but it should not be surprising that many men are willing to accept the claim that they have equal capacities in this area. Perhaps women need to make greater gains in business and politics before they can exult in their biological as well as intellectual capacities. Any woman who is awake and aware during the birth of her child and who feeds the child from the substance of her own body cannot believe that her feelings for the child are the same as the father's.

No thrill in the world compares with holding your own newborn baby in your arms and no pleasure is sweeter than feeling your breasts swell up with milk and then having them emptied by a tiny, eager, toothless mouth that occasionally pauses to smile at you. (Other than intercourse, breastfeeding is the only way that two human beings can be physically joined together; both experiences satisfy sensually, spiritually, and emotionally.) No feminist literature prepared me for the fun of dancing with a baby and discovering my ability to compose songs about him and me.

Every cell of my son's body has been made from my own. Although his father contributed half the genes, my body alone has been responsible for the growth of the fertilized egg and for four months of nourishment after birth. He will soon outgrow the small bed in our room where he sleeps. When he moves to his own room down the hall, he will literally and figuratively take a piece of me with him.

I am a new explorer in the old world of motherhood. As a thirty-three-year-old woman who had never even held a young baby be-

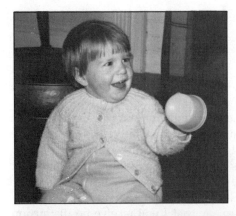

This photo of Aleksander Tamm at 13 months was used in LLL News in 1982; photo below shows Aleksander at age six with his sister Abigail in 1985.

fore her own and who had grown up on the literature of women's liberation, I had braced myself for the tedium of baby care. Every day of pleasure has been a pure surprise.

Perhaps mothering will look different to me in another year or another ten years. But today when a woman says to me she doesn't yearn for nor miss children, I must say she doesn't know what she's missing. She is like a person born blind in a society where blindness is considered an acceptable option that keeps life from being unnecessarily complicated. Thus she doesn't yearn for nor miss the sight of paintings and scenic landscapes.

I don't think any blind person should be forced to acquire sight. I don't think those who can see are superior to those who are blind. I'm just glad that I've been fortunate enough to see Lake Louise and Monet's haystacks and my own son, Aleksander.

A Working Mother

Christie Kegel
Illinois
1978

I am a working mother. I need a special kind of support because my work is special.

Sometimes my husband asks me why I don't have more time for him. My relatives and friends say I should let someone else take over for me so that I could get out more. I try to explain to them that my work takes a lot of time to be done well and that I am best qualified to do it.

Sometimes my sisters ask me why I am devoted to work they consider demeaning. They say that I will receive no distinction and that I am capable of much more. I try to explain to them that I am proud to do the work I am doing. I explain that my character, intellect, and creativity are measured daily by my work. And that I am challenged by problems that have real consequences and tangible rewards.

Many people say that I am unskilled. They say that anyone can do what I do and that I am not earning a living. I try to explain that they are mistaken.

When my family needs more money, even strangers ask me why I "sit at home" rather than find work that would enable me to contribute substantially to the family income. I try to explain that the contribution I am making is substantial. And that my baby and I belong together, full-time, no matter what our situation.

I am often resented and dismissed. I am often stereotyped and devalued. I work within my home caring for my child full-time. I am a working mother. I need a special kind of support because my work is special.

The Value of a Mother's Time

Kathleen Hoicka
Ontario
1978

Ninety-nine percent of the time I feel that my daughter, Sarah, is benefiting from the time she spends with me.

Occasionally, I wonder exactly what I'm providing during our days of shopping, visiting, and household chores that no one else

Brenda McGurk, age three, shows how she has learned loving ways to care for her "baby."

can provide. This question usually pops into my head after time spent with a day-care advocate, or after someone reminds me that I have marketable skills that I'm not marketing. By the time another mother demonstrates her child's skills at pattycake or hand-clapping, I'm devastated.

Recently, Sarah displayed a skill which astonished me. She mothered her doll! My ten-and-a-half month old child quietly sat with her Raggedy Andy doll and made very gentle sounds—"ooh, ah, oh." She turned the doll this way and that and put her mouth to its face. The next day she repeated this.

Well, I tried to teach her to clap her hands, but she prefers clapping mine together. Pattycake just gets a few laughs. But Sarah is learning how to love.

An Endangered Species?

Suzanne Carter
Louisiana
1980

A lot is being written these days about the problems women encounter in the business world. Once a woman decides to seek employment outside the home she can consult a barrage of information on what to expect and how to handle the problems which are likely to arise. Ideally, the end result is a woman who can successfully "juggle" home and office.

I think it is time more was said about the woman who, resisting the nudge of spiraling inflation, the shrinking dollar, and opposing attitudes, chooses to remain a stay-at-home mother.

Why is it that one of the world's most important careers is so underrated? Can it be that when a woman chooses to become a wife and mother she sidestepss her responsibility to make the world a better place to live? Does her decision reflect a desire to remain on the sidelines and watch the parade go by? I do not think so. What better vantage point than to take on the task of helping shape the personalities of the future leaders. Who is in a better position to allot precious time and energy to molding and shaping tomorrow's adults than the stay-at-home mothers who consider their jobs careers?

Those of us who have survived the moutning pressure and still opt to put our talents to work in the home do not consider our job boring. Conversely, it takes a great deal of dedication. We have found what we do best and do it for a living. I ask: if the present day trends persist, who will raise the children? Are stay-at-home mothers an endangered species?

To Work or Not to Work?

Jean Smith
New York
1978

To work or not to work? For me, that had never been a debate. After our baby was born, and I had rested sufficiently, of course I would return to work. I had taught for thirteen years and was employed during the pregnancy. I had permission to take the semester off that our baby was due. I would stay home that semester, then return the following semester. No baby was going to change my lifestyle. He would just have to fit in. I had planned to nurse—my mother had; I would quit at six months—my mother had. Besides, that was long enough to be tied down.

So I told myself, my husband, and my colleagues. Surprisingly, no one argued with me or tried to change my mind. (Later, my husband told me that his heart had stopped when I told him my plans; he was not pleased, but didn't want to argue with a pregnant and determined wife!) I was happy for the lack of argument because I didn't want the hassle of restating my career objectives after the baby arrived.

I quit teaching in December; baby was due in February. Therefore, I had two months to sit around, growing bigger and clumsier, justifying to myself the need to return to work so that my brain wouldn't die after being dormant from December until the following September. After all, how could diapers, spit-ups, and screeches be a challenge? Challenges were found in the hallowed halls of higher education. How I looked forward to September.

Then, on February 19, at 12:07 AM, after a twenty-hour labor, my husband and I delivered Jason Gerard at Oswego Hospital. At midnight, in the back of my mind swirled those ideas of getting this birthing over with and taking up my old routine. At 12:10 AM, as I was holding Jason Gerard in my arms and John and I were crying and blubbering about the incredible miracle of creation, I knew **at that very moment** that my destiny had changed paths. Although it took me until April to say what I knew then, truly I knew that I would be a full-time mother.

Instead of that being the end of my story, it was really the beginning, because since I had been a career woman for so many years my new lifestyle, philosophy, and attitudes confused my friends who were full-time career women with children. Added to this turnabout was my devotion to LLL meetings. I loved them! So did Jason! There I found other mothers who had chosen to stay at home—gladly, not begrudgingly. There I found other mothers who, at various times in their lives, came to know that an infant, a toddler, and "even" a newborn, is a fascinating and very social creature, who will respond from day one if someone (hopefully his mother) is there to initiate the relationship.

Jason is now twenty-seven months old, and we recently have concluded our nursing experience. What is the statement I'm beginning to hear? "So now you'll be returning to work soon." Since weaning, the pressure continues to mount subtly but persistently.

"No, I won't be returning to work!" But such an answer hasn't been enough to satisfy **me**. I don't need to rationalize nor to explain my actions. Yet inside myself I wanted to find the puzzle piece that would link everything into perspective for me.

In May as we drove on our vacation to visit friends and relatives that "piece" came to me. We were riding along, with Jason asleep and John driving, when I exclaimed to John, "That's it!"

"What are you talking about?" he asked.

"That phrase, that word that I needed to tell myself the real reason I wanted to continue to stay home with Jason. Remember e. e. cummings' poem "you shall above all things be glad and young"?

"Of course," he replied. "You know that it's one of my favorites."

"Well, the last two lines are the words I've been looking for: 'i'd rather learn from one bird how to sing/than teach ten thousand stars how not to dance.' "

My puzzle piece fits; my perspective is whole. Our little bird named Jason Gerard is more to me than rooms full of eighteen-year-olds and colleagues whose latest books are best sellers. My brain has not died; instead, through Jason, it has made room for something that will forever keep it alive.

4

A Slice of Life

A Riddle

Marge Phillips
Connecticut
1979

A six-legged creature God made me,
And yet I travel slow;
For six legs all of different lengths,
Make traveling slow to go.

I have six eyes to see the world,
But each sees a different view;
And what **one** *finds a pleasant sight,*
Another *wants to shoo!*

I have six ears, six hands, and arms,
Which constantly do battle.
Three tongues inside three different mouths,
All voicing different prattle.

Three minds within three separate heads
Do not agree on much.
What time for sleep? What food to eat?
What book to read? and such . . .

And yet all parts are stuck like glue,
None willing to divide.
Each tries to pull the rest with him,
Together side by side.

Some days are filled with push and shove,
And I cry to be free.
To shake these clinging multiples,
And only to be me.

But well I know as time goes on,
Metamorphosis will come;
And where three bodies tangle now,
I will be left with one.

Alone, at last, I'll sigh deep sighs,
Remembering with a tear,
When six arms hugged, a warm embrace,
"I love you, Mommie dear!"

My Priorities

Dianne Royka
New York
1973

To critics who wonder out loud or silently why my home is not antiseptically spotless, I have at various times reacted with excuses, jokes, and apologies. I guess the real problem is that I don't share their priorities, though because they are my friends I try to understand them. I'm really writing this for them so perhaps **they** can understand **me.**

In my house you're likely to find toys strewn about, mending undone, windows dulled by fingerprints and noses. The ironing basket is always full, newspapers and books lie in piles, and cobwebs can sometimes be found on ceilings and in corners.

But I've found time for walks in the woods and bike rides with the children. We've found bird nests, tadpoles, turtles, and recently, a patch of wild strawberries whose blossoms covered the soil like snow. We've seen the sunrise, the constellations at night, rainbows, the deer in the meadow, a male pheasant strutting in the grass, a hawk soaring in flight.

I can find time to read books to the children, nurse the youngest, write letters to friends and relatives, and run errands for neighbors. I even manage to squeeze in meetings of La Leche League, the National Organization for Women, and the Antique Bottle Club.

Our meals are sometimes served late—but they are well-balanced and nutritious. (The kids call them yummy.) The lawn isn't manicured—the many worn spots are from children's feet. Our trees are not rare, horticultural specimens, but they're great for climbing. The beds often aren't made until noon, and I couldn't care less!

I sometimes forget to buy soap or butter or coffee; but I always remember anniversaries and birthdays. I give birthday parties and have the cupboard full of homemade jam—strawberry, peach, wild blackberry. I have time to bake, and I'm not too busy to have tea and conversation with a friend who has stopped to visit me.

I read the Bible, poetry, and books about Napoleon, the Golden Age of Greece, and Neanderthal Man. I look at all the kids' school pictures and papers and hang their art work throughout our home. I always have time to hold a child who wants love and attention. Time to listen to crickets and frogs. Time to wipe noses and give rides in wagons. Time to gather seashells and listen to well-repeated knock-knock jokes.

I've caught flies and spiders for our pet lizard's dinner, watched flashes of yellow, red, blue, black, and brown as evening grosbeaks, cardinals, blue jays, nuthatches, woodpeckers, sparrows, and blackbirds eat at our feeders. I've put bouquets of weeds, dandelions, and wild flowers, brought to me by the boys, into fancy decanters. I've helped a two-year-old build sand castles, a five-year-old plant seeds, a ten-year-old with Cub Scout projects, an eleven-year-old make bird houses and boats.

I don't **care** about polishing the silver or waxing the floors or cleaning the cellar. These things will get done sometime—but my priorities won't wait.

This House Is Beautiful

Delores A. Baggett
Maryland
1976

Eight months pregnant and deep in the chill of February, I was feeling quite blue. My toddler, Joanie Kate, had wandered out to the sandbox to play. I sat staring at the pile of dirty dishes and an unswept floor.

The house always seemed a total disaster, and I was so heavy with child. Oh, how I longed for the sun to shine and for that new fresh smell of spring. Where would I ever get the energy to clean this house? When would I ever feel like doing it?

My thoughts were disrupted by a soft tap, tap. Joanie's little face was pressed against the sliding glass window as she knocked to be let in. With cold little hands and a big warm smile she threw her arms around my neck and gave me a hug and kiss. Then she went to the center of the kitchen, turned around, and inspected the room. Throwing up her little arms, she shrilled in her baby-child voice, "This is my house. It's beautiful!" And her smile lit the room like a 200-watt light bulb.

She hadn't seen what my adult eyes had been trained to see—the clutter and the mess. Joanie only knew she felt good here. No one else had ever paid me a higher compliment!

I am writing this to thank *all* little ones for their fresh outlook on what love is. Clean clothes, clean dishes, hot warm meals—yes, they are all part of feeling good and being loved—but they aren't really the important part, are they?

Turn Around, Turn Around . . .

Sheila Johnson
Connecticut
1974

One day when my daughter was four, she came racing into the house, excitedly telling me about a new trick she had learned on the swing. I listened to her, but being busy preparing vegetables for supper, I only listened. I didn't take the time to stop or even to look up.

Suddenly a scene from Thornton Wilder's "Our Town" flashed through my mind, and I could hear Emily pleading with her mother, "Just for a moment we are all together—Mama, just for a moment let's be happy—Let's look at one another!"

I turned and saw a small, round face glowing with enthusiasm and pride. To think I might have missed it!

Now I remember to look, to listen, to capture each never-again minute. In the future there will be time for all the household duties, for random wandering through the chambers of my mind; but only once will my daughter delight because she can pump a swing.

Dinner, Family Style

Marsha Harden
Ohio
1973

8:00 AM While nursing the baby check the cookbook, consider the day's activities, and select the menu

8:05 AM Decide on spaghetti, remind yourself to get the meat from the freezer

2:15 PM While nursing the baby remember that you forgot to get the meat out and ask your six-year-old to do it

2:20 PM Pick up the three cans of orange juice that your six-year-old knocked out of the freezer while getting the meat

4:05 PM Realize you should have started dinner ten minutes ago

4:06 PM Put water on for spaghetti; slice up onion and garlic

4:08 PM Nurse the baby

4:15 PM Salt spaghetti water

4:16 PM Throw away spaghetti water and start more after your two-year-old has helped by adding sugar

4:20 PM Nurse the baby

4:33 PM Strap the baby on your back, get out vegetables, look for proper pan to cook them in

4:44 PM Find pan in garage where your nine-year-old is using it to check for leak in his bicycle tire.

4:48 PM Finish scrubbing vegetable pan, add spaghetti to water, start vegetables

4:50 PM Fry partially frozen hamburger, onions, and garlic while watching vegetables and stirring spaghetti, check on milk supply, and set the table, all the while jiggling and singing to the baby

4:55 PM Reset the table, as your two-year-old has helped, but Daddy will want a fork and not need three knives

4:56 PM Continue jiggling the baby, drain and mix the spaghetti, wipe up milk the two-year-old has spilled

4:58 PM Call the children and tell them to wash up

5:00 PM Set food on table; inspect faces

5:01 PM Remove two-year-old from spaghetti and wash again

5:03 PM Kiss Daddy hello

5:04 PM Nurse the baby, being sure he is hooked up on the left side so you can eat, too

5:05 PM Thank God for all your blessings

Quickie Quiz

Suzanne Bauer
Tennessee
1974

1. What do you tell your husband with a straight face when he asks why there is toothpaste on the toilet seat?
2. Your children just dumped out the new set of 110 blocks on the floor. Without peeking, how many places can you think of where you will find them two days later?
3. There is a special television program on after lunch that you want to watch, bread to bake, supper to make, and you are to fix refreshments for the La Leche League meeting tonight. When do you think your little ones will take their naps?
4. You are going to a family reunion where you know almost all of them have heard about your "weird" childrearing ideas. You will be there about four hours. How many times will your toddler ask to nurse?
5. Janie has two brown socks, four blue socks, and four white socks. How many matched pairs does that make?

Answers: **1. Calmly explain that your four-year-old was helping the two-year-old brush her teeth and since said two-year-old is too short to reach the bathroom sink, she "spit" in the potty. (You get four extra points if you remain nonchalant!) 2. 110. Don't forget the one in Daddy's shoe, the one in the box of tissue, the one the gerbils nibbled up, and the two flushed down the toilet. 3. Never? Right! This is the day the little tykes will go nonstop from morning until you get home from the meeting. 4. At least four. Plan on his nursing for four hours straight and then it will be such a nice surprise when he gets busy with the other children for half an hour or so. (Five bonus points for nonchalance this time!) 5. None. One is on the baby, one is full of blocks, three are still in the dirty clothes, three are lost, Janie is wearing one, one is in your underwear drawer, and one is in Janie's sock drawer. (Two extra points if you can explain how that one odd sock wound up in the right place. Five extra points if you noticed that the number of socks in the question was not the same as the number in the answer. Whenever have they ever come out even anyway?)**

My Nursing Portrait

Colleen Eckel
Ohio
1982

Since my involvement with La Leche League, I have admired the pictures of mothers nursing their babies on the LLLI calendars. When my twin boys, Jason and Jeremy, were babies, I thought about making arrangements with our family photographer to have a nursing picture taken. However, two babies and my three-year-old, Drew, gave me only time enough to think, not to act. Then Tobie came along two years later and again I had the idea of a nursing portrait—but I had even less time to pursue my wish. Now two more years have gone by, and I have another wonderful baby boy, Collin. I finally made an appointment with the photographer.

The night before our appointment, I conducted a frenzied search at the local discount store for a pretty blouse in a big enough size to fit over my nursing anatomy. My husband, Jim, waited in the car with our five children. I tried on several blouses from the "larger sizes" rack. I found the proper size and then selected a blouse of a different shade than the one I had tried on. I knew I should probably try this one on also, but I could envision the baby hysterical with hunger (it had been at least thirty minutes since he nursed), and my three older boys having physical discussions. So I paid my money and left with the blouse.

The next morning I felt I had everything under control—my husband was at work, the older children were playing outside with a sitter, and my rocking chair was set up in the clean living room. I put Collin in a cloth diaper and proceeded to put my new blouse on. But I could hardly button it and then noticed that the tag was marked irregular. Then the doorbell rang and it was the photographer and his wife. Clutching the baby against my popping buttons I settled in the rocking chair. Right away Collin knew something was amiss. We were in a strange quiet room and no one was crawling over us while he tried to nurse. Then his dry cloth diaper became a wet cloth diaper which produced a damp mark on my tight blouse.

From my view of the proceedings all I could see was one large, indiscreet breast with a small baby sometimes nursing at the end of it. The photographer's wife was behind me arranging my blouse to cover my other breast and stomach stretch marks. Collin was making noises from both ends and I had a strong let-down which of course resulted in another spot on my blouse. My antiperspirant was failing by this point so I had two more spots on my "bargain" blouse. Now all this time the camera was clicking away and I was supposed to be looking down on Collin with great tenderness. This momentous occasion was topped off when the photographer's wife opened the drapes to let in more light—which exposed our scene to the neighbors who were working in their yard. Completely unnerved at this point, I settled for one last picture of me holding Collin—not nursing. This last pose will probably be the best proof so I might need to have another baby to get it right.

The nursing portraits on the calendars are so beautiful! How did they ever take them?

Values

Susan Richman
Pennsylvania
1982

This afternoon, I sat on the sofa, my little four-month-old Jacob snugly wrapped in warm blankets and nursing to sleep. Jesse, my three-year-old, was nearby inventing intricate highway games with old boards and rug scraps and myriad cars and trucks. I watched my son play, responding to his new ideas, enjoying his delight and concentration.

Then I looked at Jacob, wondering if he was sleeping soundly enough to lay down in bed. If he could be put down, then I could get to something really important: sort the heap of clean laundry that threatened to tumble off my clothes dryer or subdue the dishes that had taken up seemingly permanent residence in my sink. Maybe I could get to some sewing, make a few phone calls, or even scrub the bathtub. My mind made lists and plans.

But then I looked at Jacob, and no, he wasn't yet soundly asleep. He needed me to sit there quietly and calmly with him for a while longer. He needed my time.

And then I realized again how much Jesse needed my time, too, my unhurried time, my focused time, my freely given time. My growing child needed my time too. And little Jacob helps me to give that time, helps me to slow down my pace and enjoy these small moments of play and togetherness.

So I didn't get anything "done" this afternoon. The clothes are not yet put away, and the dishes are piled a bit higher. But tonight my house feels as a home should feel. There's warmth here tonight; there's the feeling of lives touching each other tonight, taking time for each other. For I shared time with two small boys, and that made all the difference.

The Spider and Her Web

Pat Yearian
Washington
1979

I have never been overly fond of spiders, in fact, as a child I was afraid of them. But now I have a special spider. Just outside the top corner of our kitchen window a large, brown, female spider has set up homemaking.

When I first noticed her working, I called the little ones in to watch, for it was fascinating how she carefully made her web. She seemed too heavy for those fine strands that came from within her—it seemed to be a total giving of herself. Nonetheless, it held and a web was built. Then she went to the edge of the window and was still.

The rains and strong south winds came and tore sections of the web apart. She came down from the corner and began to repair all the broken areas. Sometimes this has meant almost making an entirely new web. This has gone on day after day for weeks.

This spider has truly been an inspiration to me. Most of my time is spent with the same routine tasks—preparing meals, washing dishes, handling clothes, cleaning floors, caring for the family's needs. Making a web must be like making a home. Each connection has to hold the whole together. If a part breaks, then we give of ourselves to repair that area. In our own families the daily tasks that seem so monotonous really do make a beautiful "web." Then we may, like the spider, take moments out to just sit and wonder—so thankful to be able to share our love.

A Mother's Wishes

Gail Berke
Massachusetts
1981

I wish I had a sewing room with shelves and drawers for fabrics and notions . . . a small room where I could stop—midstich—lock the door and no one would touch my work. But I have my sewing piled high in the corner of my bedroom where my pin cushion is a discarded Winnie-the-Pooh and thread regularly disappears to become Spiderman webs or parachute cable for miniature toys. Bits of thread and snips of fabric litter the floor, and I'm never alone for a minute.

I wish I had an office with a desk and files and my own phone within reach where I could work undisturbed and ponder and write and stay on top of my work. But, I have my kitchen table that has to be cleared three times a day, where letters stick together with peanut butter and typing paper gets crayoned and becomes paper airplanes. The phone is always kept busy, usually by a teenager. I'm never alone for a minute.

My filing cabinet is in the basement, sandwiched between the furnace and the ping pong table and under the boys' dart board. I share it with Carl's household accounts, and it groans under dirty tube socks. I fold clean clothes and sort dirty laundry simultaneously, and I'm never alone for a minute.

I wish I had a room, uncluttered, neat, with flowers in a vase and polished tables. But I have toys and sneakers and fingerprints and lots of kids, mine and others, always around. I'm never alone for a minute.

I wish I had some time all for me . . . to read a book, paint my nails, think an undisturbed thought, write a letter to my mother all at one time. Instead, I'm up and down, sharing books with a five-year-old, kissing bumps, coaching a pitch, solving a ninth-grade equation, mending a doll's dress. I'm in the car, on the phone, cooking, mopping, listening, talking, busy, and never alone for a minute.

I called my mom in Florida the other night. She has a sewing room that's every seamstress' dream. She has a sunny little corner with a desk, violet-scented writing paper, and pens that stay right there. She has a tidy apartment with flowers in a vase and polished tables, like a page from a home magazine.

She asks me, "Would it be convenient to come and visit next

Photo on the right of Gail Berke and her children was used in LLL NEWS; photo below shows Gail and her family in 1987.

month? I was remembering when Dad was still alive and well and you and John and Robby were all home—how much fun we had together. I miss that crazy chaos that is a family.

"I know I just visited your brother and Veronica. The three boys were wild and woolly all the time, and the new baby was so dear, nursing and keeping us up every night. But I miss you and your kids, too. This place is too quiet. I'm alone every minute."

I wish I were twenty-two again and just starting to have my babies. I was running day and night with never enough sleep . . . endless days of diapers and teething and little nursers in our bed. Slow down time. I am never alone for a minute, and I'm glad!

5

Different Children, Different Needs

No matter how many years we have been a mother or how many children we have, we never learn all there is to know about mothering. Just when we begin to feel that we have it all figured out, along comes a new situation or another child to make us humble and remind us how much we still have to learn.

The Perfect Mother's Baby

Carolyn Butwyn
Pennsylvania
1971

Did you ever think that perhaps it is the baby's personality that determines whether he cries a lot or is quiet? Perhaps the mother's skill doesn't have so much to do with it.

We have all seen the mother-and-baby couple who seem to be in perfect harmony. The mother hands the baby just the right toy, which he takes and it fascinates him. The baby sits contentedly on the floor, playing and watching Mother walk by. Baby squawks once or twice, and Mother nurses him to sleep for a refreshing nap. We all pursue this goal, understanding baby's needs and meeting them, as if that rapport were something that grew out of mother's skill alone. But does it?

With my first baby I bumbled through, learning tremendously and getting by as most first-time mothers do. By the second baby I was a veteran and a consummate artist at mothering. I was chock full of ideals, cognizant of child psychology, relaxed, devoted, and happy; of course this baby was the perfect baby. She awoke to play happily, nursed to sleep, bright, playful, active, and docile. Who wouldn't feel like the perfect mother? Then came my third child.

Jennifer, number three, is sensitive, difficult with transitions, and a light sleeper. Barbara, number two, loved to lie in her infant seat, bed, or on the floor to watch me work. To Jennifer, seeing is holding, or else she cries. Barbara sat in her highchair finger-feeding herself and had a great time. Jennifer has to be on my lap stealing food from my plate, dropping silverware, and generally disrupting the meal. Barbara nursed to sleep every day of her life until she was two years old. Jennifer cranks to sleep while being walked, rocked, and suffered with. Where did I go wrong?

I am still the same mother; my ideals are the same, my personality the same. The household environment is easy on children. There is little sibling jealousy, lots of fresh air, activity, and interesting things. But somehow this baby just insists on being fussy. And when she gets fussy and demanding, all my skills are nothing. She cries. I have to conclude that it is her personality.

Many of the things that I do for her were unnecessary for my older two, but they work with her. And after I've exhausted my store of knowledge to placate her and she still is cranky and crying, I sit and rock and wonder: What did I do wrong? Where is that perfect mother I wanted to be? Does the perfect mother's baby cry? Is there a perfect mother?

Our Fussy Baby

Ann Carpenter
Arkansas
1984

When our daughter, Erin, was born, nothing could have prepared me for the problems we encountered. Our son, Brett, had been such a happy, contented baby that I assumed our second child would be that way, too.

Right from the beginning Erin was an extremely fussy baby. There were days when we did nothing but cuddle on the sofa and nurse. And lots of nights, too! She screamed whenever we took her anywhere, she disliked crowds, and she was very unhappy whenever visitors came to the house. For months she refused to allow anyone except me to hold her.

When my husband realized that there was little he could do to help with the baby, he cheerfully took over many of the household duties and spent extra time with Brett so that he wouldn't feel left out. Brett was wonderful, too. He brought things to me when I was busy with the baby and learned to wait for his meals until little sister finished hers.

At ten months, Erin has yet to settle into a regular schedule and still sleeps very little. However, she has gradually become a more contented baby. She now enjoys playing with her father and brother and is beginning to accept strangers better. Erin has taught me many lessons. I learned to shut out the inevitable criticism of my method of feeding and mothering my child. I had to accept the fact that it was impossible to keep a perfect house and still meet the needs of my fussy baby. I dropped all my outside activities and concentrated on my family. But rather than feeling that I had sacrificed anything, I felt enriched. I knew that in a short time I would no longer be the most important person in my daughter's life, and I enjoyed the special bond that we shared. Mothering a fussy baby like Erin isn't the easiest thing I have ever done, but it has certainly been one of the most rewarding.

A Mother Grows

Nancy Comstock
Pennsylvania
1981

When my son was an infant, I basked in the glory of motherhood. Corey was beautiful, bright, and angelic. Caring for him took a lot of work and most of my time; but love was dominant and we thrived. He responded to life with a cheerfulness that reinforced my image of myself as a mother.

As time passed Corey grew and along came his sister, Wynne. Even though I looked forward to seeing differences between them, I was not prepared for the changes ahead. Wynne was beautiful and bright, but hardly angelic. She was physically active, rolling across floors at four months and walking three months later. She hated confinement, whether in the highchair, stroller, car, or grocery cart. In spite of my feelings about screaming children, when Wynne was angry she screamed loud piercing screams. Shopping and visiting hardly seemed worth the effort when Wynne's interest waned after half an hour.

Perhaps the most difficult part was her clinging. The early months she spent in the baby carrier, since she was not happy anywhere else. Gradually she became more comfortable around other people, as long as I—her anchor—was there. But even at two-and-a-half years, it took her two days of a three-day visit to accept my sister and her family enough to let go of me.

During this time I grew enough to realize that I was responsible for neither Corey's evenness nor Wynne's fervor. The biggest difference between Corey and Wynne was simply adaptability. Corey had always been comfortable almost anywhere, while Wynne took time to adjust to new situations, new people, and new places. Too many changes at once overloaded her tolerance.

So we learned to adapt to Wynne. We took fewer trips. Family shopping nights and home-based activities were not hardships during those months. And as Wynne grew, her tolerance grew. One day a few months before her third birthday she said to me, "Mommy, you go shopping tonight. I stay home with Daddy." I knew we'd arrived at last.

We've all come a long way in the last three years, but we still have adjustments to make. In a few months a new baby will join our family, but I think we will be able to adapt.

Extra Doses of Love

Nell Ryan, Editor, 1968

I had rather fixed ideas about child care when we had our first baby. My goal was to be a good, firm, no-nonsense mother; to be scrupulously fair with each of the twelve children we then hoped to have; to love, but not to molly-coddle. The trouble was that I didn't really know how to express love to a baby.

Fortunately, I was able to nurse our firstborn successfully for about nine months and thus subconsciously supplied the cuddling he needed in those all-important early months. He weathered my stupidity. I still marvel at what a fine person he is—in spite of my mistakes.

Then came number two—Mr. Sensitivity himself, warm, loving, extremely perceptive of others' feelings but very slow to express his own. In trying to be completely "fair," I tried to hold him to number one son's pattern. It didn't work—but I continued to try for quite a while. The results were crib-rocking, head-banging, and bed-wetting. The doctors explained away the first two: "Nothing to worry about." "He just has lots of nervous energy." "He's got rhythm."

The bed-wetting was another story. "Immature bladder," "heavy sleeper," "lazy"—they said. So we tried remedy after remedy. We withheld fluids after six at night and woke him before we went to bed. Then came a new theory. The bladder needed to be stretched. So we forced fluids and measured the output. We tried many things—short of having him sleep in the bathtub. Sometimes we just ignored the situation, hoping it would go away.

Each new scheme seemed to work for a week or two—then it was back to the old routine. Funny thing, though, he was always dry during the day—and he didn't have any trouble when he spent the night away from home.

The diapers and fancy pants we'd bought for him didn't work. I was tired of wet sheets and soggy mattresses. After all, he was almost eight! But I just couldn't bring myself to resort to the drugs the doctor suggested or to try one of those alarm systems I'd read about. Then one weekend, I had a chance to go to Madison, Wisconsin and see the Primate Laboratories where the Harlowes had done their well-known research on the monkey babies who'd been forcibly separated from their mothers at birth. Not only did I see the lab, but the actual monkeys.

And what were these deprived monkeys doing? They were rocking back and forth on their "hands and knees," banging their heads against the sides of the cages, pulling out their own fur, sucking their paws. I was thoroughly shaken. Their behavior reminded me of my son's. No one could convince me that **these** babies had "nervous energy" or "rhythm!"

When I returned home, I began a concentrated program of **physical** love for the children. I'd already been working on the intellectual level—**telling** them I loved them—in words. I sat down on the rocker with each of them every day for at least ten minutes.

The second child wasn't satisfied with ten minutes. He began rushing home from school so he could sit on my lap. Sometimes it was a half hour or more. (He was a big boy and my legs would get numb.)

He had always been reticent in conversation and slow to express his feelings, even though we encouraged him to do so. I guess he was afraid that he might displease us and he didn't feel secure enough to risk that.

Now he blossomed. He talked more openly. Our relationship improved to the point that he felt he could argue with me and express real anger—something he'd never done. He even stomped around and threw a few toys. If such a thing is possible, you could say that he was "joyously" angry.

The most amazing result of all was that this eight-year-old— with the "immature bladder," who "slept too soundly" and "was too lazy to get up to go the the bathroom"—suddenly stopped wetting the bed. I hadn't set out to accomplish this. It was completely unexpected—and at first I was sure it wouldn't last. But it did.

Then I reflected on the times when we'd started new ways of helping him to keep dry. The reason these new ways worked for a while, I think, is not due to the methods themselves but rather to the increased attention he received at the time. For a brief period, he really felt wanted—and he responded.

I'm not going to conclude, just from my own experience, that all bed-wetting is due to emotional causes. But I don't think it would hurt any child with this problem if he received large, extra doses of physical love and cuddling. I say "he" significantly, because there are more boys than girls among bed wetters. And the mother-son relationship is a very sensitive one.

What did we gain from this experience? Dry beds? I certainly won't deny that it was a relief to be rid of the dampness, the smell, and the rusty springs. However, the best benefit was that we learned that we couldn't force all the children into one mold. While nine months of nursing at four-hour intervals may be all right for one child, another might require much more frequent feeding and cuddling. Trying to make one child "wear" another's living pattern is just as foolish as trying to make him wear someone else's glasses. Treating children fairly doesn't mean treating them identically.

6

Accepting Realities;
Seeking Ideals

Memos from Marian

Marian Tompson, LLL Founder, 1969

While we all want to be good mothers, let's agree that good mothering can be achieved in very individual ways. This means that everyone doesn't fit the usual description of "a good mother"—a woman who is even-tempered, gracious, and poised, always alert to her family's needs. She is not overly concerned with housework (though her house always looks presentable) and possesses that special wisdom that makes her forever fair in allotting tasks to her cheerful children. Happy in the kitchen, she prepares meals that are naturally nutritious and accompanied by homemade whole-wheat bread (which is also eaten by her cheerful children).

This kind of ideal can be rather discouraging. While we can all manage three or four of these attributes at a time, or even five on a good day, we don't all have the same temperaments, backgrounds, husbands, or children.

What we do have in common is a desire, born of love and concern, to do the very best job possible in our particular situation. And it is this desire that will provide the catalyst for improvement. We all can use the inspiration of other good mothers, but we should never expect to become carbon copies.

Appreciate your individuality.

Are You Batting .300?

Joanne Shipley
Oregon
1982

A friend and I were talking about life and looking for new perspectives to help us gain a more positive outlook. As we talked, a thought emerged. If you play baseball, you have a batting average, and it is recorded in terms of the hits rather than the misses. Most players are pleased to have an average of .300, although that is actually an average of seven misses out of ten tries, if we take a negative point of view. But no one thinks of a hitter as missing seven out of ten. Instead, the emphasis is on success, and the hitter is steadily encouraged to raise that average from an initial .000 to as high an average as he or she can get. And an average of three out of ten is considered excellent—.300!

I began to wonder about our attitude as parents when we look at ourselves and our children. Do we expect to bat 1.000? Be perfect? Do we expect our spouses and children to bat 1.000, too? And is that realistic or helpful, or can we find another perspective that will be more useful?

It seems that it might be wise to look at our successes—the one temper tantrum we handled lovingly (instead of remembering the ones that we didn't handle well), the time our child enjoyed picking up toys when we made it into a game (rather than how often the floor is a mess), the time we shared in some real conversation with our spouse in the midst of a busy day (instead of feeling overwhelmed by the days that there just hasn't been time). If we could only enjoy the fact that our three-year-old actually shared a toy voluntarily today (rather than the number of times that he or she screamed "MINE" and yanked it away) or delight in a batch of delicious bread that little hands helped to make (instead of looking at the flour all over the kitchen and the dough in a little one's hair). If we could just count up the successes, the positive signs of growth, the things that went well, and place our emphasis on these, it could make such a difference for our whole family.

My temptation has always been to try to be a perfect parent and to have wonderful, perfect children. When I look at the negative side, there always seems to be such a long way to go to reach perfection, but when I look at the positive in our family, we are already batting .100 or better and the goals that we have set for ourselves will help us come closer and closer to .300 as time goes on. I wonder if we have any right to expect that either ourselves or our children will ever bat close to 1.000? What do you think?

LLL speaks of needs, capabilities, and feelings—and I firmly believe that if our expectations of ourselves and our children really took those three things into account in all areas of our lives, we would really enjoy watching and growing as our batting averages began to climb. If we can place our emphasis on the hits, not the misses, it can make a big difference in the way we treat ourselves and others. And after all, if you can bat .300, you are a real pro!

The Ideal Mother

Norma Jane Bumgarner
Oklahoma
1978

It's one of those days when the tarnish on my halo of motherhood is showing. The baby wants to nurse *again;* four-year-old Myles and a friend are heaving trucks or atom bombs (or something) down the stairs; and eight-year-old Seth appears on the scene with, "You *never* make us any cookies!" I manage to unclench my teeth enough to snarl, "Go make your own cookies." I'm beginning to get some order on the staircase with Vincent under my arm, still squirming because he wants to nurse, when Carmen glazes the scene with a piercing five-year-old whine, "Seth always gets to make cookies; I want to make cookies." I may be a super-mom at that, because I don't hit her. I just shriek, "There's no way I can help you bake cookies right now. When you learn to read you can make cookies!" Not a scene for anyone to be proud of; but here I am.

As background on this vignette—I put out a lot of effort toward good mothering. Sometimes this effort is directed, not toward good mothering really, but toward some ideal I have of a good mother. Since my "ideal mother" keeps the cookie jar full, my kids have a perfect handle with which to hook my feelings of guilt and inadequacy. I prove the case I have against myself by looking at my friend Sue: she bakes cookies a lot. (What is really interesting is that Sue's "ideal mother" takes her kids camping! She uses our family's camping trips as evidence for the prosecution when she has her own mothering on trial.)

At any rate, I do finally get Myles and his friend to take their simulated warfare outdoors, I get the baby attached, and show Seth for the twenty-seventh time where the one-quarter line is on the measuring cup. As I sit back, I stop nourishing my guilt feelings. I take a real look at what is happening, and there is a warm flush of realization. Seth is absorbed in the profound mathematics and chemistry of cooking-baking. Carmen, after some minutes of watching Seth with envy and admiration, gets out her books and paper and crayons and starts copying words and asking me how to spell "milk" and "sugar." Something good has happened here, not out of my "ideal" mothering, but out of interaction with me, the way I really am, even somewhat short of my best.

If I had made cookies today (and I couldn't have done it without subjecting myself to extra work and pressure), I would have given them only cookies. As it turns out, they're getting a lot more. Children who cope this well with a tired, harried person (me) have a good start in their life with fellow human beings. And a child who can make his own cookies can have cookies whenever he wants for the rest of his life.

Mothering Is . . .

Mary White, LLL Founder, 1978

Mothering Is . . .

- *looking into your baby's eyes when he is five minutes old.*

- *getting to the pitcher of water seconds after your two-year-old does and then laughing all the way to the mop.*

- *squeezing your six-year-old's hand as you walk up the school steps for the first time.*

- *telling your twelve-year-old to wash the make-up off her face.*

- *seeing your sixteen-year-old inducted into the National Honor Society.*

- *knowing your husband, their father, is behind you all the way, all the time, cheering, guiding, encouraging, loving.*

- *slipping a $5 bill to your twenty-year-old as he goes back to college (knowing full well that his father has just done the same).*

Mary White with Molly, 1965

> • *standing in the receiving line at the wedding saying "thank you very much" to the guests before they have had a chance to say "congratulations."*

> • *opening the door to see your daughter (who was two when the League began) beaming as her two-year-old says, "Grandma I came to see you because I love you so much."*

> • *looking down with tears in your eyes at your newest grandchild as his mother nurses him.*

It's seeing all the wonderful things that can happen; the results of years of trying and failing and trying again, and making mistakes; and of losing your temper or being "too soft," but all the time loving them and wanting to do your best for them, and seeing them turn out better than just "all right" in spite of your mistakes.

Part Two

Being a Father
Tenderness and Love

Loving Memories

Barb Valer
South Dakota
1980

Puzzles and dolls, stories in books,
Toys and stuffed animals fill all the nooks.
Where are the children to whom these belong?
They're sitting with Daddy, singing a song.

Rocking and singing—new songs and old,
They pause for a story that's often been told.

As night draws near and pajamas are donned,
The time spent in singing has created a bond.
Daddy has etched a place in each heart.
Loving memories of Daddy gave gotten their start.

7

Time to Be a Father

"Parenthood is a very demanding job, but one with the most lasting rewards. Believe me, raising children with love is worth your best efforts."

Betty Wagner, LLL Founder, 1978

Children Open a Father's Eyes

Oscar Stephenson
Alabama
1984

Men are trained in our society to be rational, reasonable people who don't show their emotions. I believe that children come into a man's life so he can learn more about his emotional nature. Children embody joy, creativity, laughter, tears, and happiness, all of which are emotional qualities often foreign to a man. Women are allowed to enjoy these attributes and share an understanding with their children that fathers may miss when they become too involved in the workworld of facts, figures, and reason. Children see a side of life—the joy of the present moment—that we as adults often lose in the process of socialization. To a child, an ordinary walk down a city street becomes a fascinating invitation to explore the bricks in the buildings, the cracks in the sidewalk, a parking meter, or a street sign. Adults have become so goal oriented toward getting from point A to point B that we miss the joy of the journey.

Learning to Be a Father

Ruth Molnar
Colorado
1973

As I have learned to be a mother, I have watched my husband learning to be a father.

I remember when our first son, Steven, was just a young baby. He was fussing, wouldn't nurse, and I was at my wit's end. Finally I gave him to his daddy. Just having a new face to look at fascinated him. Daddy let the baby clutch his fingers—a different touch. Daddy touched Steven on the cheek—he seemed amazed at the new sensation. It was the beginning of a very special relationship.

I remember when our second son, Paul, was about two, and friends came to visit with their two-year-old. The father had been overseas and was hardly acquainted with his son. My husband and Paul initiated them into the pleasures of tender roughhouse—chewing on necks with scratchy faces, blowing on tummies.

Daddy's homecoming is the high point of our day. He is greeted with shouts of joy and the news of the day before he gets in the door. It makes him feel pretty great.

Finding Time

Robert Stewart
(With permission from Baby Talk Magazine)
1969

Calling some fathers: Don't get caught up in the commuter race as I did—it's easy to do and it doesn't pay off.

"I'm too tired tonight!" "I'm busy just now!" "It's too late!" How many times had I dismissed our three-year-old son with just such an answer when he came looking for my attention in the evening?

Once home, I'd often be out of sorts . . . still battling workday problems . . . busy with homework brought from the office. It was only natural, I told myself, that after a particularly hectic day I'd want to seek some quiet relaxation with a book or a TV show. Unthinkingly I was actually discouraging Bobby from seeking my company in addition to making him the innocent victim of my own end-of-day impatience and fatigue.

Poor Bobby! All day he had to compete for his mother's attention and affection with an eighteen-month-old sister! Small wonder that one evening, after I had told him for the second time to "Stop bothering me—I'm tired!" he backed away from me and proclaimed, "I don't like you, Daddy!"

My wife was quick to reassure me that this was Bobby's latest reaction to all forms of discipline. Nevertheless his remark stung. I vowed right then that I'd try harder to find more time to spend with my son.

Suddenly—almost magically—little "islands" of the time were found that I hadn't thought existed before. Fifteen minutes in the morning—it really isn't that hard to get up a bit earlier; an occasional hour in the evening—the "must" work completed on the train coming home. I also make "tucking-in" time a father-son routine each night. To my amazement I soon found myself enjoying these little interludes with my son as much as Bobby did.

Of course, Bobby still informs me occasionally (usually after a necessary reprimand) that he doesn't like me. Now, however, I can put such statements in perspective. And more evenings that not, there's an unsolicited "bear hug," a secret to share, and an "I love you, Daddy."

Changing the Business World

Iddy Andrews
Ohio
1980

When asked to attend a business seminar that was scheduled close to our second child's due date, my husband declined, saying that he wanted to be here when the baby was born. His boss replied, "Oh yes, I guess you must do your fatherly duty—pacing the waiting room." Bill then told him how we planned to have the baby together, as we had with our first. His boss said he felt that it would be an unpleasant experience, "too gory." Bill explained what a wonderful experience the birth of our son had been been—prepared, undrugged, and together. What a difference in attitude towards fathering!

Being asked to work late in the evenings and on Saturdays can make a man feel cheated as a father and as a husband. The success ethic can rob men of the special experience of seeing their children born and watching them grow. Maybe as more men like my husband advance in the business world, there will be more emphasis on men having time for family.

The Importance of Family Time

Sam Turner
Arizona
1978

When we first decided to have children, Phyllis and I knew we would want to adjust our lifestyle so that our activities would include our family. Since we had spent five years of married life prior to children, we were ready to change our priorities. I felt that it was worth more to see my children take their first steps or laugh or smile that it was for me to be chairman of various education committees. Through careful budgeting, Phyllis was able to give up her teaching career in order to spend her full time with our children. Although, at the time, it was a financial hardship on us, we both recognize now how important those "together years" were.

Where we once spent evenings out with others at dinner parties (no children, of course), we found delight in family games around the fireplace. Of course, it wasn't long until we discovered other couples through LLL who also enjoyed doing things with their babies. We joined a "different" bridge group, where mothers nursed without missing a bid. We enjoyed potluck picnics with our friends.

Of course, we did have moments alone. Usually after the children were asleep, we would sit by the fireplace, sigh the sighs of tired but content parents and discuss the activities of the day. We found a certain anticipatory delight in holding hands in the parking lot as we walked to the grocery store. Nothing more had to come of it. It was just the awareness that we were together; that was what counted.

Now we have two teenage daughters. What a change a few years can make! We have new challenges. Time management has become important for all of us. Our sons have made new and varied demands on the family. We are free to come and go, now that we have built-in babysitters for Robert, who is four. But somehow those years of family-oriented activities have become addictive. We look forward to evenings at home, together, with the whole family.

I must admit that I catch myself asking young mothers-to-be if they are planning to nurse their babies. It's natural these days to receive an answer of, "Why, yes! My husband and I both want to share in the birthing and nurturing of our child. He encourages me to nurse." How times have changed!

So up we grow. What a delight it is! What fun to be able to continue to share in the growth and development of our family! Our experience in La Leche League has taught us that we are not unique. Others have similar goals.

All around us is evidence that the philosophy which we subscribed to during those early years has borne fine fruit. Our children are still concerned about family togetherness, and we continue to do many things together. Most important, they know that we care about them, that we are still concerned about their activities, about their hopes and dreams of the future. We still share evenings and activities together. We still communicate. For our family, breastfeeding was the foundation upon which our future is built!

Fathering and a Career: Can a Man Do Both?

David Stewart, PhD
Missouri
1981

Can a father do well in his career and do right by his family at the same time, or is it impossible? Why do parents choose to neglect their spouses and their children for their careers? As the father of five, a university professor, and a scientist, I find it sad that many successful and famous men in my field are divorced.

The temptation to seek career and neglect family is very seductive. There is something about fame and peer recognition, something about the money, the position, the power, the praise, and the promotions offered by a career that are exceedingly enticing. One receives so much encouragement from nearly everyone to seek these things, while one receives little encouragement, if not downright discouragement, to spend time at home with the family.

What are the rewards of a career? What do you get when you attain outstanding success in your field? Well, you get fame. You get acclaim. You receive promotions. You receive salary increases. And you can also gain a great deal of personal satisfaction in a job well done. But this is only one side of the coin. On the other side you get lots of false praise. If you mistakenly accept it as real, you will inevitably suffer a big let-down.

To be a successful career person, you can never stop. The rat race never ends. The more you do, the more is expected. The pressure is never off and usually increases. Therefore, I do not believe that career success can bring you happiness. It cannot even assure you security. It can disappear almost overnight, even for a triviality. A person who opts for career first may be famous, respected, and wealthy today and forgotten, derided, and destitute tomorrow, but they who put family first reap rewards for life.

Few people do anything in their entire lives more far-reaching than raising their families. It is a rare professional accomplishment to be so significant as to make any great difference fifty years later, but the way you raise your children will make a difference fifty and even one hundred years hence.

Although you may not realize it, the effect that you have on society today is influenced for good or ill by the things that your great-grandparents did a century ago. A well-raised child is a happy child. Happy people make others happy and make good parents themselves. Generation after generation benefits. The results of the secure family go on and on.

But so also do the results of a neglected family. Deficiencies at home are manifested as deficiences in society. The root of many social problems we face today may very well be poor family life.

A perfect sample of the human values intrinsic to children can be seen in babies. They prefer to be held rather than to be housed in an expensive crib. They don't care if you're a president or a pauper. They prefer a crinkly piece of paper to an expensive toy. Their desires are so simple. All they want is to be held, to be fed, and to be secure. Compare that with the adult desires for elegant homes, big cars, and expensive entertainment. Most children respond to people for their true inner selves and not their outer shells. Success at home and success in one's career are not independent. A person who feels like a failure on his job will be in a poor state of mind to be a good parent. Therefore, a reasonable amount of satisfaction with one's job achievement is essential to good parenting.

Likewise, the person with marital or family disharmonies is not going to be the most efficient worker. The best quality of work, as well as the greatest quantity, is likely to emanate from one who operates from a secure, happy home base. Making career and parenting compatible boils down to this: First, you must determine (and this is a completely personal choice) the minimum level of achievement in your job that you can accept and still maintain your self-respect.

You can choose a level of acceptable achievement that leaves you with adequate free time for your home. By investing your spare time in your family you can be happy both in your career and in your home life. Although you may not achieve the outstanding professional status of those who choose to dedicate a larger portion of their time to their work, you are still to be counted as a success, because success is measured by setting a goal and achieving it.

Although you may sometimes feel that society or other people set the goals that you should achieve, this is not so. You alone set your goals. You may be influenced by society and your friends, if you choose to be influenced. But it is your free choice to do so or not. If you want to be a good parent, you cannot let society be a dominant influence.

Another way to accomplish a balance between family and career is this: Find out which aspects of your particular work reap the highest rates of return in terms of career enhancement and concentrate on these. Decide in your job where you can get the most effective results. Make the time you spend at your work really count. I don't spend a lot of time in the coffee room. I like to spned my free time at home. So when I work, I try to just work.

Put in your time at work as productively as possible and when the time is up, quit and go home. By applying your energies wisely and efficiently you may find it possible to excel in your career and have time at home, too. The secret of career success lies not in long hours, but in properly ordering priorities. I am a happy person and I have a happy family and that's the most important thing to me. Furthermore, I have been able to satisfy my basic ambitions in my career. We can see in our children and in our marriage the fruits of putting family first. If my job ever interfered too much with my happiness and my relationships with my wife and children, I would quit. There are lots of ways to make a living, but I have only one wife and one family.

I only do so much and no more. I do not compare myself with others. They have set their goals and I have set mine. While much of my mind, time, and energy goes into my work, beneath it all my heart rests at home.

If the right values and the right priorities are assigned to the duties at work and to those at home, I really believe that good parenting and a successful career are both going to happen—not in spite of each other, but because of each other.

Happy are they who can achieve and maintain such a balance. They will have achieved the ultimate worldly accomplishment whose true reward is itself. Careers are fickle, but parenthood is forever.

8
Father's Loving Ways

no. 4

Raymond D. Kochanski
New Jersey
1972

he cries,
and rising, she leaves my bed
for a new love.

now soothing, mollifying
she raises him up,
implanting the kiss.

she turns then her head
to me smiling,
for me to share her joy;
she bares him her breast
and brings him forth to me to greet.

The Manly Art of Supporting Breastfeeding

Lewis A. Coffin, MD
California
1975

The future father may exhibit laudable enthusiasm when his wife chooses to breastfeed their child. Secretly, he may appreciate that this will relieve him of nighttime feeding duty. His wife must be the one who gets up to nurse the baby while he nestles snugly in the sack. No 2 AM fumbling with a cold bottle and a balky stove while a hungry infant screams in accompaniment to wall-pounding from the next apartment. He probably has a warm image of himself, gently and helpfully chiding his partner-in-parenthood to wakefulness so she can fulfill her maternal destiny.

What more could be expected of him? How could there be any sacrifices for *him* to make? Well, I remember waking up at night over many breastfeeding years to find my wife plus the current breastfed baby in my bed making all kinds of sounds to each other, which might have been charming if it weren't the middle of the night. A father must groggily watch this tableaux and smile convincingly when asked whether the baby isn't sweet.

The father's role in the nourishment of his breastfed child is an important one and may involve sacrifices of another kind. For example, it is usually with some chagrin that the new father realizes that some of his territory has been invaded and occupied for the "duration." The full impact may not dawn upon him for weeks, even months. Blissfully savoring the pride of new fatherhood, it's not until he finds himself continuously faced with leaky breasts, nursing bras, and the inevitable, extremely business-like nursing pads that he comprehends who comes first, where, and for what! It is here, however, that he must put aside his personal interest and defer to the usurper, assuring his wife that good nourishment for his child comes before all else. There are some fathers who resent the trappings of breastfeeding and they may encourage the mother, even subconsciously, to give up nursing sooner than planned. Fathers who know what to expect and who are well-prepared for what is to come, rarely feel this way, and can help the mother with their patience and understanding.

From the very beginning, the father has the potential to promote a normal, pleasurable breastfeeding experience for his wife. Before birth, he can be positive about her natural ability to nurse their child. When she first puts the child to breast, he can be the

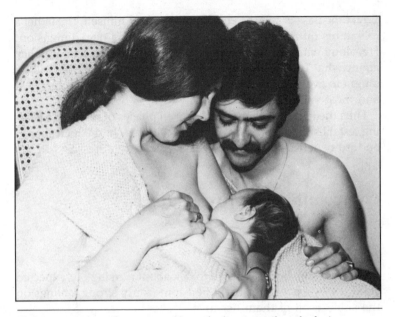

Nothing can assure the success of breastfeeding more than the loving support of the baby's father.

one to reassure her that it takes a while for most newborn babies to "catch on" to what it's all about. Thus she won't get the mistaken impression that something is wrong with her or her milk, a common fear of first-time nursing mothers. Again, in the first few weeks of nursing, the mother may experience varying degrees of discomfort from tender nipples. Here the father's sympathy, understanding, and encouragement, combined with the helpful advice of her physician and friends, can be of real help. Later on, when well-meaning friends and relatives may question the advisability of postponing the introduction of solid foods, the father can lend valuable support. He can remind her, or better yet the local "advisory board," that her milk is providing the optimum in infant nutrition all by itself. Few self-appointed nutritionists will persist in handing out advice to parents who obviously have firm convictions on the subject.

After the first six months or so, when the infant is ready to be started on solid foods, the father, whose role has been simply supportive, begins to come into his own. He can share in the actual feeding of the child. This can be a time of great enjoyment for them both.

As time passes and the child begins to feed himself, the father's role in his nutrition will become important in a new dimension. He, along with the mother, must decide upon a consistent policy about what foods the child will be eating and what he will be taught to avoid. Of course, this policy will be based on the latest and most valid concepts of nutrition.

Thus the father will have shared in all phases of his child's feeding, establishing deeper involvement with his child which should endure beneficially into later years.

Overcoming Negative Feelings

Elton J. Kerness
New Jersey
1970

When my wife, Bonnie, began to talk about nursing our expected child, I quickly realized that I had some fairly strong feelings on the subject, all of them negative.

I knew nothing about breastfeeding. My feelings were mainly based on the fact that Bonnie had not nursed our other two children. Further, I had never known anyone who *had* nursed a child. I had some vague notions that this would disturb our man-woman relationship.

I asked my wife why she was thinking of breastfeeding, who or what had influenced her decision. She said that one of her good friends was nursing her child and had talked to her about breastfeeding. This friend had also introduced her to an organization called La Leche League, composed of nursing mothers who held meetings and published materials for women who wanted to breastfeed their infants. It was after going to La Leche League meetings, talking with mothers, and reading their materials on breastfeeding that she had decided she would like to breastfeed our expected child.

I began to realize that most of my negative feelings were based on the plain and simple fact that I was ignorant of just what breastfeeding involved. Without real knowledge of the subject, I had fears of being tied down and not being able to go out with my wife, or being totally left out of her life because of the closeness of her relationship with the baby. And there was a natural anxiety about something new.

"Just read the material," Bonnie said. "Don't have a closed mind.

I believe if you read the book you will have a much better under-standing of breastfeeding and that you will feel better about it."

So I promised her I would read the book but said there were no guarantees, other than that of course I always wanted to be able to help her as much as possible.

I read THE WOMANLY ART OF BREASTFEEDING rather surrepti-tiously, for fear of being discovered by one of my male co-workers. It turned out to be an enlightening experience. The book discussed many of the fears I had expressed and gave first-hand informa-tion on the role of the father, what to expect, and the physical and physiological aspects of breastfeeding. It explained that al-most any woman was able to breastfeed, that mother's milk was best for the infant, and that the nursing mother would physically return to normal more quickly after childbirth.

After reading the book and talking with my wife about it, I be-came willing to explore further just what we had to do to make this the best possible time for all of us. When the baby came, I felt that both my wife and I were well prepared for her breast-feeding experience. We had come to realize that breastfeeding is the most natural and desirable way to feed a child.

The peace and tranquility that a household experiences when a child is nursed is a wonder to behold. Everyone is less harried, and consequently everyone can enjoy the new addition as well as each other. Breastfeeding allows both mother and child the peaceful feeding time that is essential to the health and happi-ness of any infant. It also allows more time for the other children because precious hours are not wasted with formula-making.

Our little girl is doing beautifully. She is healthy, alert, gaining weight, looks fine, and most of all, is extremely contented and happy. The benefits for our older children are also worthwhile; they are seeing nature at work.

Our oldest, a little boy of four and a half, enjoys watching the baby nurse and is truly fascinated with the fact that milk comes from his mommy to help his new sister grow big and strong. Our little girl of three is also extremely fascinated. She is more con-cerned with her own body and what it will do. Watching her mother nurse the baby, she asked, "Will I have milk in my nip-ples when I grow up?" We explained that when she is a mother, she too will feed her baby this way. She jumped the gun on us, though. One day when Bonnie was nursing the baby, in came our daughter with her doll, sat down, put the doll to her breast, and she "fed" her baby, too.

It is truly amazing that all this can be realized within the framework of simply doing what is best for your child. It seems to me that in today's society, when we are striving for a return to normalcy, there is no better way to express what is normal than by the most natural act a woman can perform—giving sustenance to her child in the way nature has provided.

Made Not Born

Beverly Sykes
California
1972

The LLL NEWS is so often full of glowing reports of wonderful nursing experiences and wonderful supportive husbands helping their wives over the rough spots that occasionally those of us with less enthusiastic husbands feel that perhaps we are alone. It may be of some consolation to know that sometimes League fathers can be "made," even if they are not "born."

When our first child was born, I was full of enthusiasm and backed by friends who had all nursed successfully. My husband, while happy with my breastfeeding, still spent much of the time playing devil's advocate and helped out in fussy times by asking, "Are you sure she's getting enough?" and suggesting, "Maybe you should try a bottle."

With the second baby we both had more confidence in my ability, and while Walt was not the sort to sit around patting me on the back and bragging to neighbors about how his son had gone three months without solids, at least the defeating comments seemed to be lessening.

When Number Three came along, we talked about his feelings toward my breastfeeding. He admitted to being jealous, but added that he was "sort of proud" of me. He also began reminding me to get enough rest and started nudging me when we saw mothers with young babies and bottles.

With Number Four he actually volunteered to help out with a Father's Night discussion. Always tolerant of my LLL activities, he had never been excited about the League, but he did attend the Father's Night and shortly afterward agreed to come with me to a League symposium, which he greatly enjoyed.

Now we are expecting Number Five. My breastfeeding is, of course, just taken for granted. The big victory for me is that he has agreed to attend Lamaze classes and be with me during the birth of this child. We've come a long way since our first baby. Walt will never be an enthusiastic League father but he's changed a great deal over the years.

Weathering Defeat

Paul Mueller
Switzerland
1983

A few weeks before our daughter's birth, my wife had waded through a voluminous amount of contradictory literature on child-rearing and chosen a course that was to determine our baby's type of upbringing. Above all else this was certain: Our child was to be nursed as long as possible. "You know," said my wife, "nursing is best from a medical standpoint as well as from the psychological: warmth, security, body contact, immunity." This all made sense to me.

It was an unforgettable experience when our Nicole slipped out of my wife's body and immediately searched for her breast. Even today when I think back to the hours in the delivery room, I say to myself, "You didn't experience that; it was all a dream, an incredibly beautiful one." If something like that really existed, it would be called a miracle.

Brigitte, my wife, took care of our little defenseless creation in a touching manner. If there was ever a whimper, she was on the spot. "A baby doesn't cry without having a reason for it," she used to say. "Crying is the only way she can communicate." Brigitte regularly got up five or six times during the night to comfort Nicole by nursing her. I started to ask myself if this could really be normal. Relatives, friends, and acquaintances all told us that their children already slept through the night at one, two, but surely at the most, three months. Our child was most likely already spoiled.

Cautiously, I tried to inform my wife of the criticism from these experienced parents. That was the wrong thing to do. There was a terrible spat which ended with my wife's decisive comment: "I'm not going to be made unsure of myself!"

Then there was the time when Nicole refused her mother's breast. We were very concerned, searching for explanations. I found one: "Nicole probably has a stomachache." The magic word was fennel tea. I filled a bottle and sweetened it a bit. Now it was my turn to take the child in my arms. Now I could "nurse" my child. And from then on, when Nicole couldn't be comforted at her mother's breast—and that happened more and more often now—I was there with my fennel tea.

One evening Brigitte cried her heart out. I tried to comfort her. "My milk is doing something wrong. There is an organization for nursing mothers, La Leche League. I'll call them tomorrow."

That was the end of the "nursing" father. LLL explained to her that the bottle should be avoided as it is easier for the child, and she doesn't have to work very hard to get the liquid. After a few days, Nicole was nursing at her mother's breast as before.

After this conversation with the LLL Leader, my wife got more and more involved in LLL. She became acquainted with a woman in our village who belonged to this organization. Every problem that Nicole had would be discussed from now on with Silvia. My advice (actually I was just passing on the wealth of experience from my colleagues) was now ignored.

More and more strange ideas that clearly originated from LLL became realities in our apartment. According to the suggestions of these LLL people, it seemed that much of the baby equipment we had purchased was unnecessary. However, I completely hit the roof when this absolutely crazy idea about a family bed came up. It was not enough that my wife hardly had any more time for me after Nicole's birth. No, our child was to practically publish the fact of our disturbed relationship by being brought right into our bed. This was too much. I won out in this round of discussion, though I must admit to the fact that our very narrow bed helped me in this matter.

Then came our vacation. I had certainly earned it. Not only was the stress from my business beginning to show on me, but also, the never-ending confrontations over these new LLL ideas were getting to me.

We rented a little cabin in Ticino (the Italian-Swiss canton), the simple kind with no electricity and such. There was only one bed and we did not bring a crib along for Nicole. The most beautiful moments of our vacation were the mornings when Nicole woke to see if Mommy was still on her left and Daddy to the right. Since that was the case, she rewarded us with a dazzling smile. On one such morning, Nicole warmed my heart with her first hesitant "Da-Da." It was a beautiful vacation.

In the meantime, Nicole had turned nine months old. Even a stay at the hospital, of course in the constant companionship of her mother, was well weathered. I have also weathered my defeats. And I have to admit that I am mighty proud of Brigitte; surely it has a lot to do with her association with LLL.

A Father's Progress

Harold Holden
Kansas
1980

When Linda was pregnant with our first daughter, Kendall, now fourteen, I was indifferent about this idea of breastfeeding. By the time Kendall was several months old, I changed from being "indifferent" to being "in favor."

When our second (and last) child, Jay, now eight, was a few weeks old, I moved from "in favor" to "proud."

Then when we were awaiting the arrival of our third (and last) child, Amber Lynn, now almost six, I shifted from "proud" to "hard to take" as far as my fellow employees were concerned. Breastfeeding isn't the normal office conversation.

Now that our fourth (and last) child, Carl John, is here, I am so happy with the way he has thrived these first five months on mother's milk that I have to remind myself that it would be easy to slip from "hard to take" to "absolutely fanatical." What a thrill it is to be a significant part of such a great thing!

Young Music Lover

Chris Cannon
Illinois
1980

"But what does the father do?" is a question often asked of breastfeeding proponents by new mothers-to-be. How broadening it must be when new parents find that feeding is just a small part of a baby's upkeep and there are a myriad of loving tasks that can be undertaken by Dad.

And think of the great fathering that takes place with subsequent births. In our family, we've found that each new baby brings a time when a father can reassess just what it is that fathering entails.

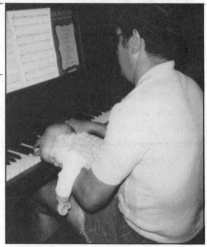

John and Cormac Cannon,
on the right, in photo from
LLL NEWS, 1980, and the
Cannon family, above, in 1985.

With the birth of our sixth child my husband, John, kept up his fantastic fathering pace, as well as the great "husbanding" I needed postpartum. However, when he offered to rock our son, Cormac, as I got the others ready for bed, I didn't expect our tiny baby to fit the scene quite so well. I had left John holding Cormac and trying some new music on the piano with one hand. By the time I had finished, John had mastered the tunes and was playing along, with both hands, and Cormac was fast asleep, still on his knee. John's only comment was, "It slows me down a bit, but he seems to like it."

Patience Pays Off

Michael Jackson
Colorado
1977

Most women I've talked to who do not breastfeed say it's because their husbands want to feed the baby too. Well, you can understand how they feel. The father loves the baby, but it is the mother who has had the unequaled experience of caring for a growing human being inside her until the miracle of birth. Up to then it has been more or less all mother and baby, and as an individual interested in caring, protecting, providing for, and guiding his family, the father has a natural instinct to jump in and DO SOMETHING. And the easiest, most readily available thing to do is feed the baby—and that means a bottle.

What the father has to realize is that whether what he has in mind is getting the father-child relationship started or helping relieve the burdens of a still-recuperating mother or just simply fulfilling his need for touching and handling his baby, all that must be secondary to the health of that child. I'm talking of both physical and mental health.

Jenny is now two years old and is as outgoing as you'd like to see in any little child. She is currently enrolled in parent-child swimming classes and is one of the better swimmers in her class, showing no fear at all of the water while other children cry and hang onto their mothers desperately. Judging from the other children's absenteeism because of illness, she's one of the healthiest tots in the class (she's only missed one class in eighteen months). And no one can deny that she's one of the friendliest—not one bit shy. In effect, what all of this points to is the incredible security she has attained through the closeness of breastfeeding. This is the mental health I was talking about.

Breastfeeding has in no way affected or retarded the father-child relationship. It *was* hard to just stand by those first few months while the baby was almost totally wrapped up in mother and breastfeeding, but since she finally shed those wraps, we have been enjoying a relationship which is like no other I could imagine. Even though Kathy breastfed her until Jenny weaned herself at sixteen months, she has found herself almost having to fight for her share of the time with *our* baby. People gladly enlighten me as to her being a "Daddy's girl," and I LOVE IT. Whether we're playing on the swingset in the backyard or she's helping me rearrange our rock garden or raking leaves, we're always laughing and having a great time. She even loves to shower with Daddy and her little blue dolphin.

Being a father is a thousand times more fun than I already knew it would be, because she is so secure in her early upbringing through breastfeeding. Daddy now gets his 50 percent of a loving child, Mommy gets her 50 percent, and baby gets 100 percent of the love and care of both.

No Other Way

Frank Pritchard
Alabama
1977

I never really gave any thought to the fact that there was any other way than breastfeeding for a mother to feed her baby. It's a good thing my wife felt the same way!

Because I have always expected that my wife would nurse our children, I never had the adjustment problem that some men have experienced when their wives have begun nursing. I help my wife when she first brings the baby home by getting up with the baby, changing him, and giving him to my wife to nurse. I try to hold the baby as much as possible so he will feel secure with me also . . . although this doesn't always work, because there comes a time that no matter how secure the baby is with Papa, Papa hasn't got what Mama has! One of the favorite things that I have done with all four of our children is to sit back in my easy chair, put the baby on my shoulder, lay my head back, and both of us take a snooze for a couple of hours.

Someone asked me once why I am so strong on nursing. Well, it is because I always follow the manufacturer's recommendations. If I buy a car that is equipped to use unleaded gasoline, I use unleaded. If the label of a product says that for best results, use by a certain date, then I use it by that date. If the directions say to let paint dry for four hours before applying a second coat, I wait four hours. So why should it be any different with a baby? Mother came from the "factory" equipped to feed her baby. There are products on the market that are "the next best thing to mother's milk," but as far as I am concerned, the "next best" just isn't good enough for our babies!

9

A Job Well Done

"Long ago I was given a definition of love that I have never forgotten. It's very simple—to love is to sacrifice—to do hard things for the sake of the one you love."

   Edwina Froehlich, LLL Founder, 1983

Memos from Marian

   Marian Leonard Tompson, LLL Founder 1978

Pity the poor father of the breastfed baby. If he can't give the baby a bottle, what else is there that's meaningful for a father to do?

   Amazingly, this is a frequently heard objection to breastfeeding, and it was very much on my mind as I attended a recent LLL of Alabama Area Meeting. For all around me were fathers and their offspring demonstrating in at least fifty ways how to love your baby without giving him a bottle.

   "Sure, I wanted to feed the baby myself," one young father admitted. "But I tried it and found that once was enough. I wouldn't want to be expected to feed him regularly." Later I sat in the ballroom as his wife, with her baby discreetly nursing, addressed the conference. Halfway through her talk the baby had finished nursing and was upright surveying the scene. By the time he was attempting to dismantle the microphone his father moved quietly forward, swooped his delighted son into his arms, and carried him off to the back of the room.

"Kelly can barely contain her excitement when her father walks in the door from work," my daughter Debbi laughed as we sat enjoying Easter Brunch. "She just throws herself at Wayne, even when I'm holding her." Kelly is seven months old now and has never had any kind of a bottle, but she obviously gets a lot of other attention from the number one man in her life.

Most fathers today want to be involved in the care of their children and feel strongly about their own responsibilities. They fill a special role in their children's lives. Let's not diminish their unique contribution by suggesting that it is only as psuedo mothers that they really make the grade.

Or as my own husband, Tom, said, "Perhaps the greatest impetus to successful breastfeeding comes from a father who enjoys being who he is and doing what he does, realizing that the family is enriched by the diversity of its members."

A Mother's Helper

Karen Hill Pearce
Nova Scotia
1974

Having recently returned home from the hospital with a new baby—our first—I was fortunate to have my mother come for the first week. At the end of that time, however, I found I still needed much help. My husband immediately saw to it that I had a part-time mother's helper, who has proved absolutely invaluable.

Although holding down a full-time outside job as well, this wonderful creature, who lived in, did all my wash in the evenings, got meals when I simply was not up to it, cleaned the house, tactfully turned would-be visitors away, handled all phone calls (these can be equally tiring), brought little goodies from the bakery so I wouldn't tire myself baking, and generally fetched and carried for me.

Endowed with a soft shoulder and a sympathetic ear, my mother's helper had a knack for making a cup of tea at the right minute, pooh-poohing all my "am-I-doing-it-wrong" fears, or ordering me off to bed—whichever was appropriate at the time.

Can you imagine the luxury of having help that gets up in the middle of the night with you to help you change the baby and washes all the dirty diapers while you breastfeed saying: "We're all awake anyway; maybe this will help us get back to sleep faster."

Now that baby is a month old and settling into a routine, I'm able to handle almost all this work myself, so I no longer need my helper's assistance quite so much. But my mother's helper is still around for moral support and help when needed. I'm lucky enough to be married to him.

The Highest Honor of All

June Schulte
New Hampshire
1979

My husband does not know I'm writing this, but I feel strongly that he deserves some sort of public recognition for all he has done.

Bill will graduate in May, but it will not be with honors. The fact is, he just barely missed honors. It isn't hard to imagine that if we did not have three children while he was in school, he would probably be graduating with honors.

For the past four of the six years that Bill has been attending the University of New Hampshire (in electrical engineering), he has also worked sixteen to forty hours per week so that I could be a full-time mother. If not for that, he would probably be graduating with honors. If it weren't for the extra hours he spent reading countless books to the children instead of himself, he would probably be graduating with honors.

Lastly, if it weren't for the time it took to attend home birth classes and prepare for our third child's birth, he just might be graduating with honors. You see, my last labor was precipitous, and there just wasn't time for the proper folks to arrive. Bill got to be midwife (or "midperson" as he puts it), and thanks to his studying he knew just what to do.

Actually, he will be graduating with the highest of all honors: "BEST HUSBAND AND DADDY EVER!"

A Father Grows Up

Ruth Sanecki
Illinois
1981

Seeing pictures of young men playing with their babies reminds me of my husband's early years as a father, when our house was filled with little ones. But it also calls to mind another picture, that of John walking our eldest daughter down the aisle for her marriage last year.

How proud I was when I saw them come into church! Anne looked so lovely, and John looked so handsome. I thought of all the years that led up to this happy day, for just as surely as the young man is father to the baby, the older man is father to the adult child.

At times during those years, John had doubts about his ability to parent our five rapidly growing children. He had sleepless nights when he wondered if he could handle the current problems of a school-aged child or if he could guide one of them through a teenage crisis or help them with college or career decisions. I saw his love for each child grow and felt confident that together we'd try to be the parents each one of them needed.

It must have been frightening for him to think of being a parent to a teen when the children were little. I know it was for me. He must have wondered if he would be wise enough to stand back and let them find their own way without trying to impose his will on them, to offer suggestions and encouragement rather than orders. He learned about them and about himself. He found reserves of patience he didn't know he had, patience to let them make mistakes and so develop the ability to judge what would be suitable for them.

As each child grew up, he grew up, too. And he grew up differently each time, for each child grew up differently. What was effective or right for one child was not necessarily good for his or her younger sibling.

I've listened to our grown-up children talk about their father's qualities and what they've learned from him. They come to him to discuss certain situations, different from those they discuss with me. They know he has had different experiences that will be helpful for them to learn from. I've seen their respect for him grow. It's like the old joke about the child at age twenty-one marveling over how much his father had learned since the child was eighteen. They've learned to admire and appreciate his hard-working, commonsense approach to life.

Now that all of them are grown and living away from home, John and I take pride in their ability to be independent. We enjoy having them come to our house often, either to visit with us or with our washer or mixer! We like to see them come with husband or wife, with boy or girl friend, or by themselves. And when they go home, we enjoy being together just as we were when we were first married.

John has made our lives richer because he is a nurturer. His quiet good humor and supportive ways have never failed us. He has helped shape our children's lives and encouraged me in all my activities. We love him, thank him, and want him to know how much we appreciate him.

In Celebration of Fathers—and Life Itself

Kay Batt
Washington
1982

As we all know, the healthy mother/child relationship is intense. It lays the foundation for future adult relationships that are strong and deep. Children who are unable, for one reason or another, to develop this close relationship find it difficult to relate to others. No less essential is the role of the father as a bridge to the outside world. Fathers are a delicious mixture of familiarity and novelty. They extend the child's world beyond mother's arms with differences in body and character. They feel different, smell different, and their voices offer a change of tone and pace. They provide love, security, and a different view of the world.

In her book *Family*, Margaret Mead states, "Even the most primitive peoples, although they have no knowledge of the role men play in procreation, *insist* that women have husbands so that children have fathers. Every people believes that there must be at least one grown man who will care for the mother, provide shelter and food, guard and teach the child, and give it a stable place in the world. For the child, the father is the embodiment of strength. Your father can let you stand on his stomach. He can lift you high in the air, or toss you up and catch you safely in his strong arms.

Because a father is tall, the little child lifted to his shoulder to look out at the world can see more than the children who must watch from the ground. Raised above the eye level of the tallest man, the child feels himself expand."

I would like to share with you a family experience in which we made some important discoveries about the father's role. Shortly before our youngest son's third birthday, I was stricken with a cerebral hemorrhage that left me on the hospital's critical list for nearly two months. I was paralyzed on the left side. Nothing worked—from a smile that would only smile on the right side, to an inability to move my arm or leg or to feel any sensation. It also robbed me of the ability to talk so that people could understand me. I could make noises but my words were scrambled and unintelligible. I was as helpless as a newborn baby.

When the hemorrhage happened, Eric was still nursing as a release to sleep and to find comfort if he was upset or hurt. Suddenly our secure world was torn apart. Evenings became very difficult for Eric. All of a sudden I was gone and he could no longer nurse to relax and go to sleep. Fortunately he was old enough to talk and understand some of the situation. My husband, Art, spent many hours each evening trying to reassure him.

My wonderful parents came immediately from Denver and they brought with them the attitudes about children's needs (or rather adults' needs) that I grew up with. They thought Art was doing a terrible thing by letting Eric "get away" with keeping him up until one or two or even later as he worked out his feelings. My mother and her sister decided that it would be best for all if my folks took the two older boys back to Denver and my aunt took Eric to "straighten him out."

I was so grateful that Art and I had talked over our feelings about family and separations, because Art knew that not only did he need the kids, they needed each other and needed to be home with him. And he knew that I wanted it that way, too. He held his ground in opposition to a most formidable force. To make a long story short, Art's stubbornness made my mother so angry she decided he could worry about the children and she would take care of my needs instead. That was a lifesaver for me.

My mother and father took an apartment next door to the hospital and one of them stayed with me twenty-four hours a day for the next five weeks. We had an inexpensive plastic lounge chair in my room that could be opened out and made up to sleep on.

It was only slightly more comfortable than sleeping in a chair. They changed shifts about three in the morning so that each could sleep in a real bed for a portion of the night. It was ironic that they were giving me the care as an adult that they considered so wrong for Art to give the children.

During this time I discovered what it was like to be a baby, helpless to meet my needs. I discovered what it was like to have someone else make the decisions about how valid my perceived needs were. During this time my parents accepted my stated needs as real and valid but that wasn't always true of doctors and nurses. I felt love welling up inside me for those who did not judge my needs but met them without criticism. I felt strong dislike and unwillingness to cooperate with those who made judgments about my needs and considered them invalid.

All my life I knew intellectually that my parents loved me, but it wasn't until they spent that time with me, making no judgments about my needs, just being available and doing their best to meet them, that I knew without a doubt that I was loved by them. It was real and tangible and a very large factor in my getting well.

For my husband it was a time of growth, too. The insistence by all that Eric was manipulating him began to erode his confidence at times. He tells of an evening that was particularly trying when he was unable to comfort Eric and began to feel sorry for himself, resentment for Eric's inability to accept the situation. Art was tempted to put Eric to bed and leave him to cry it out. He realized then that Eric's problem was real and being a child unable to change the circumstances, he needed a father who was an adult. He needed someone to care and be strong, someone who would wait out the long hours of distress with him, rather than leaving him to struggle alone.

Art tells me this was a time of revelation for him, a time of maturing to a point where the giving became easier and more meaningful. He had discovered his real value as a father. In a time of crisis he was the embodiment of strength. Art raised our children above the eye level of the tallest man. I feel fortunate about a number of things . . . not the least of which is having a husband who supported me by meeting the needs of our children when I could not.

Part Three

The Family Grows

Sharing the Miracle

Moments

Debbie Newsom
Oklahoma
1978

A moment of love
Becomes a moment of life.
A baby crying,
Softly breathing
Gently sighing.

A moment fulfilled
Of hopes and dreams
His crying ends,
Nursing quietly
His life begins.

A moment to share
Together with love,
Husband and wife.
From the beginning of love
To the beginning of life.

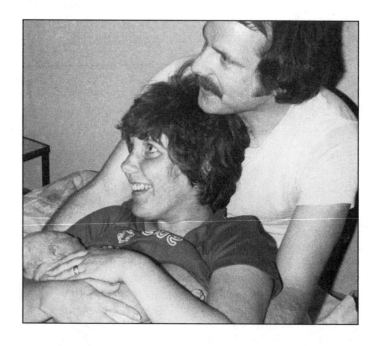

10

Love Multiplies

"The investment of time and commitment you give your child when he is young is a relatively short period of time, but the returns are forever in a child's life."

   Edwina Froehlich, LLL Founder, 1983

Birth Memories

   Sandy Martin
   Texas
   1981

To me, childbirth is a lot like a wedding. You plan and dream for months, anxiously awaiting the big moment. You play over again and again in your head how you hope things will happen. There's even practice for both. Then after months of wonder and preparation, it gets nearer to that time. All the emotions you've bottled up flood you and suddenly you're not quite sure you can actually go through with it. Only the promise of a new love that awaits you keeps you going. And then, in only a few minutes, it's happened. Your world, your life, and your love will never be the same again. But then, who'd want it any other way? You may have pictures to show everyone your moment of glory, but the real, treasured memories will live forever in your mind, waiting to be replayed any time you want to witness a miracle again.

Strongly Positive

Judy Sanders
Washington
1974

Do you recall Truly Scrumptious from *Chitty Chitty Bang Bang?* Well, how about Strongly Positive for a one-and-one-half-inch wonder? For that is the first descriptive term applied to our baby, due in September. The nurse, very soberly, said that my test result was "strongly positive." I immediately felt, "Good for you, little baby! You are not apologetically tip-toeing into this world. You are, after all, Strongly Positive!"

There are certain unexpected feelings of peace and joy when we think of this baby's coming. Gordy and I feel very special. He is grinning more than ever. He says, "This is what life is all about!"

No small part of the joy is in sharing this with our other children. John is really going to feel the change . . . he is our youngest and will be five next month. He is excited about being a big brother, finally. Our only girl, Kathleen, is eight and has had her bid in for a little sister for some years. As soon as we told the children at dinner, Kathleen had to head for the telephone to tell her best friend. And the next day she shyly asked, "You weren't just kidding, were you, Mom?" Dave, who is twelve, is delighted. Rick, thirteen, has some worries that the baby will tie us down too much. He needs reassurance also that the baby will be born healthy and whole.

We wondered just where we would put Strongly Positive . . . and then realized that by the time he/she cares about being in a room rather than in the open area at the top of the stairs, we will have one or more away at college or elsewhere. For when this little person starts kindergarten, Rick will be starting college.

John asks, "How big is our baby now?" We look at the pictures of the prenatal life of a baby. Perhaps it is because I am older than most mothers having babies that I feel so blessed. A precious life, cells dividing in the proper order, hair color and sex already determined, named Jerry or Mary Elizabeth, unaware of the love we feel for him/her. I ponder again the mystery of life. And my privileged part in it. A whole new, unique person, who will, with God's help, grow, and smile, and respond, and run, and read, and care about others. Who may marry and have children and enjoy them and feel good about himself/herself. And grow old. And leave the world a better place for having lived in it and having shared it with others . . . with love.

Have You Been There?

Jim Baskin
Georgia
1974

Have you ever heard a baby's cry? I mean the first one, when she first fills her lungs with air and bellows to the world: "I'm here, and I don't like what's happening!"

Have you ever felt the emotion, the excitement, build as you wait with your wife through each stage of labor, go with her from the labor room to the delivery room, and then watch her exert herself in helping your child be born?

Did you ever watch your baby's birth and feel the flood of excitement as you and your wife and the doctor all cry for joy that it's a girl? It's like scoring the winning touchdown in the closing seconds of a ballgame.

But even more than the exhilaration, you share something with your wife, something only a few people can ever know about. You are there, where you belong—at her side, lending strength and encouragement. You gain respect for her inner strength, a strength you never suspected she had, and you learn that she's serious about being a good mother from the start. It's a deep sharing known by few people, but once known, never forgotten.

Unforgettable Moments

Judy Sobel
New Jersey
1971

Children—I cannot help but marvel at how intuitive, perceptive, witty, and outright honest they are.

Each pregnancy, childbirth, and new baby has had its unforgettable moments. Take, for example, the time when I was near term with our third child and I awoke from a deep sleep in a soaking wet bed. "My membranes have ruptured—labor can't be far off," I thought. But as I began to make the appropriate plans and slowly opened my eyes, a little voice said, "The baby is thirsty and you wouldn't wake up, so we're giving it some water!"

A few weeks later three-and-a-half-year-old Sharon and eighteen-month-old Isaac cheered excitedly outside my hospital window, "You have milk in your bosoms again—hurray!"

"I hope you are pregnant. When you have a baby and when you are nursing, you are much nicer and calmer," Sharon blurted on one of those irritable, nothing-goes-right days last summer. And when I finally admitted that we were expecting baby number five, she sagely replied, "After waiting nine years for a sister and only getting brothers, I don't care any more what kind of baby we have as long as it's healthy."

Then there was the time David interrupted a roughhouse session and listened intently with his ear to my abdomen. "The baby is not crying—we can continue," he announced as we resumed our activity.

"You forgot about God's milk," Isaac prompted, and I stopped what I was doing to listen to the children's discussion of mammals and different kinds of milk that people drink. But what, I wondered, is God's milk? "If it takes God's help to get a baby, then it takes God's help to make human breast milk," he explained.

Together Dick and I welcomed our newest son, and together we joyously shared the wonderful news with the children. They were all excited, but each reacted differently. Michael was concise: "Mommy had a boy, and *we* have *a baby.*"

A Happy Father

Patrick Kilcoyne
Illinois
1967

The only disappointing thing about having a home delivery for our sixth baby was that we hadn't discovered the process sooner.

The term "home delivery" sounds old-fashioned, but it's still a great idea. When we decided we would have our sixth child at home, we found a doctor who would deliver the baby and we were on our way.

When I called one day and my wife said to come home, I knew this was it. Because the baby would be born at home, normal tensions were reduced tremendously. My presence had a calming effect on my wife, and she was able to cope with the situation better in our own surroundings.

Our task was much easier because it was Halloween. I dressed the kids in their costumes and sent them out with an aunt to trick or treat. In ten minutes, our new son had arrived. If you want to get a good feeling inside, try holding a baby that is about thirty seconds old. The only way one can really know it is to experience it. The most satisfying experience in my ife was to see our baby born. To try to put it into words is impossible. Nothing between a husband and wife could be more complete. In our case, what made it even better is that there was just my wife, the new baby, and me. The Maternity Center Crew was late.

Soon after the team from the Maternity Center left, the kids came home to find they had a new brother. They were a bit excited and baffled as to how it all came about so quickly. Because of being born at home, the new baby blended into our household very well.

Our oldest boy was especially proud. It isn't everyone who can tell his teacher that a new baby was born at home the night before. Perhaps I'm a bit biased about the whole thing because I, too, was born at home.

Seeing Again

Margaret Herzog
Washington
1978

Weeks race by in a blur of everyday routine. Babies, however, make the ordinary extraordinary. You see, Christopher was born two weeks ago, and I can see again.

The pace of life slows when a newborn arrives at our home; I recall this happening with Mattias, who is now two and a half. As he grew, precious little things began to slip from view in the rush of everyday living.

Now when I'm nursing Christopher I have the opportunity to be awed at the skills, physical and verbal, that Mattias has acquired. Christopher has made me aware of just how much his brother has grown. I see Mattias' delight at spreading peanut butter on his own cracker for the first time and his pride and satisfaction when he "helps Daddy." I had taken for granted a curious, eager toddler who has brought me hours of joy.

Just last night when Christopher awoke at two o'clock, I had a chance to enjoy again the night sounds. The coyotes howled in chorus, a mourning dove cooed, and other little creatures chirped and whistled as the moonlight created a soft halo around my sleeping husband and sons.

How could I be reminded of my husband Willi's understanding if it weren't for a busy day changing diapers and rocking a fretful baby? Willi smiled and thanked me for taking good care of our sons, even though he saw scattered toys and unmade beds. I have time to reflect as the baby is cuddled, which gives me time to recall Willi's compassion during labor and delivery, his gentleness when he holds his tiny son in scarred, calloused hands, his thoughtfulness in taking Mattias for little outings, and his special brand of love that brought a carnation home when he heard how blue I sounded when he called from work.

As for me, I know that time will pass and Christopher will grow as his brother has. I know that the pace of the coming days will speed up and it will be all too easy to forget about the little things that have brightened these past two weeks. But for now, I am grateful for the chance I've had to see again.

We Change, We Grow, We Learn

Elizabeth Meyer
Missouri
1983

My daughter is not a baby any more; there is another helpless one to fill that place. There is a new son to nurse, caress, and nuzzle at my breast.

But it is not the same this time. I do not sit alone all day with quiet baby sounds. I do not nap or sew or clean when baby goes to sleep. This baby son of mine does not belong to me alone during the hours of the day. Our serenity is broken; he is shared between mother and daughter.

Sometimes I want to say: "Enough, Baby, enough! I want to share some puzzle time, some singing time, some reading time with my little girl—without a baby at my breast or in my lap—as it used to be!"

I feel frustrated. I don't always want to share the time I have with each child with the other one. I don't want to be pulled in two directions, to always moderate, teach how to share, teach patience, teach compassion for one another. Sometimes I want to give my all to each child without interruption. But then they nap at different times and the frustration fades away. We are all learning to adjust to each other as our relationships adjust and expand.

Sometimes I want to shout about the love I have for this new circle we have become. As the love we have grows and we learn to live with each other, I witness the love the children have for each other. The bond between them grows. The clumsy love moves of the two-and-a-half-year-old are readily accepted by the five-month-old, for his eyes light up when he sees her. She doesn't even mind when he pulls her hair. They give to each other things I could never provide, things I can hardly describe. This baby learns faster than the first for he has two teachers, not just one. My daughter has learned to mother this baby and to mother her dolls from the example I have set. She has a healthy respect for the human body for she has seen it used as it was intended: to give life, to nurture and sustain life. When I need a moment for myself or can't quite get to the baby right now, my little girl is there with a rattle and a "no cry baby"—and he stops.

As our circle grows, there is not less love for each but more for all. At times I miss the serenity, but it is overlooked for all the wonderful excitement. We are all changing, growing, and learning. For what we lose, there is a greater gain. It may not be in exactly the same form, but it is there. It is as it should be.

What We Have Now

Jean Troy Smith
New York
1980

Almost all the stories in La Leche League publications are happy ones, as they should be. But now and again something not-so-happy happens, and those stories also need to be told.

In April, I had to go to the hospital in the middle of the night because I was miscarrying—my third miscarriage within a year. I was losing a lot of blood quickly, so I knew from past experience that I needed hospital care. My husband bundled up our three-year-old son, and we rushed to the hospital.

Around midmorning, the miscarriage was completed. Through it all, naturally, my husband and I were upset; we truly wanted another child. At various moments we had both cried, with our little boy witnessing all of this. (Both John and Jason were allowed to stay with me.)

When it was over, Jason asked, "Did the baby die?" John, who was with him at the time, answered, "Yes, it did, Jason." "Are you sad?" "Yes, we are, Jason." Then, with lip quivering, Jason replied, "But you still have me."

When John relayed the conversation to me, it made me realize that, even if we never have any more children, we have one who is lovely and wise. One who makes us realize that "more" isn't "better." That, sometimes, living for something that may never be makes us miss what is now.

Love Theorems

Alice Timmins
California
1979

It's been four years since my husband and I brought our two families together as one family. We have had many foster children cross our threshold and win permanent places in our hearts, if not in our home. However, we did succeed in adopting our *oldest* son and I gave birth to our *youngest* son in the same year. Naturally competition is high in a family such as ours, but these circumstances increased the normal "sibling rivalry." This inspired my writing the following and hanging it where all could read it:

When one more is ADDED to the family	+
Love is not SUBTRACTED from you.	−
When we give love	
It is not DIVIDED—	÷
It is MULTIPLIED.	×
Love is not an EQUALIZER,	=
Yet you cannot be GREATER THAN	>
Or LESSER THAN	<
The qualities WHICH YOU ARE,	( )
And for which you are loved.	
This then you ADD to the Family	+
Which MULTIPLIES your being needed	×
And wanted.	

With love from Dad and Mom

11

Becoming a Big Brother or Sister

"You have to keep getting the message across to your children, no matter what their ages, that you truly love them and care deeply what happens to them. If you keep giving those kisses and hugs, and do the best you can each day, you won't go very wrong in your parenting."

Berry Wagner, LLL Founder, 1979

Preparing for a New Baby

Janet Coyle
1968

To help prepare my five-and-a-half-year-old son for the arrival of a new baby, I wrote a little book entitled "The Story of Kevin." In it, I recounted all the main events of his life. I illustrated it with my own drawings, but could have used photos of Kevin or magazine pictures just as well.

In the beginning of the story, there is just Daddy and Mommy and the only thing they wanted was a little baby. How happy they were when they found that they were going to have that baby. And how busy Mommy was preparing for his arrival.

At last their baby came—and he was the most beautiful baby in the world! Daddy and Mommy loved him very much. Mommy would feed him, rock him, sing to him when he cried.

Birthdays, trips, and a move to another house were described. The book ended by telling him what a big boy he is now. He goes to kindergarten, can tie his own shoes, go to the store on errands, mail letters. In fact, he was big enough to help Mommy take care of his very own brother or sister. (I added sister "Susan" when I came home from the hospital.)

One night when I had been home for about five days, he awoke, crying miserably, and I was unable to learn what was wrong. I took out the book and began to read (at 2 AM!). At first he wasn't at all interested, but soon he realized the story was about him, and his little face slowly brightened.

Now, six months later, the book is somewhere amid the junk at the bottom of the toy box and is dug up occasionally when feelings are hurt. I think it was well worth the time and effort I put into it, though to be quite honest, I loved every minute of it!

The Little Mother

Kathy Grantham
Mississippi
1982

With the arrival of our son Douglas, our family relationships have been in a new period of adjustment.

As a very selfish only child, I spent a lot of my recent pregnancy silently feeling sorry for Kate, my daughter. After all, I could imagine myself at five having to share my mama. I would not have liked it one bit. Of course, I knew that love multiplies, not divides, but how exactly could I have more love when Kate—well, I mean, she's special. I know others may not see her exactly in the same light, but what do they know? They aren't her mother!

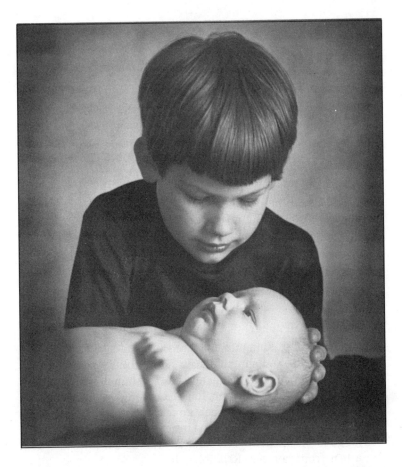

When Douglas arrived and looked up and smiled (newborns can smile, you know, but only their Moms and Dads can see it), I realized my love had expanded and everything was rosy—until we got home.

Suddenly Kate and I were having lots of conflicts, not the ones I had expected and for which I was prepared. Rather, Kate and I were having a tug-of-war over who was the baby's mommy. In one of our lighter discussions she told me that she'd promise me all her babies when she grew up if I'd just give her Douglas now! She seemed so full of positive feelings for Doug, I worried. Everyone said to expect jealousy—where was it?

Finally it sank into my brain that Kate's possessiveness really made logical sense to her. If *she* was Douglas' mommy, she didn't have to share me. I was just hers and she had a new toy—the baby.

Since then, I have talked to Kate about how we had fun "before Doug" and that I'm sorry we have had to change some of what we do. I have encouraged her to comment and "remember when" and we have talked about how Doug has limited the time we can spend with "just us—not even Daddy."

Now, after four months, Kate has finally realized it's okay to have negative feelings about her brother as well as positive ones. She knows that we understand and love her even if she sometimes wishes Doug weren't here. Yet she's learned to wait for Mommy— Doug comes first when he's crying and hungry. On the other hand, she and her dad are developing a new, closer relationship. And as she said the other day, "It's hard work being a mommy, but it's even harder the most being a sister."

On the Brink

Marga Raudsepp
Ontario
1980

Our middle child, Raja, almost three years old, always so easy to get along with, so loving with our new baby, so *reasonable*, was begining to act strangely! First, she'd ask for something: "Mummy, I want a banana." "Go take one, Raja," answered Mummy blithely. "But I *want* one." "Yes, my sweet, go take one!" "But I *want* one!" "I said you *may* have one!" Raja, in tears, "But I want one!" Finally, I go to the kitchen, get a banana, and hand it to Raja. Brushing a tear from her eye, Raja takes it.

This kind of exchange took place many times each day, every day for nearly three weeks. At times I got so frustrated, I'd almost scream my words at Raja: "YES! YOU MAY HAVE SOME YOGURT!"

Then mercifully, the pattern broke, Raja showed *me* the way to solve the problem. She added another line to her standard plea: "But I *want* some!" It now went like this: "Mummy, I want a grape!" "Go take one, Raja." "But I want *you* to give it to me." There it was. So simple. I couldn't see the forest for the trees. (I think we, as mothers, often see too many trees!)

My mother-in-law had chuckled at Raja's behavior and said Raja wanted to be argumentative, even to the point of creating an argument where there was none. But I couldn't see the reason for it. Especially not with Raja. She got an abundance of hugging,

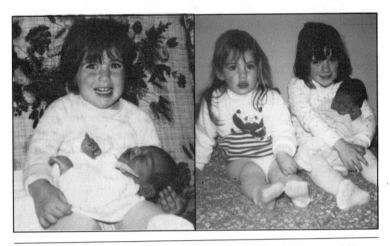

Siblings are special! Vanessa Speed holding Kate, in 1983; Vanessa and Kate with Zoe in 1986. (Story on page 8.)

cuddling, and playing from both her father and me. She was her older brother's favorite playmate. Still, those three weeks she'd been clingier than usual, constantly asking to be picked up, carried, and held in my lap. I don't know why I hadn't connected these actions with her strange protests sooner, but now it all began to fit. Baby Laine was eight months old, crawling, and walking around the furniture. This sudden mobility had occurred almost overnight . . . just three weeks before. The baby was on the brink of toddlerhood, and the former toddler was becoming a little girl. Before going full steam ahead, however, and forever shedding her toddler role, Raja wanted to know that her mummy wouldn't forget her, now that so much was happening around the house. A few steps backward now and again are needed to reaffirm one's status before assuming a new role in the hierarchy of growing up.

Grandma to the Rescue

Liliane Johnson
New Jersey
1980

When my second child was born in September, pandemonium broke loose in our home. It had been a difficult pregnancy, in-

cluding emergency surgery during the third month. To compli-
cate matters, I discovered three-year-old Mandy had pinworms
when David was only three weeks old, so I spent the next two
weeks keeping the house spotless. By Christmas, Mandy and I
were badly in need of an understanding referee.

Grandmother and Grandfather visited for a week over the holi-
days, and quite literally rescued us. One night, after my night owl
had finally fallen asleep, I asked my mother-in-law if she had any
suggestions. Fortunately she did, and I'd like to share them.

- **Don't try to be a supermother.** You can't do everything. Mandy
has to learn to adjust to the new baby in her own way and in her
own time. You can't do it for her. Just try to be understanding. Hug
and cuddle her when she allows, but don't force attention on her.

- **Quit organizing every moment with her while baby is sleeping.** Let her take the initiative once in a while. By always approach-
ing her with your idea of an activity and giving her complete
attention every time the baby sleeps, you are overcompensating.
You are harried and not much fun. And she thinks there must be
something dreadfully wrong if you're going to so much trouble to
correct the situation.

- **When the baby wakes, pick him up.** Then unless the baby needs
to nurse immediately, tend to all Mandy's needs (activity, toilet,
food, and drink). Then sit down to nurse David and don't allow
her to interrupt with tantrums or violence. Go to another room if
necessary.

- **Establish routines she can count on**—a story before bed or a quiet
time in the day with you alone. Apart from this, just go about your
business and allow her to participate as she chooses.

- **Make her feel special.** Give her special corners for her toys in
every room and put surprise snacks in the refrigerator she can reach
for herself.

- **Provide her with a playmate**—at home if she isn't ready to be
separated from you yet.

- **Don't expect her to be older than she is.** Also expect her to regress. Let her wear diapers and take the pressure off. Hold her during the night when she has nightmares. Make sure you keep your
promises, because she needs consistency and stability more than
ever right now.

- **Most important**—tell her you love her at least once a day.

Not once did my mother-in-law say, "You spoiled her by giving her too much attention before the new baby's arrival, so what do you expect?" or "If you'd given her the attention she needed when she was little, you wouldn't have this problem now."

Grandmother and Grandfather weren't even on the plane before I started implementing my mother-in-law's suggestions. In three weeks Mandy was singing around the house again, and although we still have some problems to work out, I think we can manage until Grandma's next visit.

Big Sisters Are Special

Margaret Utt
California
1983

Our first baby, Heidi, now four-and-a-half, was a tremendous joy to us, and yet Kirsti's birth and growth have been that much more fun because we've been able to share it all with Heidi. Heidi watched with me in the doctor's office while the nurse confirmed my pregnancy, and she was the one who told the delightful news, "Mommy's pregnant," to Daddy over the phone. She looked with fascination at photographs of babies the same age as "ours" in the book, *A Child Is Born*. And she loved going with me to doctor's appointments so she could listen to baby's heartbeat.

We tried to prepare Heidi realistically for life with a baby. Together we noticed newborns on shopping trips, and I would point out how they mostly slept—or cried. We talked about how babies put everything in their mouths, and she became used to keeping tiny toys up high even before Kirsti was born.

My husband, Charles, and I felt very strongly that Heidi should be present at the birth. She would be three-and-a-half when the baby was born. Interestingly enough, it was our doctor who suggested it first, as she had just had her fourth baby at home with her other children present. The doctor gave us the name of a book to read to Heidi to prepare her. Heidi was enthralled with it, and we had to read it daily. My mother planned her vacation for the baby's due date and came all the way from East Africa to be here for the birth. Charles' mother wanted to see her grandchild born so much she endured a twenty-four hour bus ride to be here. Luckily, then, Heidi had two grandmothers to take care of her during the labor and birth.

We never made it to the Alternate Birth Room where relatives are allowed, as complications set in just after we arrived at the hospital. My mother saw them take me into the delivery room, and she called my mother-in-law who brought Heidi and held her up in the doorway to see the birth. The nurse started to protest, but she was too busy trying to set up for a possible cesarean. Kirsten was coming too fast for that, and indeed both mothers and Heidi saw her actual birth from the doorway, just a few feet behind my head. As planned, Heidi was the one who told her grandmas the baby's name—she had kept it a secret with us until she saw the baby was a girl. The look of awe and wonder on Heidi's face as she saw and held her brand-new sister for the first time will illuminate my memories for the rest of my life.

Many skeptics worry that witnessing a birth will traumatize a child. I can only say Heidi witnessed a birth where things were definitely going wrong, but she wasn't at all upset by it. For several months after Kirsti's birth, Heidi begged to see the birth pictures at least once a day. She loved them and would tell the story of the birth over and over again as she lingered over each picture. If the birth had "traumatized" her, I'm sure she would not have cherished the birth pictures so much.

She was thrilled when we brought Kirsti home, and we all gave Heidi lots of attention and complimented her greatly on her "Big Sisterly" skills. Every diaper change required big sister's help with the tabs on the disposable diapers. She insisted we bathe Kirsti with her (we floated the little inflatable bathtub inside the big tub with Heidi). She wanted to hold Kirsti endlessly.

With time, Heidi found things only she could do for the baby. She would sing specially composed songs to her sister and delight in bringing her toys. Kirsti has always had special smiles and laughs only for her sister. Shunning her mobiles, she would stare at her dancing, magical Big Sister obviously thinking, "What a wonderful toy a sister is!"

Jealousy? Sibling problems? I'm sure there will be. But in the first year the sisterly relationship has been very positive. We feel that much of Heidi's easy acceptance of Kirsten resulted from her complete involvement in the pregnancy from the start. We don't believe that every child should be present at their sibling's birth. But we do feel it should be an available option and that we parents know, if we'd trust our deep feelings, whether our older child should be at the birth. How wonderful it would be if all doctors and hospitals gave us this option! The relationship, the bonding, between big brothers and sisters and the new baby is very important, and can be wonderful, as Heidi and Kirsti have shown us.

12

Love Across the Generations

Special Insight

Lynn Wannberg
Utah
1980

My husband's grandmother is one of those terrific ladies who, when any of her grandchildren or great-grandchildren are crabby or out of sorts, picks them up and sympathetically soothes them and says to their annoyed parent, "Be kind to him. It's probably his teeth, and you know how teething hurts."

This is a ritual we go through from three months to five years. I finally pinned her down and asked if she really believed it's always teething pain that causes the baby or toddler to misbehave or cry.

From her years of wisdom she said, "Of course not, but as adults we seem to need reasons for our children's behavior. If we believe the child is in some hidden discomfort because of vague teething pain, we are much more sympathetic to his need for attention than if we don't see any obvious reason for his whining."

How right she is. I've seen her magic work on fathers who would have gladly thrown the eighteen-month-old out the door just a few moments ago, now walking around the yard patiently inspecting the shrubs, giving that individual attention the baby needed all along to help distract him from "teething pain." What special insight grandmas have!

Old-Fashioned Ideas

Barb Krahn
Wisconsin
1980

I recently had a long, involved talk about babies with my grand-mother, who is over ninety. This was new ground for us. I never brought it up for fear of upsetting her with my approach, and she never mentioned it because she was sure I would disagree with her "old-fashioned" ideas.

My mother was born seventy years ago at home, where almost all babies entered the world. Back then most doctors made house calls. While the doctor and close women friends attended to

Grandmother's needs, Grandpa boiled water in the kitchen (yes, it really was done) so that any instruments that might be needed could be sterilized. None were needed, and my mother's first experience after birth was to nurse. Demand feeding was the rule, and schedules were unheard of. Grandma's sisters stayed for the first month to do the housework and to help take in Grandma's wardrobe so that she could wear the same dresses she had worn during her pregnancy.

Solids were begun late (she didn't remember exactly when) by using mashed foods. Solids were considered a supplement to nursing. My mother nursed until toddlerhood.

When my grandmother realized that I not only accepted her ideas, but agreed with them, she went on to talk about the importance of mother and baby being together. She mentioned that not only does the child need the mother, but the mother needs the child. "Attention and love cannot spoil any child," she said. Seventy years ago, children usually went everywhere with their mothers, including to work. My grandmother proudly told me, "If I was invited to a friend's house and Margaret was not included, I didn't go. They had to include us as a pair." Considering babies to be babies for only the first year is overlooking a lot, she felt, and perhaps we should still consider them babies at two and three, and sometimes extending beyond three.

With all this in mind, I want to thank all mothers and grandmothers who have passed this "old-fashioned" legacy of mothering on to their daughters and granddaughters.

A Changed Attitude

Kathy Heidemann
Illinois
1982

My daughter, Jill, is now three months old, the first baby in the family in a long while. Because of this, a "ladies only" afternoon luncheon was given by my grandmother in Jill's honor. About a dozen or so ladies attended—many great aunts, aunts, and older ladies who are friends of the family, as well as my mother. Things were going fine, till breastfeeding came up. Many of the older ladies who had never been married were appalled at the idea—especially breastfeeding in public. (I had been advised earlier that I should feed Jill in the bedroom.) One comment led to another and before I had a chance to defend my position, the entire group of ladies were discussing the disadvantages of breastfeeding.

I sat politely, like a good little granddaughter, but all the while feeling terribly intimidated—until my Great Aunt Maita told this story. She and her husband were German-born Americans, and when their son was born they decided to return to Germany so they could visit relatives and show off their new baby.

But their visit was untimely. World War II broke out and they were in the middle of it. Although they had American passports, Hitler didn't pay much mind; they were German-born. They drafted Great Aunt Maita's husband for the German army and she was told she could leave the country. Maita ended up on a boxcar with her new son, not knowing where the train was headed. There were dozens of people in a single car, no place to sit, no sanitary conditions, only one dry sandwich per day with water. Thank God, Maita had decided to breastfeed. These conditions continued for several weeks, and if it hadn't been for breastfeeding her son would not have survived; she knows that. Maita herself became sick and undernourished as did her son—but they survived. At this point in the luncheon everyone was quiet, many recalling the memory of Maita's first husband who was never seen or heard from again. Maita had tears in her eyes as did several of the others.

Great Aunt Maita had come to my defense. It took a lot out of her to tell that painful story she had tried so hard to forget, but she had done it for me and my baby Jill. At that moment, in the stark silence, I was so very proud to be a breastfeeding mother.

The subject was changed quickly and the afternoon rolled on. Later that day I breastfed Jill in the living room *in front* of the ladies, and not a negative word was said. Although I know many of the ladies will never approve or accept breastfeeding, they now tolerate our feeding time, and for me that is enough. To this day, no one who was at that luncheon has ever made a negative remark.

Sweet Memories

Mary Lou Mullins
Michigan
1984

While I was expecting Christopher (now ten months old), I could hardly wait to relive those beautiful moments of nursing. I had nursed Scott (now four-and-a-half years old) and then, two years later, gave birth to two tiny girls who did not survive. Nursing Christopher brought back so clearly the special memories of my experience nursing Scott.

Then I began to wonder how long these memories would remain so clearly in my mind. Would it be ten, twenty, or maybe thirty years? Perhaps I should start a diary.

About this time, I made an emergency trip to see my grandmother. Christopher was then five weeks old. During the week Chris and I spent with her, she talked of her nursing experience with her only child—I was amazed that she remembered it so clearly. Those sweet, gentle memories were sixty-five years old! It didn't end there either. She also remembered pulling the chair over to her mother's side so she could nurse. That memory was eighty-four years old!

I met many of my grandmother's friends during my stay. My grandmother would proudly announce that I was nursing my baby. Immediately, I'd notice a change in them. Their faces would soften, and they would completely relax. Then they would share with me their own nursing experiences. It was so beautiful. Now I know—these wonderful days will stay with me always.

A Precious Photograph

Kay Wallin
Illinois
1983

Recently, my husband's Aunt Eleanor, who is in her late seventies, was sorting through an old box of pictures. She ran across a very special picture of her mother, Anna Wallin, nursing her younger brother, Norman, who is now my father-in-law.

Aunt Eleanor knows how important nursing is to me and my children, so she sent the picture to me. Needless to say I was thrilled when I opened her letter and found such a precious keepsake. What a beautiful gift to hand down from generation to generation! I find it interesting that someone was thoughtful enough to take this special picture.

Anna Wallin is remembered as a warm, loving woman who always had time for her children. Eleanor can remember her mother nursing her young siblings. The love that she gave to her babies almost a century ago still lives on through her children, grandchildren, and great-grandchildren. When there are family get-togethers, the feeling of love is everywhere.

The picture I received of Anna nursing her son was sixty-five years old. Today I am nursing our third child, Eleanor, who was named after her great-aunt.

It's a good way to mother, even in the 80s!

Live and Let Live

Cathy Thomas
Tennessee
1980

When my husband was in Vietnam, I went to live with my in-laws with our first daughter, who was three months old. I remember feeling I would just explode if grandmother said one more thing about using a bottle, and I even had my "telling her off" speeches all rehearsed in my mind. But I knew this wouldn't really help our situation. And despite my bruised self-confidence and growing resentment, I knew that my mother-in-law and I still shared at least one common bond: our mutual love for her son, my husband.

I kept remembering my psychology teacher telling us, "Much of human behavior is motivated by the need to protect one's own self-image." In other words, we all need to feel good about ourselves and if someone makes us feel bad about ourselves, it is a natural reaction to defend our self-esteem by attacking the offender. Boy, could I identify with that because I felt that was exactly what she was doing to me; but could it be that she too felt that I made her look bad to herself?

I tried to put myself in her place and imagine what she might be feeling. My thoughts went like this: she has devoted her whole life to the love and rearing of her three sons. She did for them what she felt was right, with the support of her doctor: nursing the first two a short time and the baby (my husband) just a month. He did just fine on the bottle, she thought. The boys grew up and each one chose another woman to be the center of his world. I was the most recent offender, the baby snatcher. It occurred to me, "That's got to be a hurtful process—to see a son grow up and away and then cleave to someone else when it was her mothering and nurturing that enabled him to do so in the first place!" She could comfort herself in knowing she mothered him well, as her son is someone to be proud of. Then her baby suddenly had a wife and baby of his own. And on top of that, I had the audacity to succeed at what she had failed at: breastfeeding. Could this mean that her daughter-in-law was a better mother than she? Could she have been a better mother? Certainly it was too late to wonder about that.

It became very clear to me that both of us were caught up in a vicious cycle of attack and defense of our mother images. I tried to think of ways to break the cycle. I came to the conclusion that it really was not *what* I was doing that bothered her, but *how* what I was doing was making *her* feel about herself. I no longer felt the need to defend myself with endless explanations of why breastfeeding was better. I decided that I needed to let her know in some way that I thought she was a good mother even though there were many points on which I disagreed with her. After all, this woman raised the love of my life, and his strengths and wonderful qualities are a direct result of her good mothering. I remember saying to her one day, "If my children grow up to be as responsible and considerate as Kent, I will have done something to be proud of." She smiled, and the day went better because I was not defending my actions. The verbal attacks began to come far less often. When I did get a "Well, in my day" lecture on, for example, delaying solids, I was careful to listen to all she had to say. Then I tried to make a non-threatening comment—such as, "I know what I am doing must seem very strange to you, as it is different from what was recommended then, but I feel comfortable with it. It makes me wonder what new changes I will be facing when my children are grown." I tried not to say, "You are wrong and I am right," which would certainly invite retaliation. I tried to offer an acknowledgment that methods are different, an understanding of her questions, and finally agreement that changes are hard to accept.

I was sure at this point that she was not going to change her opinions. My attempts to enlighten her only seemed to increase tension between us. Like all relationships, it took working at (and still does) and the sacrificing of my normally outspoken nature, but the resulting respect and friendship were well worth it. She learned to respect my need to be me without feeling it threatened the worth of her own mothering experience. As for me, I could enjoy being with her without the anger and rage I once felt.

It is my hope that writing this down will serve to remind me to "live and let live" when it comes my turn to be the mother-in-law!

13

Families in Other Cultures

*"No matter what our cultural or religious background,
no matter where in the world we were born, no matter
how different we might be in many respects,
breastfeeding parents have something in common."*

Edwina Froehlich, LLL Founder, 1983

The Welcoming

Delores Friesen
Ghana
1975

Having a baby in Africa is doubly fun, since children are so desired
and loved here. Our first daughter, Rachel, was born in Blooming-
ton, Indiana, but came with us to Nigeria when she was six
months old. Her sister, Ingred, was born in Ibadan, Nigeria, at
a large university teaching hospital.

For our son's birth, we chose a private Ghanaian clinic where
the doctor is happy to have fathers participate, and my husband
was with me for the first time. It pleased our Ghanaian friends
greatly that Jonathan was born in Ghana.

I still hear occasional comments, such as "I didn't know Euro-
peans could nurse their babies," or "Where's his food?" Every
baby's cry here tends to be interpreted as a hunger cry, so it is
not hard to follow a demand schedule. In fact, in Nigeria, when

Ingred was small, people sitting near me in church services or meetings often said, "Nurse her, nurse her."

A few weeks after Jonathan's birth we invited friends and neighbors for an outdoor naming ceremony. We adapted the traditional customs to suit our own beliefs and had a wonderful time celebrating his birth and receiving additional names from those who came. A lovely motherly Ghanaian widow, who had no children of her own, took the elder's role and introduced Jonathan to the world and to life by placing his foot on the earth, giving him the symbols to taste, and introducing him to our assembled friends. Here are some excerpts from the ceremony.

You are welcome! Akwaba! Welcome! (If the following words refer to you, please join in saying them.)

> *We are here as friends: this is a time to celebrate together.*
> *We speak and act for the family and for friends far away.*
> *We are here because we are neighbors.*
> *Sharing everyday troubles and joys: trying to live in love.*
> *We children are here because the baby*
> *Belongs among us; we will play with him.*
> *We are here as mothers—and grandmothers—*
> *We have seen it all before—the joy renewed with each child.*
> *We are here as fathers.*
> *Proud of our children, knowing the responsibilities.*
> *We are here as Brothers and Fathers and Sisters. . . .*
> *We all belong to God's family. . . .*
> *Parents say: We bring this baby: he too has a place.*
> *We invite you to share our joy and to help in our responsibilities.*
> *All: You are welcome! Akwaba! Welcome!*
> *An elder asks: What name is the child to be given?*
> (Names and their meanings are given. The baby is carried around so that everybody can greet him, using any of the names.)
> *You are welcome! Akwaba! Welcome!*
> (The baby is carried to the threshold of the front door and his foot placed on the earth.)
> *The elder says: The earth is the Lord's and the fullness thereof*
> *The world and those who dwell therein.*
> (Baby is carried to a nearby table where there are some everyday things.)

*The elder says: Here are symbols of the good things of life,
symbols of what man is seeking after.*

*Water is for refreshment, the quenching of our thirst, the
satisfaction of our desires.*

*Salt is for seasoning, to save life from dullness and drabness,
to freshen things and to preserve the good.*

All: We wish you the good things of life.

*Elder: But the symbols of man's desires are also symbols of di-
visions among men. Oil is for peace, the peace which comes
after discord, the peace which God gives in the midst of
confusion.*

Milk and honey are for the sure Promise of God.

*Milk speaks of the care a child receives from his parents and
the daily care of the Heavenly Father.*

*Honey symbolizes the sweetness of life, that special quality
that gives joy and meaning to life. The sweetness of life has
to be shared with justice for peace.*

*(The symbols are passed around for everyone to taste
and share: by so doing, we celebrate the gifts of God
that are a part of our life, and we accept responsibility for their use. . . .)*

Close and Cozy

Ellen Davis
British Columbia
1982

After a ten-year absence my husband, Mas, recently returned to
visit his family in Japan. However, this time he had a wife and
an eight-month-old baby boy in tow. It was my first chance to see
my "in-laws" and to learn about mothering in Japan. My husband's two sisters both had young children and I also talked with
several young mothers in the neighborhood. They were a little
surprised that a North American was nursing her baby.

At once I noticed how much the Japanese carry their children.
Strollers are rarely seen. Babies perch happily on their mother's
back in cloth baby carriers. Baby goes everywhere with mother:
cycling to the food stores, off to visit neighbors for a cup of mild
green tea, or down to the big modern department stores. There

are special coats and capes that fit over mother and baby to keep them cozy in winter. The fashions are adapted for keeping mother and child close.

I was most impressed with the local department store in Kawagoe, near Tokyo. There was a large nursery adjacent to the baby department, equipped with a kitchen, cribs, and toys. Mothers could take a break from shopping and chat with other women, if they wished. Also an impressive variety of clever baby items were available: socks with non-skid soles—these had hundreds of rubber dots on the bottom; fine wool diaper covers with stick-on velcro fasteners—no pins to fight with and so easy to adjust to fit. The Japanese really treasure their children and have employed all their ingenuity in making baby clothes and accessories.

However, the custom that changed our lives was the Japanese practice of sleeping with baby on the tatami mats. I had tried to sleep with Shawn in Canada but was afraid he'd fall out of bed. In Japan we felt warm and safe sleeping on the mats and it was easier to nurse him in the middle of the night, too. The day we returned to Canada my husband headed for our bed and took off the legs. We added another single bed next to it and voila, the family bed Japanese style.

Products of the State

Nancy R. Sherwood
Poland
1981

I am an LLL Leader living in Poland. Since this is a Communist country and La Leche League views would be considered political, I don't have an active LLL Group. In fact, I don't have very many Polish friends. My husband is a consul at the American Consulate here in Poznan (the only other consulate in town is Soviet). As we are American diplomats, most of the local people avoid us rather than risk the surveillance and possible harassment that associating with us would bring.

There is a common belief that life is too "stressful" here in Poland for most mothers to be able to nurse their babies. The consensus is "breastfeeding is nice—if you can do it." Doctors do tell mothers that breast milk is the best food, and all babies do nurse while in the hospital. However, a strict four-hour schedule is observed. If the baby is fussy before four hours are up, he is given a pacifier and told that crying is "not permitted." Often the pacifier is dipped in sugar so that baby won't refuse it. Night nursing is altogether discouraged. When the baby wakes at night, he gets tea, juice, soup, or formula. Most of the women I have spoken to say that by the time they leave the hospital they have stopped breastfeeding.

Women are given a one month mandatory paid leave from their jobs. One problem with this is that it's not uncommon for the woman to enter the hospital days or even weeks before she actually goes into labor. This is because there is a shortage of hospital beds, and there's a chance that otherwise the woman won't get a bed. (I don't know what happens then!) The minute she enters the hospital, maternity leave begins. Beyond the one month paid leave, mothers are allowed up to two years unpaid leave. After that if the mother chooses to stay home, she loses all medical care privileges for herself and her children. (The medical care in Poland is socialized—free to workers.) This means that only the husband is bringing in money, and the family has to pay for expensive, private medical care. Also, certain food supplements for children are not available to the non-working mother.

On the positive side, mothers of children under twelve years old get off work two hours earlier than everyone else. Most of this time is spent standing in lines—lines are a block long for meat, as there are always shortages. In the winter, there are also lines wherever fruit and vegetables are available.

When women enter the hospital to give birth, their husbands are not allowed to visit. Period. Husbands are always standing on the sidewalk in front of the big maternity hospital here. Their wives lean out the window, and they call out to each other. I go past there all the time and witness this heartbreaking scene.

Once the mother is home, the father does share in child care—feeding the baby, taking it out in its buggy, hanging diapers on the line. Generally, even though both the husband and wife work, the wife is expected to do the housework, shopping, and cooking as well as child care.

Pacifiers are universally used to soothe the baby. Babies are walked in their buggy a lot and rocked in their buggy when fussy. In the year that I've been here, I have only once seen a baby taken out of its buggy to be soothed. That was after at least ten minutes of vigorous buggy-rocking by both parents and attempts to push the pacifier into the baby's mouth. Parents do talk to their babies in soothing voices, but I have never seen a pre-walking baby being carried in arms. They are always in buggies. Babies that can walk are either in strollers or are walking—they do not often get carried.

Nursing older babies is unheard of among the current generation. People are not upset that I am nursing a two-year-old. They are just amazed that it can be done. Generally, people say that my daughter's still nursing is probably why she is so nice, smart, and healthier than most Polish children. One older woman saw me nursing Courtney when she was about eighteen months old. The woman put her hands to her breasts and said she nursed her babies for two years, as had her mother before her. She said her two-year-old grandson had only been breastfed for six days. I don't speak much Polish, and this woman didn't speak any English, but she had tears in her eyes at the sight of Courtney nursing. I have not seen a single baby being nursed since I've been here, though I know nursing couples do exist.

Poland, being a Communist country, sees children as products of the State, rather than part of a family. I think the state pushes "equality" for men and women and institutionalized care for children, so the State will have the supreme authority—not the parents, who are "just" individuals. As a result, everyone is equally oppressed. I think most Polish women would prefer to be home with their children. It is so different than what we are used to in the United States. It's hard to believe it's real, even though I live here.

If a woman were actually to publicly espouse League philosophy here, she would probably be labeled "dissident" and be subject to harassment and perhaps even prison.

Parenting on a Kibbutz

Donna Ron
Israel
1984

The author of this article lives on a kibbutz, a collective farm in Israel. Parenting customs follow long-established traditions and new ideas or beliefs are not readily accepted.

Without the silent but positive support of my husband, Zimry, I could never have accomplished what I have as a mother. Ein Harod, our kibbutz, was a much different place to be a mother seven years ago—*not only* because of me, *but also* because of him.

I was almost revolutionary here in many ways. And Zimry, although not always agreeing with me (and at times even disagreeing), went along. He once surprised me by acknowledging that we started many of the things that are being done differently here today.

When Yael was a baby, babies here were fed every four hours. No one nursed more than five or six months, and very, very few nursed for as long as three months. Most women did not even go to visit their babies and young children in the "baby house" very often because their work was considered more important. People would go places and leave their babies and children home alone or in the baby house. I was the first person to bring my baby into the communal dining room.

Zimry once had to defend me in front of a committee that met to discuss the way I was feeding Yael. They started the meeting by saying that I couldn't feed her every two hours. He asked them if they thought Yael was developing well (she was a healthy, beautiful baby). When they said, "yes," he asked why I couldn't feed as I wanted. After a discussion of about one-and-a-half hours, they closed by saying that they would continue recommending their infant-feeding practices of the last forty years. Zimry said, "Just because you've done it for forty years doesn't mean it's right."

Zimry is from a culture where women nurse only behind closed doors, yet he has accepted my feeding Yael and Beni on the airplane to visit my parents and in other places. While I breastfed Beni in Rockefeller Center, he walked around with Yael. Zimry was raised in a culture where babies and children slept in the children's house at night. There were many reasons given for this custom; one was that this way parents did not have to be "bothered" by their children at night. Zimry grumbles about it, but he ends up sleeping in our regular bed with me, Eyal, and Beni. *All* the children on our kibbutz now sleep in their parents' houses.

Zimry has criticized me when the house was a mess and I was just sitting, holding, and nursing the baby (whichever baby it happened to be at the time). But one day he came back from working in the cotton fields; Beni, who was just past two at the time, had been with him. He said, "You know, Beni is not like the other children. He is different, very special. The other worker's child who was in the cotton fields just cried all the time. Beni asked questions and looked and learned."

When Zimry was with me for the birth of Eyal, he was the first husband from his group on the kibbutz to do so. Husbands being with their wives during childbirth is a new development here. Zimry was a pioneer and gave me an experience I had always dreamed of having.

When Eyal was a baby, I took him to work with me. The usual procedure here is to leave the baby in the baby house while mother goes to work from the time he is six weeks old. The mothers usually go to nurse or bottle feed their babies every few hours. I was working at the kibbutz switchboard and I decided it would work out to keep him with me instead of being separated. Zimry gave me his silent support and this was totally revolutionary in our community.

It is very difficult amid the daily tensions and struggles of working and raising children to express to our spouses how much we need them, love them, and appreciate them. But I know in my heart that Zimry is truly a helpmate and a partner and that without his belief and trust I couldn't have raised our children as I wanted.

Mothering in Guatemala

Bette Jo Stevens
Guatemala
1982

When our second child, Eric, was one month old we moved to Aguacatan, a small Indian village in northwestern Guatemala, where we lived until he was seven months old. Babies there are nursed on demand. The mothers (or older siblings or grandmothers) carry the babies on their backs, "in minch," most of the time. Babies sleep either "in minch," in a hammock (which is gently swung when the baby starts to toss or turn), or in the family bed. Whenever a baby cries, people usually say "El quiere chiches." Translated that means "He wants his mother's breasts." Babies are nursed anywhere and everywhere.

All a mother needs for her baby in Aguacatan is a shawl or two to carry him "in minch" and to keep him warm, a hammock, old sugar bags for diapers, shirts, and a little hat. How different it is from all that we think we need for babies in the United States.

A very interesting thing about the people of Aguacatan is that despite their difficult lives (i.e., most of the people have to carry to their homes all the water and firewood they use), they are generally an exceptionally cheerful and generous people.

When I came to Aguacatan, I thought the people would be impressed that the "gringa" nursed her baby just as they did. They weren't. People didn't seem to notice that I nursed him as I walked down the street or when he was fussy at the market. I think that giving him a bottle would have gotten a lot more attention.

Eric usually sleeps between me and Michelle (our three-year-old). But sometimes he sleeps in the small hammock above our bed. A few times when Michelle was needing attention and he was starting to wake up, I was able to take care of Michelle and rock him back to sleep without ever getting out of bed. Hammocks are great for people of all ages.

When in Doubt, Nurse

Carol Ann Passmore
Colorado
1978

When Heather, my second child, was born, we lived in university housing and had many neighbors from other countries. Nursing Heather around these neighbors led to several interesting experiences.

I dropped in on Beena, a neighbor from India, and was urged to stay for dinner. When Heather began fussing I realized I was wearing a shift that zipped down the front and could hardly nurse discreetly. Beena's husband, Misra, a very formal person whom I scarcely knew, seemed to be watching my discomfort. I decided that whatever his expectations, he'd just have to accept this strange American custom. As I settled Heather on my somewhat exposed breast, Misra beamed. "My mother nursed me until I was four," he said.

While visiting a woman from Malaya who had three small sons, I began to nurse Heather. My neighbor was astonished and said, "I didn't know Americans did that." I assured her that many Americans did nurse. She had wanted to nurse but failed. She questioned me for an hour.

My third experience made me a confirmed "nurse anywhere" mother. I knew that my German neighbor was an open admirer of the female figure. I also knew Heather was tired, irritable, and would indulge in much shirt-waving, side-switching, and very little nursing. Dieter watched with amusement as I tried unsuccessfully to divert Heather.

"Go on and feed her. People everywhere else nurse until their babies are at least two. Americans are causing non-Westerners to quit nursing and that's terrible, particularly for Third World countries."

I settled Heather to nursing as I listened to the lecture I could have delivered. Since then I've had no problems. When in doubt, go ahead and nurse.

Part Four

Meeting Baby's Needs

An Investment in Love

For Rebecca

Lee Ann Elias
Ontario
1982

Your tears are rainbows
within
prisms in the half-light
of neon signs.
They hover on your lids
before spilling down your cheeks.

I've been told that
you are too young to have tears,
but if you do, they are good for you.
You will be spoiled by my arms,
too much love.
Ah, but you are too young
to have learned to listen
for footsteps in the hall.

Some people would chastise me
for carrying you during the day,
seeing only my aching back,
not a quiet child, happy mother.
Some would criticize a cluttered
kitchen; dustballs under the bed.

They do not know the peace
that is mine
as I cradle your head
in the crook of my arm.
They do not see the looks,
the smiles, we exchange
when sitting idle,
content,
satisfied,
giving each other what we need.

14

When Baby Cries

"The tiny baby's wants and needs are the same.... If he's crying, he obviously needs something.... If he stops crying when you pick him up and hold him, just keep on holding him and be happy that you are there to satisfy this need."

The Womanly Art of Breastfeeding, 1958

Notes from Grandma

Betty Wagner, LLL Founder, 1977

From time to time I hear of parents who are worried about "spoiling" even before their baby is born. It's always amazing to me that they have such a concern. How can they think that one so small and new can be spoiled? A newborn *is* brand new. His brain is new. His feelings are new. His demands are new to him and to his parents. His brain has only a few facts, discovered while still in the womb. You can describe his brain as like a new, unprogrammed computer. It will only have in it what he has experienced. Before birth he may have an understanding of noise, light, and rocking. After birth he quickly learns of wet, dry, faces, singing, hunger, and pain. At birth his little computer brain is ready to receive input from his parents.

School begins at birth. Baby is learning and parents are teaching. You teach by your handling, tone of voice, responsiveness, facial expression, care; all in all, by your giving of tender loving care.

Crying is the only way he can let you know he needs something. He doesn't yet know about you—your feelings, problems, weariness, frustrations, hunger, and anger. His only concern, his only understanding, is himself. It's true at any age—in order to understand others we must first understand ourselves.

So think it over. How can you spoil someone who doesn't understand anything yet? First teach the important lessons, love and trust. Then when your baby/child understands, gently teach discipline. You will be living with this baby/child for years and years. You have lots of time. So relax, enjoy, have fun with the baby, and you will be teaching your baby the very best lessons of all.

Happy Babies Make Happy Mothers

Mary Kuster
Illinois
1982

When David was around two months old, I attended an LLL Couples' Meeting with my husband. The discussion was on not letting your baby cry. I asked how a person could get anything done around the house following this philosophy. The Leaders answered that people were more important than things, and it is possible to get things done in one, two, or three minute stretches. I decided, "What the heck! What have I got to lose? I might as well try it because I'm certainly not too pleased with the way things are going now."

The next morning I began my new regime. When David cried, I picked him up, I rocked him, I nursed him, and his disposition changed almost overnight. It went from "What a temper that baby has" to "What a sweet baby," "Is he always this good?" and "I've never seen such a happy baby." His little personality just blossomed. And happy babies make happy mothers. I relaxed, began to enjoy him, and our nursing relationship became more fulfilling. I certainly became an LLL believer after that. It scares me because I think I might very easily have become the kind of mother I didn't want to be. The example and the support I received turned the tide in the right direction. I will be forever grateful for this help.

Babies Do Cry

Jan Wojcik
Florida
1970

We League Leaders try so very hard not to color motherhood with only shades of rosy pink. And yet—somehow—new mothers are a little surprised to discover that babies do cry and get upset and can create some very real pandemonium.

The picture of a little baby being always and instantly soothed by its mother's breast is a lovely portrait indeed. And it is the rule rather than the exception with a breastfed baby. "Don't let your tiny baby cry," we say, and we mean it. And then we get a phone call. "My baby cries a lot no matter what I do!" There is a feeling of failing at motherhood if a mother can't keep her baby happy. There are doubts as to whether or not the mother's milk might be the cause of the baby's distress. And because we stress that a mother should meet all her baby's needs, there is a concern that the baby may develop psychological problems as a result of prolonged periods of unhappiness.

Why does a baby get so upset that nothing (nursing, rocking, walking, music—nothing) calms him and restores serenity to the household? Immature nervous system? Immature digestive system? Tenseness in the home? Only occasionally can we pinpoint the cause. Most often we just have to accept the fact that the baby is upset and work from there.

Naturally, a mother becomes upset when her baby cannot be comforted. She feels rejected. She feels angry at the baby because he isn't cooperating and at herself because she cannot find the cause and eliminate it. She feels she has failed her baby and herself.

How many times have you heard a friend say, "That baby just cried and cried. I did everything a mother could do, and he still was not comforted. So I just put him in the crib to cry it out."

This is the temptation. What difference does it make whether the baby cries in mother's arms or in the crib?

A lot.

Think how overwhelmed the baby must feel. Something is wrong. Probably the baby doesn't even know what it is. All of us would be frightened if we were crying uncontrollably and didn't even know why. Wouldn't we feel better if someone were around to reassure us? To care that we were upset? Wouldn't we feel rejected if our husband were to say, "Go in the bedroom. I don't want to be around you until you regain control of yourself." Don't we want to be loved in times of stress as well as in times of happiness?

Perhaps our suggestion should be changed to, "Don't let your tiny baby cry—alone. Comfort him. Speak quietly to him. He needs your presence **more** when he's upset." As for emotional problems resulting from periods of unexplainable crying, well, I don't think that a baby who feels absolutely sure of his parents' love will grow up with problems. And what better way to demonstrate your love than by comforting him in times of stress?

It's hard on the mother. We know that. And we sympathize. But the peace of mind that comes from meeting all of a baby's needs more than compensates. And that includes the need for consistent love—even when the baby's not being particularly lovable.

Empathy Is . . .

Miriam Sullinger
Missouri
1980

I am teething and I am miserable. My gums are swollen and they ache. At night, my jaw throbs and keeps me awake. Even my stomach is upset. I don't feel very hungry, but eating seems to soothe my mouth. I have this vague feeling of dissatisfaction.

I am grumpy and fussy because I don't feel very well. No, I am not a baby, an infant, or a toddler—I am a thirty-five-year-old mother with two young sons!

My wisdom teeth are just now coming in and they are making me wise! Wise to the "whys" of how a teething baby feels. I now understand why a baby who is teething is so fussy—he is truly miserable. I now understand why a teething baby seems to want to nurse continuously—he needs soothing. I hope that I will never again get up in the middle of the night feeling so irritated with my young one that I could cry, too. I hope that I will have all the patience and understanding needed for a suffering or confused child—even in the middle of the night!

Thinking about teething from this new perspective may help other mothers to try to be more patient with their children when they are fussy. I know how hard this can be, and I am so thankful for breastfeeding which gives a closer rapport between mother and child.

What Is a Perfect Baby?

Ellen Greist
Kentucky
1977

At a recent League meeting, our Group got into a discussion of baby-mother attachment. While each mother's experience varied, it boiled down to the fact that our breastfed babies all demanded a great deal of our time and attention in one way or another.

What struck me most about the discussion was not the described behaviors, but our attitudes toward these behaviors. When referring to a baby who slept a lot and was generally undemanding, I kept hearing the terms "a perfect child" or "such a good baby." The word "demanding," which we tended to use about our own babies, was negative; we rarely said our baby "asks for" attention or "needs my company," or "is very sociable." We almost always used the term "demand," which conjured up the picture of a little dictator lording it over his serfs.

By the end of our meeting we began to realize that all of this points up yet another instance of our society's confusion regarding the nature of humanity. A baby is naturally active and curious. A need for physical as well as mental closeness and security is normal. Generous amounts of holding and touching are necessary for a baby to thrive and develop normally. That "perfect" eight-month-old who seems to "sleep all the time" or is content to lie quietly in a playpen for many hours may be withdrawing from a world containing too little of the warmth and stimulation he needs.

Isn't He Smart!

Lynette Albritton
Tennessee
1982

I often come across mothers who are frustrated with a baby who seems to cry for "no reason." After three babies I have learned that this is normal, but it doesn't seem to help to tell a mother this. Since I am a "retired" speech pathologist, I rely on my training to reassure them.

My instructors at school told us to be alert for the child whose mother reported that he or she was "such a good baby." This was considered an indication that there was some problem. Since all babies need to be held, the smartest ones would be yelling the loudest when their needs were not being met.

There are no hard and fast rules concerning children, but when a mother tells me her baby cries a lot and likes to be held, I comment, "Oh, how wonderful! Isn't he smart!" Then I relate the information about "good" babies.

Imagine a conversation between one of these mothers and a neighbor or relative as the mother relates this "sign" of intelligence after it is suggested that breast milk may be the reason that the baby cries!

The Tables Have Turned

Sue Powers
Ohio
1982

My three-and-one-half-year-old twins are at the age when I trust them out of my sight, but I still need to know where they are. When I stick my head out the door to call them, I expect an answer if they are within calling range. I get frightened when I call and no one answers with "Here I am" or "What?" My fear turns to anger when I discover they were behind the garage all along, too busy to answer my call. As we were acting out the above scenario for the umpteenth time today, I thought of how the tables have turned.

When Troy and Shawn were small infants, I was often told that letting them cry it out would let them know who's boss. Like most first-time mothers, I tried this several times before realizing I was ignoring very real needs. My babies did not know that I was just in the next room and that I would be back—just as I did not know Troy and Shawn were just behind the garage. As infants they experienced those same feelings of fear and anger when their cries for me went unanswered as I have experienced when I think I cannot find my small boys.

An Investment Pays Off

Judy Good
Ohio
1979

I had a most dismaying December. I spent it flat on my back with pneumonia. Since I usually enjoy vigorous good health, I kept thinking I would get well in a few days; but I was astonished to find out I just couldn't get up, and I didn't even care.

Four of our eight children are married, and we have four grandchildren—add grandparents, aunts, and uncles and you'll realize my Christmas list is long. December is no time for a mother to be sick and there should be a law against it!

The day was saved when our grown-up daughter, Jeanne, came home from the Dominican Republic for a visit. She took care of her sick mother, cooked and cleaned for our family of six, finished the shopping and wrapping, decorated the tree and house, and did the holiday baking.

When I tried to thank her, she told me she had been happy to do it.

I thought back to the time when Jeanne was a baby and we lived in a student housing project with thin walls. Jeanne had colic and she cried and cried. I walked her, rocked her, and nursed her endlessly. The only time we slept was with Jeanne lying on my tummy while I dozed in exhaustion.

Next time you're kept awake by a fussy baby, maybe it'll help to think about how my investment in love paid off. It is a wonderful blessing to have grown-up children to pitch in and save the day! Thanks to Jeanne, our Christmas was relaxed, and Santa came on schedule.

15

No Substitute for Love

Memos from Marian

Marian Tompson, LLL Founder, 1965

Well, it won't be long now, mothers. Soon we will be truly free of all motherly drudgery and ready to make our contribution to the "outside world." For piece by piece, "mother" is being taken out of mothering.

I first got suspicious when they started playing a mechanical heartbeat sound over hospital loudspeaker systems to soothe lonely little ones. Then a newspaper article about "mother heart," an invention of Hiroshi Majima of Japan, brought it all into focus.

For "mother heart," a pillow designed to bring "slumber in peace to squalling infants," is actually a life-size electrically warmed foam rubber breast with a real heartbeat. It feels and sounds, claims the inventor, like a mother's real breast. "A baby grasps hold of the soft, warm, right-size facsimile, puts its mouth on the nipple and its cheek against the electrically turned-on heart."

Children not only fall asleep quickly but there is far less bed-wetting too, a byproduct no one had anticipated.

Makes you thoughtful, doesn't it, and a little hysterical too? Given a few years and enough TV exposure the "heart of the home" might come to mean a throbbing lump of warm foam rubber to a whole generation of children.

The only problem though, as I see it, will be convincing our breastfed babies. . . .

The Real Thing

Laurie Labak
Colorado
1980

Before our first child was born, my husband and I weren't sure how we would handle a newborn's fussy crying spells, so we bought a recording of *Sounds from the Womb*. The heartbeat and other internal sounds of a mother's body were supposed to soothe a fussy newborn. Now, four years and three children later, we have never used the recording. A breastfed baby has no need for a sound recording to put him to sleep. His own mother's heartbeat and warm breast are what he needs.

Likewise, other products of newborn technology have come on the market to comfort a fussy baby. The waterbed crib is unnecessary if you just take the baby to bed with you. So are the super-fortified, ultra-convenient formulas, since breast milk is best, and electric food grinders become superfluous when at six months a breastfed baby wants more than pureed mush.

I could go on and on. A new baby's special needs for nourishment and warm body contact cannot be met by devices and designs of modern science. Mother love, the breast, and an old rocking chair will do just fine.

Toys

Shirley Collins
Indiana
1974

I saw a commercial on television today that made me think of something I'd never thought of before but is so obvious. It was a commercial for a roly-poly face with a squeaky nose and mirror inside. They showed how much a baby loves playing with his mother's face—pointing to her eyes, nose, and so on. The picture then flashed to a baby playing with the above-mentioned toy with the same enthusiasm. The implication was that it was as exciting and pleasurable for the baby to play with and touch the toy as the mother's face.

Then it hit me—the reason for most early infant-development toys. They are a substitute for mother. They're designed to keep baby happy in his crib or playpen, leaving mother free to do "more important things."

Psychologists today talk about the importance of early education. The crib has become a school. But think about it for a moment. What do these toys really accomplish? Aren't all the things they are supposed to do things baby learns better from mother?

Think about some of the various early infant toys. First, motion toys, such as mobiles and wind-up crib ornaments, designed to give the baby a sense of motion, exercise his eyes, and introduce him to a variety of shapes and colors. A baby carried around by his mother doesn't need these toys. As he is carried, he gets a **real** sense of motion. As she moves from room to room, baby is constantly meeting new colors, sounds, and smells.

Next, the texture toys, mirrors, crib gyms, rattles, and toys calling for baby to manipulate something, which teach him to differentiate objects by touch and teach him that he can elicit a response from the environment by his actions. Actually, texture toys replace what a baby feels if he is held regularly. He feels the contrasting textures of mother's (and father's) skin, hair, and various clothing. The mirrors and manipulative toys replace the interaction between mother and baby. Instead of smiling or frowning in response to Mommy or Daddy, he reacts to his own image in the mirror. Rather than receiving vocal or action responses from people, he manipulates inanimate objects.

Then come the cuddly toys and noise-making and musical toys. These obviously substitute for mother's soft arms, her voice, lullabies, and peek-a-boo games.

So don't feel your baby is disadvantaged if he rejects the latest infant educational toys. He has something much more exciting, stimulating, and educational—YOU.

And More Toys

Kathy Emerson
Southern California
1984

As I was tidying up one day, I tried to dazzle my six-month-old with some shiny rattles. They did not interest him for long, however. While I threw the toys into a box so the rug would at least be clear (if not clean!), I started contemplating the myriad objects he already possesses at such a tender age. Despite our tight budget and conscious effort to limit the supply, the room is quite crowded already with stuffed animals, books, puzzles, building sets, cars, balls, and various other sources of stimulation and (supposedly) education. However, what my son noticed most was a swag lamp that began gently swinging when I turned it on. The simple motion caught his eye and continued to hold his attention. He preferred looking at a swaying light instead of the expensive gadgetry I'd plopped down in front of him. Another example is one of my older son's favorite toys—a large metal spool (the kind that bulk chain and wire comes on from the hardware store). It was given to him by a thoughtful clerk who "figured the little tyke could put it to good use."

I have also realized that my children would much rather help me do the dishes than play with their toys. Although it takes twice as long, David at three really can help rinse and stack the dishes, and baby Gregory loves to be in the backpack watching. And while I might not think they're learning anything watching this repetitive chore, I wonder. Will they "learn" anything if I force them to be by themselves with some lifeless, albeit fancy, object? Won't they learn all that basic stuff about motion and such just from daily experiences?

Perhaps what my children really need to learn in this technologically oriented society are the simple lessons about love and caring. And maybe when they're adults, they'll remember the silly songs we used to sing while we washed dishes together. As I look to the future when my children are grown, I want them to spend time **with** my grandchildren, not money **on** them.

Not the Same

Marilyn Lathom
Virginia
1977

In this day of technological entertainment sources such as television and records, it's easy to let them do a great deal of babysitting for us. But we need to remember that these aids can't replace mothering. My four-year-old daughter put it quite succinctly one morning. After listening to one of her record/books, she came to me and said, "Now **you** read it to me, Mommy." When I asked with surprise if she didn't like the way the man on the record read it, she replied, "But he isn't **close** to me like you are when you read it to me."

A Substitute for Mother

Beth Lamb
Illinois
1984

My nursing relationship with my first child, Vanessa, started out very well. I began giving Vanessa bottles of juice when she was five-and-a-half months old. I saw bottles everywhere I looked, and it seemed like the thing to do. A few months later, we received the big news—my husband was being transferred to faraway Chicago. Life had never been so busy, and Vanessa started wanting the bottle more and more often.

At fourteen months of age, Vanessa surprised me by refusing the breast. She wanted only the bottle. I took full advantage of this situation and let her have it as often as she wanted; frequently she took the bottle all by herself. I was expecting my second child, and my pregnancy seemed like a good reason to stop nursing anyway. After all, it was not unusual to see children at stores or in the park with a bottle, and I never gave much thought to any possible problems.

When I was three months pregnant, I started to attend La Leche League meetings again in my new town. I read a paragraph or two in one of my Group's library books about the possibility of the bottle being used as a mothering substitute. This was very hard for me to accept. I decided that it might be true for some but not for me. After all Vanessa had nursed for over a year, which was longer than I had originally planned to nurse her.

Nathan was born at last. The birth went quite well, and as time went on we became very close and very much in tune with each other. I was so sensitive to his needs and just adored him. But what absolutely overwhelmed me was how distant I felt from my daughter. Something was missing between us. This was very difficult for me to accept, since I prided myself on my doing a good job of mothering. I began thinking about all the times she had been left alone with a bottle so that I could attend to household chores. I also reflected on the changes I had seen in Vanessa. Though she had started talking early, her speech development had seemed to slow down. She had been a sociable toddler, but she had recently become withdrawn. The more I thought about it, the more aware I became that the bottle *had* become a mothering substitute. I had come to rely on the bottle to give her the comfort and security she needed, and our relationship had

Beth Lamb on the left with her family in 1984 and below, in 1986, with the addition of Aaron.

suffered for it.

After I realized the mistakes I had made, I set out to make things right. I held Vanessa as often as she wanted and gave her plenty of focused attention. She continued to use the bottle for sucking, but she stayed on my lap instead of going off by herself with it. Housework went much more slowly, and fewer chores got done, but eventually we regained our close, loving relationship. If anything we became even closer than before. Vanessa became much happier. Her personality just blossomed, which made me feel wonderful, and she began talking more. Also, my two children became the best of friends.

Needless to say, my son has never used a bottle. At the age of seventeen months, he is still nursing regularly, and we both enjoy this special relationship.

An Insidious Invasion

Henny Breen
Canada
1983

When our first child, Sarah, was born, I was very concerned that nothing would get in the way of mothering my baby. Therefore, I avoided the use of bottles, soothers, walkers, jumpers, and swings. However, I never realized till recently, now that Sarah is almost three and I have another daughter seven months old, that I had allowed the worst culprit of all to take over mothering for me, and I'm ashamed to say, get in the way of mothering my children. Television—an insidious invader in our home—has finally been controlled.

Possibly my experience will sound familiar to other mothers. It started when Sarah was very young, I enjoyed nursing her while reading a book or while watching television. However, as she got older, it became too difficult to nurse and read at the same time as she constantly tried to grab the book. Therefore, I watched television. As Sarah was my only child at the time, I could nurse her leisurely while watching television, playing with her during commercials. Thinking back, I realize now that I allowed a lot of my activities to be centered around television programs—Sarah's baths, diaper changes, those long nursing periods, housework, and preparing meals.

Then, when Sarah was old enough to enjoy television herself, I would encourage her to watch it. While she was captivated by the television, I could get my housework done, prepare meals, or peacefully care for my second child. I had discovered the "built-in babysitter." Even the baby would enjoy sitting beside her older sister watching television while I did housework!

This whole addiction came to a head when I found myself denying my children's needs because of television schedules. I couldn't read or play with Sarah till my program was over, and then hers would be on. I rushed her to bed at night for fear of missing a certain program. I began to realize that television was controlling our lives in many ways. My husband and I decided to unplug the television set and move it to the study where it can't be watched. The advantages to our family have been numerous: leisurely meals, more time to spend with the children, Sarah has to develop other ways to entertain herself (which is to her advantage developmentally), long interesting conversations with my husband (instead of quick messages during commercials), and time to read and develop my own interests. How I regret all those wasted hours! Our family life has been enriched enormously by curtailing our television viewing to only one or two hours a week. Sarah may watch television for half an hour per week if she asks, which she rarely does any more because she is too busy playing. To watch television now requires real effort because the heavy, portable set has to be moved to the living room.

It was difficult for me to write about this as I had to come face-to-face with my shortcomings as a mother. However, I feel it may be of some benefit to other mothers to hear of our family's experience.

16

Keeping Baby Close

Memos from Marian

Marian Tompson, LLL Founder, 1972

Almost everyone seems to agree . . . a baby does need a mother for optimum growth and development. The importance of her presence from the first hours after birth and continuing through the early years is being acknowledged and stressed. With mother close at home and always available when needed, the child is much more likely to grow up secure and with a good feeling about himself.

We know, as nursing mothers, how well breastfeeding fits in with this need of our babies. We have to be around; we enjoy being there; and as we respond to their needs with our bodies as well as our minds, we find ourselves experiencing a unique relationship that affects us as much as our babies. Lucky babies—lucky mothers.

For just as baby needs unrestricted mothering, so does mother need unrestricted care of baby to really get to know him and in knowing him to become aware of what motherhood is all about. With this awareness she also becomes secure in her role, gains confidence in herself, and develops a very healthy concept of self.

And while babies do eventually wean, the insights gained earlier continue as the basis for the ever-changing relationship between mother and child. It's a relationship that may have to undergo enormous amounts of strain at times; but this strain is surely eased by the closeness and sensitivity that go back to the beginning.

As you may gather, these are purely personal reflections. Philip, our youngest child, is eight years old now. While I felt at the time that mothering our children through breastfeeding was giving them a good start in life, I'm becoming more and more aware that it also gave me the best possible introduction to my role as mother.

Notes from Grandma

Mary Ann Cahill, LLL Founder, 1980

With the nuclear family the predominant unit in our society, mothers and babies are pretty much on their own. Mother is usually the only "motherly" figure with baby consistently for much of the day. Dad is a welcome addition part of the time, but it seems only natural for baby to keep a close eye on his mainstay, Mom.

So the question comes to mind, would a little one readily accept substitute mothering if our households were large and there were loving aunties and grannies as an everyday part of family life? Can it be that our system of isolating mother and baby develops this intense dependency of baby on mother?

It's easy to think there's something to the oft-heard advice to new mothers, "Leave the baby. He has to learn to get used to others." It's easy to think that, until one is part of a large, diversified family and can see firsthand how a baby responds in an extended family.

Extended is how I think of the nine of us in the bilevel on Paradise Lane—we go down the line, spanning half a century in ages, covering three generations and two distinct families. There are the four youngest Cahills and Mom; and living with us are the Stroms—our daughter Teresa, her husband, Carl, and their two children, Daniel, six, and Angela, almost two.

From birth Angela has enjoyed the good life, surrounded by doting aunties, grandparents, and a big uncle. (Uncle Joe, who has been known to come home at two in the morning, sometimes finds a wee one up and jogs around the house to lull her to sleep.) What child could be more familiar or "used to" the prospective substitutes or sitters who could fill in when mother is gone?

Angela is used to us, of course, but there's no doubt about it, none of us is Mother. There's no mixing up where the bond binds. While there's always someone ready to play, read a story, or just hold Angel Baby, it's obvious to us when the games with Auntie Fran or the stories with Grandma have worn thin. Like a little magnet, she's looking for that one and only Mommy. Nature, not circumstances, dictates the young child's need to be with Mother. No matter the many loved and loving others surrounding this little person, her internal emotional system is geared to the steady reassurance of Mom's presence. There's a lifetime ahead for "getting used to others." More important in the early years is being able to count on **one.**

A Need to Get Away

Becky Coerper
Maryland
1982

When Jeremy, my son, was a newborn, I couldn't imagine leaving him, partially because he was nursing frequently and also because I knew that the smell, the touch, the sound, the look of his own mother were the most familiar landmarks in a sea of strange and new experiences.

A few months went by, he was still nursing often, and I couldn't bear the thought of the anxiety he might feel when his eyes could not find me nor his cries summon me. I wanted him to be able to take for granted the security of my presence whenever he needed it, so that he could be free to explore his world and practice his growing repertoire of skills.

When he was a year old, I still wasn't quite ready to leave him with a sitter. He was walking, climbing, enjoying others' company (and still nursing), but he still seemed to need regular "Mommy checks." When he was about to try something a bit beyond his capabilities, or toddle out of sight after some unknown treasure, he would often turn first to catch my eye and get a nod of approval or smile of encouragement.

Now at sixteen months, he embarks on expeditions of great daring and imagination: to the shed to inspect the boat, up the hill after his rapidly vanishing daddy, across the lawn to play with the neighbors' toys. But before he goes, he stops and gives me a wave "bye-bye." It still seems important to him to make, and be secure in, that contact with me.

Nighttime, too, has its special ritual. After he's been asleep for an hour or so, Jeremy will often waken with a start and cry. I go to him and say, "Wanna nursie, Jere?" The crying stops, he says, "da" (translated "yes"), so we cuddle up and he nurses off to sleep again.

So, Jeremy still doesn't know what a babysitter is. My husband, Kip, and I have left Jeremy a few times (they can be counted on one hand). But it's always been during the day, and he was busy and happy playing with other children.

The road to this seemingly unique place has not been without thorn and mire. When Jere was quite young, friends said, "I'm worried about you. Don't you ever get away by yourself?" Others, surely meaning well, would inquire, "But what about you and Kip? Don't you need time away?" Recently I've been hearing, "You really should get him used to a sitter and take some time away for yourself." And it doesn't help to read in books and magazines that are by and for mothers that it is an absolute must for the well-being of mother and baby to have "away time."

Kip and I have done lots of thinking and talking about Jeremy's needs and about how we want to meet those needs. We've been uneasy about not knowing how our joint absence affects Jeremy's understanding of his relationship to us and his ability to deal with his world. Besides, I really like him and enjoy spending my days with him. Is there anything wrong with really savoring the slowed pace, the perpetual motion, and discovery of a toddler's world? Sure I get tired of it sometimes. Then I pick him up and we visit friends, or he has some time alone with Daddy.

We've been spending endless hours these days reading picture books. I point out the objects, name them, and if they are animals, make the appropriate noises. Today while we were reading, unprompted, he roared at the lions and meowed at the kittens. I was truly surprised and delighted at this new skill mastered and new concept learned. I wouldn't miss that for the world! I guess I'll wait a little longer before I call that sitter.

Mother's Morning In?

Brenda Toomey
Alabama
1984

Mother's Morning In? Well, it's actually something that started out with about six of us and has grown to include more mothers and babies each week. We meet each Thursday morning to sew, talk, mend, nurse, and watch our little ones play.

In our section of the country, Mother's Morning Out programs are very common and widely used. Mothers drop their babies off at the nursery and return later to pick them up. At our church the program is free. When I first started going on Thursday mornings, many of the church women didn't actually leave, they just met in the parlor to visit while their children played in the nursery. I kept my Jamie with me, and even though I was one of the few who did, I felt accepted by the other mothers.

Because of this practice, several of my friends began to come and keep their own babies with them. Our church parlor, although warm and inviting, holds little attraction for two- or three-year-olds. So as our little ones grew, we looked for another way to continue to meet and keep our babies happy, too.

We found it! An unused room was available complete with toys and low tables and chairs. Not only did our church gladly let us meet there, they have even provided us with a coffee pot. Now our group often numbers ten mothers or more, each with one or more children. It's been a perfect solution for us—getting away from the house, meeting with friends, even getting a little needlework done, and all while our children play at our feet.

Music and Mothering

Valerie Hess
Colorado
1984

I had just begun work on my Master's degree in music at a university in northwestern Indiana. After six years of marriage, John and I were pretty sure we couldn't have children, though we hadn't had it officially confirmed. Well, you can imagine our surprise and dismay when we discovered that my "flu" was really pregnancy! After we got over the shock, we decided that we were pleased, though the future, especially my degree, seemed uncertain.

The baby was due in August, and we decided to proceed with my second year of graduate school under two conditions: no babysitters and the baby had to do well breastfeeding. I had heard of La Leche League, but I didn't think I could call them until after the baby was born. Many problems would have been avoided had I known otherwise.

Maggie and Valerie
Hess, 1982

In August, ten days before the next semester and six days after our last childbirth class, Margaret Johanna Hess (Maggie) entered the world.

Maggie was the hit of the music department. John worked out his schedule so that he worked forty hours in three-and-a-half days, mostly on the weekends, so he could be available to watch Maggie. But most of the time Maggie went with me. She nursed in class, in a quiet corner of the library, in the student union. The only thing I couldn't do was nurse her while practicing or taking a lesson, but John was there then.

During the second semester of that final year, Maggie got to the point where she didn't want to stay with Papa while I rushed out for a night class, yet she was too active for me to take to class. After a few distressing days of John trying to comfort her and me worrying about her all through class, we arrived at a solution. I spoke to my professor, and Maggie, John, and I all went to school together those two evenings each week. John would take her out in the hall if she got too disruptive, but just knowing I was available kept her content much of the time. John loved the lectures, and it gave us more to share during a time when we often felt like ships passing in the night.

At my graduate recital, Maggie stayed up and later entertained guests at the reception. At my orals, she and Papa were nervously waiting in the student union for me to finish. She helped write papers, she came to rehearsals, and she loved the few concerts that we managed to get in. In May, she was featured in many of her mother's graduation pictures. Yes, I made it—we made it. I will never do it again, and I don't recommend it to anyone, but there were many positive things about the year. I owe a big "thank you" to my husband, to my professors, and to Maggie's wonderfully mellow and flexible personality.

Accent the Positive

Rona Mandell
Ohio
1975

I'm a great believer in accentuating the positive. When my baby was only a few months old, someone said to me, "You never go anywhere without her, do you?" I answered, "I always take her with me." She said, "That's what I said!" But it wasn't, was it? I like my way better.

Early Childhood Separations

Rose Mary Fahey, Editor, 1967

A most interesting study has been going on at the University Medical Center in Cleveland, Ohio, according to a report published in the magazine *Pediatrics* by John H. Kennell, MD, and Mary E. Bergen, MSW.

A team of pediatricians, psychiatrists, and child psychotherapists have been observing and recording the effects of early childhood separation from the mother in a study that followed thirty-nine children in twenty-one families from the last months of the first pregnancy for the next six years.

An outstanding finding was that every child studied, up to the age of about two and a half years, showed marked reactions to separations from the mother—"no matter how close or how distant the mother-child relationship might be, no matter what the type or length of separation or whether it was the first or fiftieth."

The investigators concluded that such reactions are naturally or biologically determined and are not affected by what the mother does or does not do to avoid them.

Several myths debunked by this study are that a child won't be anxious about separations unless the mother is anxious about leaving him, that a second child becomes independent of the mother more quickly because she is more casual with him, that a child can be "taught" independence by "not giving in to him" when he resists separation. All false, this study indicates.

Though the study is most interesting and indicative, a question might be raised about the child's reacting to separation "no matter whether it is the first separation or the fiftieth" and no matter how it is managed. The data indicate that **all** of this group of children had in fact been separated from the mother fairly often as small babies. None of them had experienced the security of the continual loving presence of the mother during early babyhood. The study therefore does not prove anything about the child who has experienced such security. Our observation has been that such a child, usually long before the age of three, is not troubled by the occasional brief absence of the mother when he is left in the care of other familiar, loving members of the family.

On the other hand, our observations certainly bear out the conclusion that the child under three showing "separation anxiety" (whimpering, clinging, and so on) is **not** manifesting spoiled behavior but a perfectly normal biological reaction. Our own motherly instincts tell us the remedy: avoid the separation until he is ready for it. Saves wear and tear on everybody.

Opportunity of a Lifetime

Pamela Brugman
Minnesota
1982

Pregnancy was lovely! It was our first baby, and I quit a challenging career in order to sew sleepers, kimonos, and diapers. Dreams of the future were a part of my daily routine. My husband, Sam, was in a contest being sponsored through his job. The first place winner would be flying on an all-expenses-paid trip with his wife to Switzerland. This, too, was part of my dreams.

June brought the birth of our beautiful daughter, Sadie. We had a natural, calm delivery, and her birth filled her Daddy's eyes with a sparkle I had never seen before. We were proud parents and extremely happy. Everything was going according to my dreams, everything—until one day in August.

Sam called home from work and I could tell from the bubble in his voice that something important was on his mind. He had won, and we would be going to Switzerland! It was too good to be true. I immediately called our doctor, and he confirmed exactly what I wanted to hear. Sadie was three months old, a perfect age to travel. Since I was breastfeeding there would be no danger with foreign water or warming bottles. She would have me to comfort and nourish her. With a few quick calls, I located our birth records and arranged for passport pictures for all three of us. I called our family and friends to relay the good news and then made myself sit down and catch my breath. That's when the phone rang one more time.

It was Sam, and this time he told me Sadie was not invited to come along. I reacted defensively and told him to tell them if she couldn't go, I wouldn't go. I called my La Leche League Leader, and with her help I found all the information to provide evidence to the contest officials that my daughter should not be separated from me at this time.

The next day my husband called the contest officials. He is a gentle man, and he usually leaves the writing, reading, and speech making to me. I was very proud to hear a man of his nature expounding on his happy daughter. He told them of the benefits of nursing: natural immunities, lack of digestive and constipation problems, and the importance of bonding achieved through breastfeeding. He sounded convincing, but it was not enough.

Meanwhile, I had called Sadie's doctor again. He advised me on formula, explaining how I could keep up my milk supply so that I could return to nursing after the trip. The only problem would be whether Sadie would want to go back to nursing. My emotions were mixed, and I was in a turmoil. I did not want to leave my baby, yet I thought the resentment we would feel if we didn't go could be worse than the short time I would be aching for her while in Switzerland. Sam had worked so hard for this trip. I didn't want to take that away from him or make him feel tied down because of our baby. I made a decision. No matter how much we loved our daughter, I would cheerfully go along with whatever decision he made. He decided we would go and that Sadie would be fine with Grandma.

As I sat for my passport pictures, tears flooded my eyes. I saw Sam holding Sadie, and I thought about the day we would walk onto the plane and wave good-bye to our baby. Few words were exchanged between the two of us as we drove home. I felt torn between my love for my husband and for our daughter. It was probably the longest night of our five-year marriage. Sam spent the night in his easy chair, refusing to talk or come to bed. He wanted to be left alone to think.

As the sun's early light was appearing through our window, he came to tell me we would not be going to Switzerland. He called the contest headquarters to tell them, "Sadie is more important than Switzerland." They were astonished and tried to change his mind. They told him that he was passing up a $4,000 dream, an opportunity of a lifetime. He replied that we would never again have this precious opportunity with our daughter either.

Our daughter is now eight months old and crawling. She has grown, and so have we. Our decision has strengthened our marriage in a way that a dream-like vacation never could have. We do not miss the Swiss Alps; we delight in the view of our daughter as she reaches a new height and stands alone for the first time. Ten days of honeymoon bliss could never compare to the tender love exchanged in just one afternoon of nursing our baby to sleep. Happiness is a fragile thing, so easily dreamed away. Would the beauty of Switzerland's setting sun glow brighter than the happiness in my heart as I gaze at the downy head beneath my cheek? Would a vacation opportunity of a lifetime lift my spirits any higher than the sun that blessed my baby's face this morning? I will never know for sure, but I don't believe so. I have no regrets, and my time is too valuable to waste it dreaming of Switzerland.

17

Baby on the Go

"Babies were not often taken out in public in [the League's early] days. Many times our baby was the only one present at a so-called 'family type' affair. The few baby carriers available were sling-type gadgets made to help support an older baby on mother's hip. I'll never forget when Mary White and I ordered our first Gerry Carriers designed for babies of mountain-climbing parents. We never did use them to climb mountains since Franklin Park is pretty flat, but they sure made it easier to take baby along."

Marian Tompson, LLL Founder, 1981

Mothers soon learned the value of baby carriers.

Kangaroo Mother

Suzette Pruitt
New Mexico
1977

When I first used a baby carrier nine years ago in San Francisco, I seemed to be the only one in town who had one. But through the following months, then years, baby carriers became a common sight in the Bay Area.

Now I can again be seen on my errands with my new baby riding peacefully in a baby carrier. This time, though, I'm in a small town in New Mexico where babies are usually carried in plastic infant seats, and I am again the only one in town to carry my baby this way.

Shopping must be done at a leisurely pace, so I can answer questions from every other person. I never cease to be amazed at the many people who say, "I thought that was a doll!" As he blissfully sleeps away, people ask me, "Are you sure he's comfortable?" Then, "But aren't you uncomfortable?" I can tell that my assurances of our comfort are often met with disbelief, but I realize that those asking probably do not believe as much in the benefits of holding and touching as I do.

When I'm told, "I've never seen a contraption like that before!" I sometimes feel like delivering a lecture on the many civilizations where women keep their babies on their bodies all through infancy and how they don't have the social and psychiatric problems our society has. But mostly, I try to hold my tongue and let my baby's good-naturedness speak as an example of the benefits of the carrier. Though he's still only a few months old, he's already received many compliments on being "such a good boy!"

I sometimes get somewhat irritated at the people who can't resist jiggling the arm or leg that hangs outside the carrier, even when he's asleep. Of course, he generates more interest than the babies carried in infant seats, and he's already quite well-known around town. If I shop without him, strangers (I thought) say to me, "Where's your papoose?" or "Did your baby outgrow his 'thing'?"

One of the funniest comments I've had, though, was from a middle-aged lady who spied me and ran over to me giggling, "Oh! Are you a kangaroo?" As I stood, taken aback, trying to think of a clever answer to that one, she explained that she'd once seen

Photo of Suzette with Zack that was used in 1977, and the two of them again in 1986.

a cartoon of a little boy posing that question to a lady attired similarly.

A "fad" that has practical and pleasurable implications soon catches on, though, and I've been getting inquiries for order forms, so I won't be the "only one in town" with a marsupial baby. I hope before long to be just "one of the crowd."

Square Dancing

Paulette Fick
Missouri
1876

In planning for our daughter's birth nearly a year ago, I looked forward to slowing down my outside activities and relaxing in the joy of a new baby with my family surrounding us in the warmth of the fireside hearth. Alas, the best of intentions broke in the wave of reality.

The school-age children had activities that required mother's presence, and my husband's business required a few social evenings. It was my husband who set the pace and decided that Marita should be wherever I was. It was he who paved the way for us whenever possible, such as the time we were invited to St. Louis for dinner and the Muny opera—he simply asked our hosts if we might bring the baby along, and they said "of course."

Square dancing is one of our pleasures, and we belong to a club that dances biweekly. It's great exercise, so I danced until a week before the baby was born. When she was six weeks old, we bundled her up and took her with us to the dance. The group meets at a church that has a small nursery with cribs and a rocking chair, a quiet place for nursing. There were always any number of willing arms to hold her while we danced a tip or two.

There have been many family outings that Marita has fit into with ease. Snug in her carrier, up front where I can keep a watchful eye on her, she has accompanied us to the zoo, 4-H activities, county fairs, picnics, vacation trips, and the home town centennial celebration. Taking her with us has been a good experience for all of us—it is such a simple way of life.

Wilderness Camping

Linda Schreiner
Washington
1972

Hiking, backpacking, and tent camping in the mountains and along the rugged ocean beaches of Washington have always been favorite activities of ours. When our son, Peter, now almost two, was born at the very start of the summer camping season, we knew we would find a way to continue our wilderness outings with a new nursing baby.

Camping with the baby was not the complicated, expensive production I thought it would be. We found that a little extra planning, plus disposable diapers and a baby carrier, were the only really necessary additions to our regular camping gear. We did invest in a portable crib, but the baby quickly outgrew it, and I'm not sure it made things any easier. Most of the time he slept with us on the ground in our zipped-together double sleeping bag; it made middle-of-the-night nursing warmer and easier.

We began camping with Peter when he was five weeks old, and since then he has been over rugged mountain trails, splashed in mountain streams, and slept in his backpack over many miles of ocean beach. We have taken him camping in all weather—from stormy, rainy early spring to hot, sunny summer to frosty autumn. As long as the baby is properly clothed and protected, we have found that we can go just about anywhere. Of course, we have the benefit of an ideal climate in western Washington: mild temperatures year-round, fairly predictable (always expect drizzle) weather, and very little potential danger from large animals, snakes, or insects. But where conditions are not so ideal, common sense should dictate the necessary precautions to take.

Plan carefully, be realistically prepared, then relax and have fun. The beauty, peace, and adventure of the wilderness are there to be enjoyed, now, **with** your little one.

Mother of the Bride

Barbara Sobey
New York
1984

Holly, my twenty-one-year-old daughter, recently got married. She is the oldest of our eleven children. My two youngest children, Danny, nine months old, and his two-year-old sister, Cindy, are both nursing.

We decided early on that we wanted our babies with us during the ceremony. They go to church with us every Sunday, but if they get restless, I take them outside. If they had to be taken out of the church during the wedding, I certainly did not want to be the one to leave, nor did I want either grandmother to miss the ceremony. Because our other children were all in the wedding party, I found a babysitter for the first time in many years. A family friend, Kathy, was hired to come along with us on Holly's wedding day and help with the two little ones from 11 AM to 11 PM. On the morning of the wedding, we all had our hair done by a friend who came to our house. This saved spending a lot of time at a beauty salon. Kathy helped the bridal party dress while I nursed the babies. While I dressed, she dressed the babies.

In church, Kathy sat in the second pew with the babies and grandmothers. In the middle of the ceremony, just as I was getting weepy, I heard a familiar sound—the hiccups. Kathy took Danny outside where the fresh air soon cured him.

Just before entering the reception hall, I took the two little ones into a small quiet room, nursed them, diapered them, and spent an additional fifteen minutes playing with them. Then I took them into the reception and to their own table. We had a special table placed against the wall behind ours. Kathy sat at that table, with Danny in his stroller next to her; Cindy and four of our younger children also sat there. Danny watched the action on the dance floor for about fifteen minutes, then fell asleep for the remainder of the reception. Cindy, who is used to dancing with her older sisters, got up and danced the night away. She provided the entertainment for those who could no longer dance. Kathy watched out for the others and assisted them with their meals. I was only a few feet away if any of them needed me.

I enjoyed myself knowing that my babies were close by, and yet because I hired Kathy, I did not have to constantly keep an eye on them or worry about them.

Most people commented on how wonderful it was to see the entire family present. In fact, when the minister asked, "Who gives this woman?" my husband answered, "We all do."

Second Honeymoon

Leilani Eveland
Georgia
1979

When Jenny was five months old, we planned a vacation to Hawaii. Three weeks would be spent with relatives who live there, but my husband and I planned two days in a hotel on the beach as a "second honeymoon." We had always taken Jenny with us wherever we went so it just seemed natural that we take her with us now. Our friends thought we were crazy, but as it worked out, we would have missed so many special moments in those days without her.

Paul and I arranged to have Grandma come and spend the afternoons with Jennifer up in the hotel room while he and I bathed in the warm Hawaiian sun under the palm trees. It was heavenly to have a special time together, just the two of us. When Jennifer wanted to nurse or just needed the closeness of her mother and father, Grandma would signal by waving my red shirt from the hotel balcony. We'd go up and spend some time with Jenny, then I'd nurse her to sleep and we'd return to the beach.

We spent the late afternoon playing with our daughter and strolling on Waikiki beach. In the evening, I nursed Jennifer to sleep . . . so peaceful and contented she was, so happy to be with her mother and father. Grandma came up to the room while Paul and I went on the sunset sail out to Diamond Head. It was so romantic! We returned just a few minutes before Jennifer woke up to nurse again. What perfect timing! Grandma left saying she'd be back the following afternoon. So, you see, we had our time together, but without shutting out baby. She needs us so much, and a breastfed baby is so portable and easy to please.

The Only Way to Travel

Jane Neiswender
Bolivia
1984

My husband and I have just recently returned from twelve rigorous weeks of survival training in the jungles of Chiapas, Mexico. We are missionaries, and our ten-month-old son, Josh, was born in Bolivia just two months before we were due to come back to the United States on furlough. I had planned on breastfeeding him, and now I'm so glad I did. Not only could we travel for long periods with ease because Josh had his food whenever he needed it, but I have learned that a breastfeeding mother needn't think she has to stay home, she can go anywhere and everywhere.

Our travels included an all-night train ride, a dusty, night-long bus trip over winding, rough roads, living for six weeks in a thatched-roofed, dirt-floored adobe hut, hiking, getting up at odd hours, living for four weeks in an isolated area where we built our own shelter and cooked on our own homemade mud stove, then two more weeks living in an Indian village in a small, primitive hut. What an adventure! People ask how we could have possibly done all this with a small baby. It was difficult, but breastfeeding made it a whole lot simpler.

Bugs, snakes, primitive conditions, and unsanitary water were our constant companions in Mexico. We really roughed it, but all the while Josh thrived and grew on breast milk. By the time we left our Mexico survival training, Josh was eating solids but still nursed frequently. I saw to it that I got good food and enough liquids. Despite our new surroundings and sometimes hard physical work, my milk supply was fine. (This is an answer for those who will tell you that unless you take it easy you'll lose your milk.) Another important advantage was that Josh was receiving valuable immunity to disease. Many times on hikes, the only food he had was breast milk, and it satisfied him.

At ten months of age, Josh still enjoys nursing, and it gives him the security he will need for our future travels. I really believe it is one of the things that has helped him to adjust so well and has kept him so healthy. I'm thankful that God so wisely and lovingly created mother's milk so that mother and baby can begin their lives together with a unique closeness and security in each other. So mothers, **don't** feel tied down by breastfeeding, it's the **only** way to travel!

Island Jungle

Louise Thornton
1969

Many people dream of going to live on a South Sea island but how many people would dare go with an eight-month-old baby? My husband and I dared and never regretted it an instant because our son Charles was a breastfed baby.

My husband, George, was an Assistant Professor of Psychology at Colorado State University when the Peace Corps invited him to spend the summer training volunteers for work in Micronesia.

Micronesia is made up of thousands of small islands located in the Pacific Ocean between Polynesia and Japan. It is a Trust Territory of the United States. Many of the people still live in grass houses, cook over open fires, catch rain water to drink, and exist on fish and coconuts.

The idea of living the primitive life excited us, and George accepted the job "with pleasure." Family and friends expressed concern for our son's welfare but we weren't worried. Because he was nursing we didn't have to worry about pure water, sterilizing bottles, or bad food. And the Peace Corps assured us that should an emergency arise, medical aid could reach us quickly by helicopter.

At the end of June, we flew to Rota, an island ten miles long and three miles wide rising from white sand beaches to a flat-topped mountain covered with dense green vegetation. Coconut palms sway softly in the breeze. A coral reef surrounds the island so the huge ocean waves break several hundred feet away from shore leaving a calm lagoon at the white beaches.

The villagers, called Chamorros, were very friendly and tried their best to make us comfortable. Most of the Peace Corps staff lived in one concrete building that had been divided into tiny rooms by cardboard "walls." A dilapidated old crib had been found for Charles. That plus twin beds left little standing room in our cubbyhole. The living conditions were not private, but no one complained about Charles. On the rare occasions that he did awaken at night, he was quickly silenced with his ever-ready favorite snack.

Because of the hot, humid weather, clothes were kept at a minimum. Charles spent most of the time in his birthday suit.

The natives tried to cook foods that would please our tastes, so selecting solids for Charles was no real problem. Nursing, however, was still his mainstay. With all the traveling he went back to nursing more often and for greater lengths of time. That was fine with me. I had nothing else to do but care for him.

We spent many hours playing on the beach or in the ocean or taking long walks. The sight of the blonde American lady with the white-haired baby on her back was almost always cause for a parade. I felt like the Pied Piper!

The native women seemed impressed that I nursed Charles. They thought all Americans used bottles, so many of them had stopped nursing and started using bottles and powdered milk. This was quite expensive and led to more infant illnesses because of poor sterilization techniques. I hope Charles and I were a good influence. While almost everyone had attacks of "island stomach," Charles suffered no more than minor discomforts. He even cut teeth with no problems.

When our time on Rota was over, the three of us traveled on

to Japan for two weeks. We lived true Japanese style—sleeping on mats and eating raw fish—which would have been out of the question had Charles not been a breastfed baby. He just slept with us on the mats, ate whenever appropriate food was available, and nursed the rest of the time.

After Japan we went back and toured other Micronesian Islands before finally returning to the States in late September. We had spent four months traveling, most of the time in cultures alien to ours, and had a glorious time doing it. We think we owe our once-in-a-lifetime experiences to three factors: Charles was a breastfed baby. We could travel light, not weighted down with baby bottles and sterilization worries; Daddy believed in nursing as firmly as Mommy did. He was so supportive, in fact, I did not even feel the need to take **one bottle** along for emergencies; We had a backpack for Charles. He practically lived in it all summer and he loved it. So did we!

Now we are expecting Baby Number Two. Wonder where we can go next summer?

Part Five

The Nursing Relationship

Closeness and Comfort

Pierced

Judy Brown
California
1973

Like an arrow
piercing my heart
you lie
diagonal
across my breast
molded to me
attached to me
taking life from me
giving life to me
making me feel so
important so real
so universal so
eternal so damn good

your eyes, I never
looked into such eyes,
watch my face
while your hand
holds mine
caresses
lets go
falls limp
like a plump starfish

I drift and flow
at rest bound
to you freely
taking
love given without restraint
only asking
I be there
loving you myself the world

you are an arrow
my heart is pierced
the wound will never heal
God willing.

18

The Joys of Nursing

"I don't think any of us were really prepared for the effect that breastfeeding would have on our lives. Childbirth as an event was over in a matter of hours, but breastfeeding went on for months and years. And something magical happened when we put our babies to our breast, and it changed us and the way we viewed our lives at a very basic level. Breastfeeding, which in this day and age is a conscious choice, became a mechanism for raising our own consciousness. It expanded our vision and heightened our sensitivities to all things that affected us and our families."

    Marian Tompson, LLL Founder, 1981

I Didn't Nurse My First . . .

    Mrs. Raymond Larrow
    Massachusetts
    1965

I had ten children but never nursed any of them because I was told that my Rh negative blood factor would prevent it. When I asked my obstetrician about the possibility of nursing my eleventh baby, he said, "Fine, there is no longer any question of Rh negative mothers not being able to nurse." He also cited research which showed less chance of a nursing mother developing breast cancer.

So I decided to nurse my eleventh baby and find myself at a loss to explain why I am glad I did. For only a great poet could express in words what this pure intimacy between my baby and me means to me. Who could put on paper what it means to have my baby's eyes gaze into mine so tenderly as I am nourishing him and fulfilling his needs so completely? Who could explain the need that my baby has of me and the sense of need that he thereby establishes in me?

Now I realize that it was an impossibility for me to have experienced the same purity of emotion while bottle feeding. Statistics and convenience mean nothing to me compared to the joy which I am aware of while breastfeeding and that I never experienced until I had my eleventh baby.

But enough of the "maternal instinct" side—now for the practical aspects. I had many doubts about the practicality of nursing in such a busy household as ours. I am now assured that nursing can only lead to good in the home.

How convenient it is in the morning! My eleven-year-old boy is always the first one up. He changes the baby and brings him in to my bed and I am all set for another half hour.

My three preschoolers have plenty of attention. As soon as baby is hungry I sit down on the sofa and they collect their books. And since I am able to hold the book, which is something children always seem to want an adult to do when reading to them, they really feel that I am paying close attention to them.

And I am so pleased that my older sons and daughters are being made aware of the fact that a woman's breast is a beautiful, necessary part of the body and that there is such peace in the home when baby is at mother's breast.

I am far from an authority on breastfeeding having only nursed this baby of mine who is now only four months old. However, I do feel a bit of an authority on "practical marriage" and I am certain that marriage is off to a good start when husband sees how necessary mother is to his own flesh and blood, and when mother realizes that **only she** can give that new baby what he needs.

Enjoy Your Baby

Wilma Sheard
Illinois
1959

After three bottle-fed babies I am finally a successful nursing mother. The striking difference is the tremendous feeling of satisfaction that this baby has given me. Up till now I have always been completely baffled by the phrase "enjoy your baby." I did not even feel close to them until they reached the age of five or six months. Not so with my breastfed baby. At three months, she and I are already great friends. To see those big blue eyes looking up at me as she contentedly slurps away, I feel as though I have finally arrived at motherhood. It's such a lovely warm glow that nursing imparts. Her nursing times are islands of peace in the otherwise hectic, chaotic day. And the nicest part of all is that this warm glow seems to be endless. It spills over into my relationships with all the rest of my family, and there's always some to spare. It's a tragedy of our highly civilized society that so many women miss such a tremendously rewarding experience.

Learning to Love

Carolyn Farrell
Pennsylvania
1973

So much has been said about how a breastfeeding mother teaches her baby to love by the love she gives him. In my case, I think I learned more about loving and feeling and caring than my babies did.

I didn't have a deeply loving relationship with my parents. They weren't bad parents; I just never felt close to them—generation gap, I guess. My older sister was born six years before me and my younger sister was born five years after me. Because of the wide differences in our ages, we never shared a great deal and so never felt close. I don't remember having a close friend during high school or college either. When I talk about a close friend, I mean one who is **more** than compatible, one with whom I could strongly identify, a kindred spirit. My husband always felt that my inability to have strong, deep feelings for another human being was just part of my emotional character. He felt I was a loner.

The birth of my twins aroused no special excitement in me. I brought them home from the hospital anxious to undertake the new experience of raising children, but they seemed like strangers to me at that time. My contact with La Leche League had sold me on the values of breastfeeding and so with LLL's guidance I proceeded to breastfeed my twins.

It didn't take long. I soon began to experience **intense** feelings of love for the babies. I found it upsetting to be away from them for more than a few hours. Every move they made, every discomfort they felt, every pleasure they had, reverberated in me. I had never experienced feelings this intense, this wonderful, for any human being before.

Before long I found that it was possible for me to have deeply loving adult relationships too. I am relieved to know that I am capable of loving fully, as so many other mothers seem to be. There always was a certain vacuum in my life. I am grateful to my babies and to breastfeeding for helping me to become the fuller, happier human being that I now am.

What Nursing Means to Me

Lyn Abruzzi
Kansas
1972

To understand what nursing means to me, it is necessary to understand what I was like before I had a baby. I was a senior in college when I became pregnant. Neither my husband nor I had planned to have children for many years to come, since I had expected to teach biology after graduation and to pursue a Master's degree. We accepted my pregnancy with a mixture of regret and curiosity—hardly joy. As the months passed, however, the swelling of my belly and the quickening of the life inside me aroused us with excitement over the new child to come. Still, feminist that I am, I was determined not to let a child stand in the way of pursuing a satisfying life for myself (which, in my mind, didn't include being a full-time mother). I was sure that I would in no way let this child alter my plans.

How naive I was! I certainly had not counted on that motherly instinct which creeps up on us after a child is born. My husband

was firmly in favor of breastfeeding, and I was too, so little Matt got a good start in life. I really believe that without the easy, necessary closeness between mother and child that nursing brings, my motherly instincts, so deeply buried within me, would have emerged more slowly and less fully.

Although I have taken several courses since Matt was born and plan to obtain a Master's degree eventually, my priorities have changed to the point where I cannot seriously occupy myself with these matters until my children are of school age. Just this past summer, when Matt was one year old and I was taking a course, I found that I really enjoyed playing with my son and tending to his needs more than studying the subject.

Through the closeness that breastfeeding brings, I have discovered that mothering is hardly the least of my satisfying roles in life. I feel like a butterfly emerged from the cocoon—what a metamorphosis!

A Sense of Continuity

Princess Grace of Monaco
1971

I had never considered anything else but breastfeeding when I had children. And when these children came, two girls and a boy, I breastfed them as I always intended to do, simply as something which was to me wholly normal and right. I had never thought about it as anything extraordinary for me to be doing—neither as a working woman, which I had been in a so-called glamorous profession, nor as the wife of a ruling Prince.

It seems to me that the closeness to the child resulting from breastfeeding is somehow an extension and affirmation of that very love that has resulted in its being there. A man and a woman have united to create this little being that one is holding to one-self and nurturing. And this nurturing is to be treasured for its relationship that is to end all too soon, the very first of many partings.

The breastfeeding of the child by the mother is a temporary extension of the closeness and security the child knew whilst still sheltered within its mother's body. We are giving it a sense of continuity that will remain with it, in one form or another, throughout the rest of its life.

Sweet Smells

Norma Jane Bumgarner
Oklahoma
1976

Five years ago, when my mother-in-law was holding my daughter, she asked, "What did you put on her—honeysuckle?" No, it was just the lovely fragrance of baby hair rinsed clean, not shampooed.

With a tiny baby in my arms again, I am reminded of the pleasures for mother built-in to these little people. One that pleases me most is the sweet smell of the breastfed baby, especially before he begins other foods.

It is fun to try going completely natural and experience the baby's body perfume. For baths, rinse his body and hair in clear water without soap, which leaves an odor behind. Leave off all the powders and creams and lotions. Dress him in clothes that have been washed without perfumed fabric softeners and use cloth diapers rather than the perfumed disposables.

And then enjoy! Smell his breath and find out why those delicate blossoms used in bridal bouquets are called "baby's breath." Smell his hair and his silky skin. Discover another way nature encourages us to hold our little ones close.

The Miracle of Love

Marcia Behrendt
Wisconsin
1968

Love is expressed by closeness. The newborn knows instinctively that he is loved when he is held against his mother's breast. "The mother loves with her breast. The infant loves with his mouth." Even if he does not respond immediately, he feels secure when cuddled in his mother's arms. It is reminiscent of when he was held in utero only a short time earlier. Good mothering through breastfeeding is accomplished through the miracle of love.

As Natural as Breathing

Margaret Rewolinski
Wisconsin
1977

One day I was at my mother's with my three children. I had just put Andy to bed and Tim was outside with Grandpa. Joel was sitting a bit away from me in the living room playing with a pile of toys. I had become quite engrossed in an interesting conversation with my sister, when I suddenly thought of Joel (who is quite a dickens at climbing and getting into things) and looked toward the toys. He was gone! I quickly and anxiously inquired of those in the room, "Where's Joel?" but received only a couple of incredulous stares as an answer. I felt a bit foolish as I looked down and realized that Joel had crawled into my lap moments before and was peacefully sleeping and nursing there! It seems as if nursing has become as natural as breathing for me.

The Only Way to Go

Mary West
Maryland
1969

My friends know why I nurse my baby. I'm lazy! Strangers say, "Oh, my dear, brave child! All those night feedings, and you can never let anyone else take over the chore." Then I look patient and long-suffering, and it would come off very well if my husband didn't choke and start snickering.

Be honest, now. Advantages of breastfeeding to Baby David are many, but the real goodies are mine. Okay, so he's happy and healthy from nursing, but who reaps the benefits of having a contented child? Me. And who watches TV, nursing David while Daddy does the dishes? Me.

Boy, do I have it easy! My friend struggles to pacify her hungry child on a shopping trip. I ease my feet up in the fitting room while baby has a snack. Afterwards I can have an ice cream cone (since my baby borrows a few calories) while my friend drinks black coffee and moans about her postpartum bulges. On the way home, my friend's baby is again frantic with hunger and though her car is very up-to-date, it has no bottle-warmer.

Speaking of bottles, you won't catch me burning my fingers or breaking my back sterilizing those things. I did it with Number One son. We bought the powdered stuff. It took half an hour to mix, about forty utensils, and unfailingly globbed the nipple at feeding time. Talk about frustration, sweat, and toil! The nights I stood over the stove with a frantically screaming baby, begging the bottle to heat! When it finally did, I had to sit up, shivering, half-awake and resentful, until Billy finished eating. Now I just lean out of bed to get David, then snuggle up under the blankets with him nursing. Do I prop my eyes open until he's done? Nope. Total time awake: fifty seconds.

Our older son doesn't mind having a lazy Mommy. No indeed. His mommy doesn't brush him off with "Mommy's warming David's bottle." I have a free hand to cuddle my "big boy," to hold a storybook, to sketch a lopsided kitty, to hand him a drink.

So, feel free to consider me a martyr, bless me for my motherly goodness, applaud my dogged courage for nursing, but don't try to convince me you're right. For us lazy types, breastfeeding is the only way to go.

19

In Special Circumstances

Nursing My Twins

Patti Lemberg
Texas
1976

When I first told my husband that I planned to nurse our expected child, he hit the ceiling with an emphatic NO. Our doctor, however, was glad and suggested that I attend La Leche League meetings for the education and moral support. She also suggested that Mac and I attend Lamaze classes in prepared childbirth, which we did. I shared my LLL reading material with Mac, and by the time we learned we were expecting twins, he was convinced that prepared childbirth and nursing were "the only way."

So we were all ready when the boys were born. Due to a little too much "help," not enough privacy, and too little time allowed with each child, they didn't nurse well in the hospital. But once home they settled in my arms and began nursing like real champs.

They nursed about every two hours for twenty minutes at a time and slept one four- or five-hour stretch a day. The hardest time for me was the six-week growth spurt, when each of them nursed every forty-five minutes. It was a bit much, but I just took the same attitude I had taken during the last weeks of pregnancy: "Next year this time they'll be toddling around, so cute—I won't even remember this day."

The women in the League Group helped me enjoy my babies with their relaxed, patient attitudes. I had been raised "never to leave the house with dirty dishes in the sink," but I learned to do this—and more! The first two months we had diaper service; we used the playpen for a clean laundry depot for the first four months; Mac took over the shopping duties for the first year; and so on. Our priority list: babies, Mom, Dad, food, laundry, with house cleaning bringing up the rear. (Mac really felt as if he was first because he had a happy wife and healthy, happy babies.)

By two-and-a-half months the boys had settled back to nursing every two to three hours and twice each during the night. (Six hours equals a "night" for a wee one.) The only problem was that David was an early bird and Alan was a night owl.

Between six and seven months, we voted to adopt a four-hour schedule. But this, too, passed, and now at seventeen months they usually nurse only at sleep-related times.

The most important advantage I have gleaned from the whole nursing experience is confidence. I know my way of mothering is good and that makes me happy, which in turn relaxes me into a patient frame of mind, which can't help but increase my intuitiveness, which induces loving guidance rather than instant hysteria, fostering positive results, which breed pride and confidence! It's a lovely merry-go-round. Now, with two toddlers running in and out, complete with sand and soil, it only takes me about three hours to clean house—including stops for getting drinks, kissing bumps, and loads of "help." When you're on the confidence-patience-relaxation-pride merry-go-round, it all seems simple!

Three Times the Joy

Laura Brizee Smith
Colorado
1984

My third pregnancy went well; the only surprise occurred in my seventh month when we learned we were going to have twins. What a shock! How would I ever handle twins when I already had a five-year-old and a two-year-old? As the final weeks rolled by, we became more and more excited about the idea of having two babies. I kept active during my pregnancy because I felt so good.

At last the great day arrived! At the first twinge of labor, I rejoiced because soon I would be rid of the monstrous figure I had developed. I was so anxious to keep my labor going strong that when we left for the hospital, I decided to walk. The hospital was about a half mile from our apartment. Since it was 9:00 PM, my husband drove slowly behind me in his pickup truck to ensure my safe arrival. It must have looked awfully strange to see a man slowly cruising behind a very pregnant lady as she walked down the street. A woman pulling up to a stop sign saw this and came to my rescue. She drove in front of my husband's truck and asked me, "Honey, is that man bothering you?"

My labor was twenty hours long, but at last I was off to the delivery room. After a few pushes, we were looking at our daughter, Anniki, five-and-a-half pounds. We held her for a few minutes but there was more work to be done as baby number two was impatiently awaiting her entrance into the world. Three minutes later we were looking at another little girl, Heidi Jo, four pounds. We were so excited to have two healthy little girls! They were quickly whisked away to the nursery for the usual cleaning and examination. My husband was putting his camera away, the nurses were cleaning up, and the doctor was waiting for the placenta to be delivered when I heard those incredible words, "I think there is another one in here!" The nurse checked for a heartbeat and sure enough, baby number three was still hiding in my body. A few more vigorous pushes and we were looking at five-and-a-half-pound Rebekah. What a shock to realize that within seventeen minutes I had given birth to identical triplet girls! Now I know why they call it the recovery room! I had just walked to the hospital carrying fifteen pounds of babies. We were grateful that everything went smoothly and all the babies were healthy and strong.

The real fun started when we called friends and relatives to tell them the happy news.

"We had the babies," I would say.

"Oh, what did you have?"

"Girls."

"Ah, two little girls. How sweet."

"No, three."

"Pardon me?"

"I said we had three little girls."

"What?"

"I said we had triplet girls." The response to that ranged from total silence to hysterical laughter.

Soon I asked the nurse to bring my babies to me so that I could nurse them. I was told, "Oh, you can't nurse triplets." I somewhat agreed but at the same time I wanted at least to try. After I put the first baby to my breast and held her as she gently drank her fill, I knew I would be nursing them all. It felt so natural and it was what I wanted to do.

All three babies were totally breastfed for the first six months, after which they were slowly introduced to solids in addition to the breast. It has been over a year and a half now and all the babies are still nursing without ever having been supplemented with a bottle.

I always enjoy taking the babies back to the hospital where they were born for the nurses to see their progress. I let the nurses go on and on about how healthy the babies look and how strong and alert they are. Then at the precise moment I let them have it with, "Did you know they are breastfed babies? I never did give them any formula, just the breast. In fact, they didn't even have any solids until they were about six months old." I must admit, it is a little calculated on my part, but I love the surprised looks. What follows is always the same—"But you look so good!"

Some people are critical of my nursing the girls. Nursing one toddler is bad enough, but nursing three of them is outrageous! That doesn't discourage me from continuing, because I know I am giving the very best I can to my little girls. I made the decision when they were born that they would suffer no lack of bonding, security, nutrition, individuality, or comfort just because they came in a group of three. I have heard many mothers of multiples express fears about not giving equally to each baby. I feel the reason I have never worried about that is because they are breastfed. One gets to be held and nursed by Mommy. When she is finished, the next one climbs up on my lap and she has the same comfort as her sister did. When the second baby is finished, there is still plenty of warmth and comfort for the third baby. That way they are equally satisfied. Breastfeeding my triplets as well as my other two children was the wisest decision I have ever made in my life and I continue to reap the benefits from it.

Oh, how that day has changed our lives! We can't go anyplace without stopping traffic—we practically need a parade permit. My husband designed and built a stroller that would carry the three babies and still be maneuverable.

People say the funniest things when they see us. One woman asked me if the triplets were identical. When I told her they were, she asked their names. I told her, "Anniki, Heidi, and Rebekah," She said, "Those aren't identical." One time a little old lady came strolling by the park where I was sitting on a bench watching the two older children playing. The babies were in a baby buggy all wrapped up with another blanket over the top of the buggy for extra warmth. She asked if she could take a peek. After pulling the blanket back she just stood there frozen for the longest time, then exclaimed, "Oh, my God, there's three of them!" Here is a classic. A pregnant woman was walking through the shopping mall when she spied all of us and started over to see the girls. Her husband grabbed her arm, pulled her back, and said, "You better not get too close; it might be contagious." A young boy expressed it perfectly when he asked me, "Did you have all three of them in the same litter?"

An organized household is a thing of the past. The days of fancy meals and eating off anything but paper plates are few, and no more small economy car for us. The prospect of getting a full night's sleep is out of the question.

In spite of the problems and hard work involved, there is such love, laughter, and joy that it helps smooth over all the sleepless nights, the unmade beds, and the mountains of laundry. If we had it to do all over again, would we? ABSOLUTELY!

A True Miracle

Kathleen Vasek
Illinois
1982

Little Rosie's birth came as a complete surprise—she arrived early one July morning two-and-a-half months before her due date. Luckily we made it to the hospital just in time, because our three pound seven ounce premature daughter needed lifesaving techniques immmediately. She was transferred to the Neonatal Intensive Care Unit at Loyola Hospital the same day—she had severe hyaline membrane disease and could not breathe on her own.

I insisted on being discharged from our local hospital the next day, and Jerry and I went straight to Loyola. As I stroked and talked to this tiny newborn all hooked up to IVs, monitors, and a respirator, the reality of the situation began to sink in. The doctors said they did not know whether she would live or die.

On the third day I rented an electric breast pump. After nursing my first daughter, Polly, I knew there could be no other way.

This critically ill baby would need mother's milk even more than a healthy, full-term infant.

The hot, sticky days passed by slowly for the rest of the summer. I sat at the kitchen table and pumped my breasts—crying when I was alone, laughing when I was solemnly observed by my two-and-a-half-year-old, Polly, and her neighborhood playmates. And, incredibly, the baby slowly began to improve. After a month, Rosie started to get partial-strength breast milk through a tube inserted down her throat to her stomach. Gradually she began sucking with a premie nipple on a little plastic bottle. She was gaining weight and her apnea spells became less frequent. It was clear that little Rosie was going to survive.

The photo on the left, used in 1982, shows Rosie at one and a half with her sister Polly; photo below shows the Vasek family in 1987.

I became increasingly anxious to nurse her and was no longer satisfied to bring my bottles of mother's milk to the hospital. At last, when Rosie was about eight weeks old, came the happy day; the nurses told me that I could try nursing her. At first she didn't seem to understand, but before the nurse even returned, Rosie was nursing vigorously. I sat and rocked her and she nursed, and it was just as I had imagined so many, many times during those long weeks.

Two weeks later Rosie came home from the hospital, and our family breathed a sigh of relief. She was still so tiny it was necessary to nurse her every two hours around the clock. She also still had breathing problems and had to be watched closely while nursing, because sometimes she'd get so intent on her feeding that she'd forget to breathe and start to turn blue. Rosie's first year could not truthfully be described as "carefree," and she has some ongoing problems. But what a little doll-angel she is—so happy and easygoing, with a terrific sense of humor! To see this delightful child and know what a difficult beginning she had is to see a miracle of God and modern medicine.

At nineteen months, Rosie is a happily nursing toddler, I will always remember that hot, humid summer, sitting at the kitchen table without my baby. I have talked to other mothers with severely sick infants in the hospital who are discouraged and tired of the breast pump, and I try to encourage them to keep at it, because I know they will eventually tell themselves a thousand times over that it was definitely worth it!

Nursing My Adopted Child

Judy Uhey
Kentucky
1984

It's been several months now since Rebecca has come to share our love and life. We feel so blessed. We have four other children, one of whom we adopted several years ago at the age of six. They range in age from thirteen to nine years of age.

I remember very well the night we talked, prayed, and decided we wanted another child. It was a night of joy and excitement as we sat together dreaming of our baby.

The adoption process is a long and very thorough process. There were physical examinations and blood tests, reference letters, paperwork, home study, and weeks and months of waiting for the approval. I remember the day we got the "Yes, you've been approved" phone call. Joy and excitement prevailed for hours in our house!

Then one day I came across an article in the local paper on "Breastfeeding an Adopted Child." This sparked my interest and rekindled my memories of that old feeling of closeness I had experienced nursing our three oldest children. When I returned home, I contacted my local La Leche League. Within a day I had papers and pamphlets and books on relactation and induced lactation. I found my thoughts were totally occupied with the idea of being able to nurse a baby to whom I had not given birth.

My husband and I read the material and discussed all the aspects of breastfeeding the baby that eventually would come to us. We had no way of knowing when the baby would come or how old the baby would be. My husband didn't want me to feel like a failure if it didn't work out, but finally he said, "Why not? Let's try!"

For the next few weeks my prayer was for an ample milk supply and for a baby who would accept the breast. Most of the articles cautioned against getting so caught up in the amount of milk you can bring in that you miss the whole point of nursing. I decided it didn't matter how much milk I could produce, that the most important thing to me was the bonding process that naturally happens when you nurse a baby. Whatever amount of milk that came would just be an additional plus.

I set up a schedule for myself and followed it faithfully. Every two hours during my waking hours I would use a hand pump or the hand expression method, five minutes on each breast. The pump and hand expression would be enough to send those messages to my body and brain saying, "Make milk!"

Then one day about four weeks later as I sat using the hand pump, I noticed drops of colostrum (pre-milk) on my nipples. I was so excited that I could hardly wait to share this news with my family! With exploding joy and excitement I exclaimed, "I've got drops! I've got drops!"

I continued to use the hand pump every two hours, then one day my friends surprised me by renting an electric pump for me to use. Within just a few days of using the electric pump, my drops went to streams of beautiful, rich-looking milk. I was able to pump about a half-ounce every two hours. Then, after two weeks I was up to one or two ounces every two hours.

Finally we got the "This is the day" phone call from the adoption agency. The baby we had been waiting and praying for was ready to join our family. My husband and I were on our way to pick up our new baby daughter.

Holding Rebecca in my arms for the first time filled me with joy and awe. Feeding time came quickly and I was full of anticipation as I offered Becky my breast. She nursed beautifully, as though she had been nursing all of her two-and-a-half months of life.

I felt relaxation flow over me and I just settled back and enjoyed holding and nursing my baby. My husband sat close beside us, just beaming and watching so tenderly. That is a moment of my life that I'll treasure forever.

Rebecca has continued to nurse well these past few months. She still takes some formula from a bottle each day, and this has worked well for us. At this point, I don't have enough milk to completely nurse her at all the feedings, but I've come to know that the amount of breast milk that Rebecca gets really isn't the most important thing, it is the beautiful bonding and closeness that comes with nursing. Through all the work and waiting, nursing my daughter has been and will continue to be one of the most fulfilling experiences of my life.

It Was Worth It

Marion Blackshear
New York
1973

A number of people—doctors and mothers—have asked me, "Is it really worth all the effort to breastfeed an adopted baby?" I can say a most emphatic "yes." How else would I feed him the times he didn't feel well? What could I have done to comfort him back to sleep in minutes? What better way to insure a deeply loving relationship with our adopted son after knowing it with our three biological children?

It had been eight years since the birth of our last child when two-week-old Peter nursed on my empty breasts for his first feeding in our home. He also had formula, which was gradually decreased as my milk supply increased. At two-and-a-half months he was completely breastfed.

At Peter's bedtime nursing around fifteen months, he liked me to talk about the happy events of the day. So in this atmosphere of love and happiness I decided to tell him in simple words his adoption story. He couldn't have understood it all, but he stopped nursing, smiled from ear to ear, and patted my cheek. With a big lump in my throat, I felt Peter's own story was full of love and security for us both. He has since asked to hear "Peter's Story" again several times when he is nursing.

20

Nursing Discreetly

"Of course, one of the drawbacks to breastfeeding twenty-five years ago was that nursing in public was unheard of. You didn't even nurse in front of your relatives! It was LLL Founder Mary White who showed me how it could be done when she sat next to me while we did a panel on parenting at a church function and to my great amazement discreetly nursed her new baby. Today, though, we have no less an authority than the 1980 edition of The Book of Modern Manners *to reassure us that nursing in public is not only acceptable, but that 'those who disapprove should do so silently.'"*

Marian Tompson, LLL Founder, 1981

She's an Expert

Beverly Sykes
California
1970

I'm sure that anyone who has ever nursed a baby has found herself at some time in a situation where discreet nursing was called for. Having now nursed three babies, I am beginning to feel like an expert.

My "baptism by fire" into public nursing came when our daughter (now three) was tiny. We were attending the funeral of a gentleman who had been a member of the Knights of Columbus, an organization whose uniform includes plumed hats, epaulets, and swords. When Jeri began to get fussy, I discreetly retired to the foyer of the funeral parlor to nurse her, as I thought, in quiet. Suddenly a parade of Knights in full panoply filed out of the chapel to gather in a circle around me! After that, I figured I could nurse under any conditions.

By comparison, the rest of Jeri's nursing life was fairly quiet. She was nursed at wedding receptions, church services, in the University of California Physics Department, on an excursion boat, and in the back room of a photo shop surrounded by camera equipment (a shopping trip had taken longer than expected).

Six-month-old Paul is our "star-spangled nurser." He nursed through half of his baptismal ceremony. He has been nursed on just about every form of public conveyance—car, plane, train, helicopter, bus. He was fed in front of the Smithsonian Institution, in the Senate Wing of the Capitol Building, on the New York subway, in Central Park, at an ordination ceremony. At the moment man first landed on the moon, Paul was nursing—as he was when man left the moon. I could go on and on, but the baby is hungry. . . .

"She Nurses"

Dorell Meikle
British Columbia
1980

After a week of camping we decided to go into the nearby town for a meal. When we arrived, we learned to our dismay that everything was closed except one very posh-looking restaurant. Although we were wearing clean clothes, we felt the week's worth of grime under them, and we certainly did not look our best.

As we approached the restaurant a few well-dressed patrons entered. Should we or shouldn't we? With nowhere else to go, we finally decided we would. Upon entering, we were quickly and quietly ushered to a table next to the kitchen, which was actually partitioned off from the rest of the dining area. Mops stood beside us next to the entrance to the kitchen. From within we heard the clatter and noise of the kitchen staff. I was feeling particularly unwelcome when I noticed a small well-dressed man appear at the kitchen door. He stood, hands clasped at his waist, and leveled upon us the most disgusted glare ever to cross a human face. He turned and left, only to reappear shortly again. His nose clearly appeared to support his opinion of us.

I was becoming progressively more nervous and upset. The children seemed to be acting worse than I had ever seen them behave. I could hardly wait to be done and out of there, but before the older children had quite finished eating, the baby began to fuss. I knew what I would have to do or face a screaming baby. Nursing, on the other hand, would probably put the capper on it. I knew our well-dressed critic would see me removed from his establishment for this ultimate desecration of his premises, yet what choice did I have? Baby had begun to cry.

Between the man's appearances, I picked up the baby and positioned him at the breast. A hurried check told me I was well covered, and I was ready for the onslaught. I looked up and there he was again. Fear gripped me. His eyes grew large as he looked down from my face to the baby. His arms opened wide in shock— suddenly all motion slowed for me—he literally leaped six inches off the floor and calling to his staff in the kitchen, he cried out in a strong French accent, "Look, look, come here." Slapping his chest with both hands he added, "She nurses, she nurses." Suddenly his nose quit "testing" and his face turned into the greatest smile I have ever seen. The cook and his helper rushed from the kitchen to see what he wanted. They were taken aback by what he showed them but smiled awkwardly at us and disappeared back into the inner domain. "I not see since old country," he said excitedly. "You'll have healthy, strong baby, lucky baby," he beamed.

We rose to leave at that moment and he rushed over to our table with fruit from the large centerpieces which decorated the other tables. He followed us through the restaurant and out to our old, dilapidated truck, pressing more fruit into my arms.

"For the children, for the children," he said, and waved as we pulled away.

A Need for Understanding

Martha Davison
Michigan
1982

Every Wednesday evening our church provides a program for children ages two through fifth grade. Many children from our own congregation as well as from the surrounding community attend.

My husband and I were asked to teach a fourth and fifth grade class. At the time, our daughter, Kiralyn, was five months old. We were delighted with the program and eager to teach together. Kiralyn, of course, would accompany us in the classroom. We are a nursing couple and felt leaving her in a nursery or with a sitter was unnecessary. Kiralyn was very happy and enjoyed the children just as much as they enjoyed her.

Several weeks into the session, the directors asked me not to nurse my baby in an area of the building where I could be seen by the children. They were concerned that the sight of a mother breastfeeding her baby would cause "irreparable psychological damage" to an older child. It was my understanding that they felt nursing a baby "in public" was improper.

I was very disappointed and saddened to learn that such attitudes are still held by some people. After a great deal of thought, I resigned my teaching position.

Kiralyn is my first priority. As with most breastfed babies, she nurses for a variety of reasons. She may be tired and bored or playful and happy. Or she may be hungry. Whatever the reason, her needs come first. Kiralyn is a happy, healthy, and secure child because her needs are met when and where they occur. When we are in public, I nurse her discreetly.

I feel strongly that all children benefit from seeing a mother responding to her infant in a nurturing and loving manner. Many children today are growing up in homes where love is not openly expressed. To witness the loving and caring relationship between me and Kiralyn was surely an asset to our classroom.

In addition to breastfeeding being the most nutritionally sound method of feeding a child, nursing Kiralyn is a testimony to my belief in the importance of good mothering.

Leaving the classroom to nurse my child would have only served to perpetuate the myth that breastfeeding in public is wrong. It is a biological fact that a woman's body is fully equipped to adequately nourish her infant. Children need to be educated to the fact that breastfeeding is a virtue.

It was comforting to not be alone in this situation. Another nursing mother, also on the teaching staff, chose to resign over this issue.

We stay home now on Wednesday nights. I hope that all nursing mothers will be able to stand firm in their beliefs when their convictions are questioned. I look forward to the day when breastfeeding is totally encouraged and accepted.

Memos from Marian

Marian Tompson, LLL Founder, 1979

Was Aldous Huxley right? Are we fast on our way to that Brave New World where the natural became obscene and the unnatural was considered normal?

In New Jersey, Barbara Damon lost her family membership to a community pool because she breastfed her two-month-old baby, Michael, at the poolside while watching her other two children. Although she had a large towel around her shoulders covering both her and the baby, she was told by a lifeguard that breastfeeding was offensive to others at the pool and she would have to nurse her baby in the ladies' washroom. Mrs. Damon refused, her family's membership was revoked, and she is suing the community. The pool's Health and Safety Rules now state that: "...there will be no showing of the human male or female genitals or the pubic area or the buttocks or breasts. . . . Breastfeeding is prohibited unless arrangements are made . . . in advance, in which case, breastfeeding may be permitted in a location determined by the manager, providing the location is not in view of the public. . . ."

In Iowa City, when Linda Eaton returned to work after a maternity leave she found herself facing an ultimatum from city officials to give up her job as a firefighter or to stop breastfeeding her son, Ian. On those days when she had to spend a twenty-four hour shift at the fire station, Linda planned to have Ian brought to her twice a day, during her personal free time, so she could nurse him in seclusion in the women's locker room. But this was not acceptable to the fire chief and a resolution was immediately passed by the City Council forbidding breastfeeding in the fire station. A spokesman for the firefighter's union, which supported the chief, gave as their reason the fact that firefighters are supposed to exhibit *good moral conduct!*

The Outcome

Judy Torgus, Editor, 1980

During the same week in March, both Linda Eaton and Barbara Damon were awarded settlements in their court battles over their rights to breastfeed their babies. Linda, the firefighter from Iowa, was awarded $2,000 in damages, plus court costs, and the right to continue having her son brought to the fire station to be breastfed. Barbara, whose case involved discreetly nursing her baby at the community swimming pool, was awarded a $7,500 settlement (most of which will be used for court costs). In addition, the city has agreed to build a canopied structure where *all* babies are to be fed, whether they are being breastfed or bottle fed. This structure will provide a clear view of the kiddie pool.

Both of these women have faced many obstacles in their struggle to stand up for the rights of nursing mothers—hoping their efforts will make it easier for other mothers who want to breastfeed. Linda hopes her situation will allow breastfeeding relationships to increase and flourish. "The babies deserve the best," she writes, "and the women also deserve to enjoy mothering." Barbara expresses a similar sentiment, saying she hopes her case will help other mothers to be comfortable discreetly nursing their babies in public. We applaud these mothers for their perseverence.

Out of the Stalls and into the Booths!

Cynthia Byers Walter
Virginia
1984

Recently I was dining at a family restaurant in a local shopping mall with my in-laws, my husband, and my two sons, ages four months and two-and-a-half years. Periodically during the meal, the baby would fuss and I would discreetly lift the hem of my blouse and feed him.

When we were finished eating, I handed him to his daddy and made a trip to the ladies' room. The stall was occupied, and another woman holding an infant was waiting. The mother revealed that she was waiting for the toilet stall to be free so she could nurse her baby there. When I told her I'd been nursing my son for the last hour at my table with no one noticing, she replied that since her table was at the busy front portion of the restaurant, she could not breastfeed comfortably at her seat.

Across the mall from the restaurant was a bookstore selling "girlie" magazines. How odd, I thought, that the exposure of the female breast in those magazines is condoned for the purpose of titillating men (or should I say boys?), while the slight exposure involved in breastfeeding is considered scandalous.

When I told my husband of the incident in the restroom, he was even more upset than I was. He said it was time nursing mothers "came out of the stalls and into the booths!"

La Leche League has done a splendid job in the last twenty-five years. The advantages of breastfeeding are widely recognized and physicians now encourage new mothers to nurse. At the private hospital where my children were born, 90% of the new mothers are breastfeeding when they leave the hospital. But as long as women feel unable to perform in public the motherly task of feeding their infants as nature intended (discreetly, of course), our task is not over. Until it is, the function of the female breast will still be defined for the general public by the publishers of *Playboy* and *Hustler.*

Many illustrations of breastfeeding show nursing couples in rocking chairs or in the family bed, photographed through gauze in very private settings. I love those photos, and perhaps they do depict breastfeeding as it most often occurs. However, they do emphasize the romantic aspects of nursing over practical considerations. There ought to be more photographs of women nursing children at sports events, on buses, at the beach, in restaurants.

One of the arguments used against breastfeeding is that it "ties the mother down." As long as women feel they have to stay at home to nurse their infants, or worse yet, seek out the privacy of bathrooms, this myth will persist.

La Leche League and other organizations have convinced the people who count most—the mothers—that breast is best. Our next step is to educate the public so that we need not feel ashamed to nurse our babies in restaurants, any more than we hesitate to feed our toddlers.

This is a radical letter for me, but breastfeeding is a compelling issue. Sometimes it takes radical measures to overcome social attitudes. Everyone in La Leche League knows that nursing in public can be done discreetly. If we act on our convictions, others will know it, too, and accept breastfeeding as the normal way to feed a baby, both privately and publicly.

To My Son, with Love

Marilyn Wortley
Manitoba
1972

What, now?
When the dinner is burning
and the pork chops need turning?
When the guests have just come?
When the housework's not done?
When we're all in a hurry,
Running late, in a flurry
and we really must scurry?
What, now?

What, here?
In the bus? In the pool?
At the church? At the school?
It really is ridiculous
Your nursing is ubiquitous
and always most conspicuous
What, here?

What, still?
How can I explain it
When people complain it
Is really disgusting
That you should be "busting"
At your age?
Too old for your mother,
Too young for another—
An outrage!
And how to stay modest
When you are so honest
In your admiration
Of your feeding station;
When you lift the curtain
Just to make certain
That both are still there?
You do this anywhere
And plainly don't care
How many may stare.
What, still?

21

Growing Away from Nursing

*"The breastfeeding baby and its mother build a
relationship with each other that is based on their
mutual needs. This relationship changes gradually as the
needs of the nursing couple change. . . . If we consider
nursing only as a means of nourishing the infant...then
we can readily see why it would be desirable to bring
the nursing to an end at an early date...But, if we view
the nursing experience as a whole—if we see this
important, intimate relationship as a vital part of
motherhood—then it is hard to see how setting an
arbitrary time for terminating this relationship should be
encouraged."*

   Edwina Froehlich, LLL Founder, 1959

Each at His Own Pace

   Dale G. Blumen
   Rhode Island
   1982

I've always believed in the wisdom of taking our cues from our
children especially in regard to weaning. This practice helps us
to remember each child's unique developmental schedule and to
better meet his/her needs. But I had never considered the possibility of weaning as an adult experience, until I fractured my knee
and became almost immobile for several weeks.

During this time, my family all pitched in to take care of my physical and emotional needs. At first, this required almost constant "doing for mother." Eventually, the knee splint was removed and I had permission to go downstairs once a day. However, I did not have confidence in my ability to use crutches for negotiating the many steps in our house. So I was very reluctant to leave the bedroom level. My family seemed to understand. No one "forced" me to go downstairs; instead, they continued to bring me meals on trays, as they had done before. As I gradually began to notice improvement in my knee, my confidence began to increase. One day, I was ready to go downstairs—and did so with a minimum of fear and discomfort. A first step in "weaning" myself from the safety of my bedroom was accomplished with the support and encouragement of my "tuned-in" family.

Now I am in the process of "weaning" myself to one crutch. But there are times, especially on my outdoor excursions, when two crutches simply feel safer. I realize that this may appear to be a step "backwards," in much the same way that a nursing toddler who occasionally returns to mother for a quick "snack" or a hug may appear to be "regressing." But I am certain that in being allowed to progress (and "regress") at my own pace, I will master "one-crutch" locomotion and then eventually, "no-crutch" locomotion. Along with our little nursing people, it's comforting to know that outside aids are there for the occasional times I may need them.

The ups and downs of my recuperation have given me additional perspective on the long-term course of human development. Initially we wean from the breast. Eventually, we wean from total dependency on our parents. But whatever our age, we never wean from our need to be understood and appreciated as individuals who progress in various developmental tasks at our own pace.

All She Wants Is Me

Sheila Davis
Alabama
1982

I have two older children besides my little Valerie. With each pregnancy, my mother would try to convince me to breastfeed by telling me how much closer you feel nursing a baby. Each time I would reply, "I can hold my baby just as close feeding him a bottle as I could nursing him."

Well, I have no idea what prompted me to nurse this last baby, but during the whole pregnancy, I felt very positive about nursing.

Being an active person, I needed several weeks to adjust to the demands a nursing baby can place on a mother . . . especially one like Valerie. I think she could have nursed twenty-four hours a day. But after we got into our routine, we both loved the time we spent together. As a matter of fact, I came to really look forward to being able to stop and nurse her. I suppose nursing gave me the excuse I needed to stop and rest.

I enjoyed nursing Valerie for about eighteen months, but then I started feeling confined. My husband kept talking about a week-long trip—"just the two of us." And I started feeling a need for freedom to do what I wanted to do. So, since Valerie had cut down on her nursing time, I decided to "help her along." Oh, I tried everything to distract her. Then when that didn't work, I just told her that we weren't going to nurse anymore.

Sometimes she would get so angry at me she'd beat her tiny fists on me and cry. Then often I would go ahead and nurse her, but sometimes I wouldn't. This went on for a couple of weeks, with her asking to nurse less and less frequently.

But I had the grouchiest baby of anyone around. People had always mentioned how even-tempered and good she was. But now my baby had turned into someone I couldn't relate to. She began having tantrums and hitting and biting anyone who crossed her. Once cheerfully independent, she became a "clinger," clutching at my skirt and whining all the time. She seemed afraid to let me out of her sight.

A few weeks later, she came down with a virus and started demanding that I nurse her. I tried to tell her that my milk was gone, but she wanted to nurse anyway. Thinking that she would nurse for a minute, get discouraged, and quit, I allowed her to nurse. She nursed for forty-five minutes.

Since I obviously had very little milk, it dawned on me that all she wanted was me. So, after a lot of deep thinking, I told my husband if she needed me that badly, then she was going to have me. And I will continue to nurse her until she wants to stop.

Oh, by the way, I've got my good-natured little girl back!

Respect His Needs

Mrs. Mark Latterman
Michigan
1971

When my boy was born sixteen months ago, I looked forward to the nursing experience. (I had nursed my little girl for only five months and felt unsuccessful in the endeavor.) But I hoped he would want to wean to a cup by twelve months; holding a gangling nursing toddler sounded repulsive to me. That feeling has long since disappeared.

The announcement of bedtime or naptime to Gregg brings outstretched arms and a smile, because he knows it's nursing and rocking time. The sigh he usually gives as he starts nursing matches mine when I look down at the little bundle in my lap. His in-between snacks vary in quantity and in length from day to day, but regardless of how many or how long, he always seems to be totally recharged after each nursing.

A couple of months ago, when he was getting up every two or three hours insisting on nursing, I just wasn't sure I was doing the right thing. Would he ever give up the feedings and sleep through on his own? How much do you go along with the child and how much do you try to pattern him after your life? (You certainly can't discuss this problem with most of your friends, because they're upset that you're still nursing during the daytime.) However, now that he only wants to nurse (usually) once a night, I'm assured that he will give up feedings on his own. In fact, I enjoy that one night feeding, because eight hours is a long stretch to not hold him even once! And also I think we did and are doing the right thing when we go along with his desires—he's such a good-natured, secure child. He knows we are there if he needs us and the dark isn't scary.

Nursing an older baby helps you grow as an individual. Perhaps it would be more convenient for you if your baby wanted to wean at twelve months, but when he doesn't, you have to make a personal decision. Whose needs come first, and what do you do about them? Reading about how long babies nurse in other countries helped me to see how arbitrary societal pressures can be. There is a limit as to how much voice a baby should have—most of the time we do need to set his boundaries. But in the area of nursing, a baby should have his needs respected.

"We" as in Weaning

Miriam Doell
Colorado
1970

At a year and a half, Desiree was still nursing casually to get to sleep and for special comfort when it was needed. We were very relaxed about it right up to the time that I had to leave the children with my parents for five days while attending a conference.

The children and I spent a weekend at my parents' home prior to my flight to the conference. Danny and Desiree fit beautifully into the routines of the rambling parsonage. Desiree's occasional nursing sessions, though, had my parents concerned. My father stated plainly that nursing was meant for only *one* year.

We were all wondering about the five days ahead. Although I knew Desiree was quite independent and would go to sleep for babysitters, I had moments of doubt. But it had to be; on the morning of departure I hugged Danny, kissed the back of Desiree's neck as she ate a bowl of cereal, and took off.

On the third day at the hotel, Mother rang me up to inform me that all was well. Danny was proving himself to be a big brother and a big help. As for Desiree, "Papaul (my dad) has a scheme worked out to get her to sleep."

Seeing the children two days later at the airport was a thrill all its own. Danny never quit telling me how glad he was I was back. Desiree squealed, "Mamma!" and grabbed the front of my suit. "Num-a-nuh!"—her word for nursing.

My father roared, "Oh, no," in great dismay. "She was supposed to forget all about that."

I realized that returning was probably going to be a bigger problem than leaving. The problem was caused by my parents' good-natured warnings not to dare to nurse Desiree again after she had gone all that time without it.

Demonstrating just how his getting-to-sleep technique worked, my dad displayed both pride and humor as he maneuvered an old faded stroller back and forth in the long living room. Pillows piled in at precise moments balanced the nodding head. Tipping the stroller back on two wheels whisked her off to sleep. Triumph for Papaul!

But naptime next morning brought me face to face with the problem again. Rocking her was simply not enough. She clung to my neck, sobbing "Num-a-nuh!" over and over. My heart almost at the breaking point, I thought about it. Why was I refusing her? To prove to my parents that she was a big girl? What kind of reason was that? After my unexplained absence, she really needed me a little more; how could I deny her? I made my decision and joyfully let her cuddle and nurse to sleep for that morning nap.

Sleepily she broke her nursing hold a little to smile up at me. I smiled too, knowing that I wouldn't have to lose this loving hold so abruptly. But I dreaded breaking the news to my parents.

I needn't have worried. Shortly afterward we were all in the car returning to our home six hundred miles away. Naptime on the road grew into a fussy stretch, and Desiree's cries for "num-a-nuh" crescendoed. When she quieted as I matter-of-factly nursed her in the back seat, my dad glanced in the rearview mirror.

"Well, well. I guess that's what she wanted," he observed mildly. Then he added, "I guess the good Lord really knew what He was doing." And my mother smiled in knowing approval at the baby and me. Mark that moment with a special star for all of us.

He's a Big Boy Now

Lois Entwistle
New Jersey
1975

I smiled as I overheard our four-year-old John proudly insisting to his father the other day, "But, Dad, I'm a BIG boy!" How independent, how satisfied with his accomplishments, how secure and loving a little (BIG) boy he is!

What a long way he's come (and how much we've grown) since his birth. John was a shock, compared to our other placid, happy babies. He seldom slept, was happy only in my arms or a baby carrier (which we used well into his second year), wasn't happy left for even short periods of time with even the most loved family member, and spent most of his first few years in my arms or by my side. He seemed to need more intense mothering than our other children. Of course we gave it gladly, firmly convinced of the importance of meeting his needs as fully as we could, but there were many times when I was overtired, times when it was difficult to keep from becoming filled with doubts. But it was easier to take him everywhere, to carry him around, to tuck him in bed with us, because he was so unhappy when we'd try other ways.

In moments of tired doubt I'd wonder, "Are we just taking the easy way out, when perhaps I should be more inventive in seeking other ways of mothering him?" When he continued to nurse into (and out of!) toddlerhood, it again was so easy; but occasionally doubts would creep in once more, "Will he ever really wean? Will he forever rely on me to mother him to sleep?" Whether from my own "laziness," or busyness, or the firm conviction that we should meet his individual needs, or a combination of the three, these questions remained unanswered as we continued to mother John at his own pace. Each year has become easier, and very gradually he has weaned himself, not only from my milk, but also from his need to be with me every moment and to sleep in my bed. He has developed into a happy, self-reliant, very loving four-year-old.

I remember hearing years ago at an LLL meeting a comparison between a woman who gave up smoking when she was ready to and the child who weans himself when HE is ready. The speaker had pointed out her feelings of resentment and frustration at being pushed and her subsequent feelings of pride and self-satisfaction when she gave up smoking on her own. The question was posed, "Might not the feelings of a child who is pushed to wean, or allowed the freedom of deciding for himself, be much the same?" The simile stuck with me and came in handy when doubts would crop up as to whether John would *ever* decide to wean on his own. And, of course, he did! It was not all smooth sailing, but as I watch the pride John takes in his BIGNESS that he accomplished at his own pace, I am filled with gratitude that LLL was there to guide us and help us find the real meaning of "gradually and with love."

Still Interested?

Therese Niesen
Minnesota
1970

When I told my doctor that my toddler was still nursing, he asked, "Do you think he'll still be interested in the breast when he's eighteen?" I replied that he most probably would, but it wouldn't be mine!

I Thought She'd Nurse Forever

Emmy Reese
California
1969

Larky was one of those babies who was born to nurse. It was her only comfort when hurt or frightened and the only thing that soothed her into a very reluctant sleep. When not nursing, she was hyperactive, and I think she just couldn't turn off and relax any other way. I made half-hearted attempts to wean her, hoping that she would help by being ready, but she really never was until she was an older toddler. I was quite sure it was the right time then.

At eighteen months, my family doctor had strongly suggested that I wean her "cold turkey," although he thinks that nursing a baby is "very important." Our pediatrician decided I was crazy. (He's also a close family friend, so that hurt.)

Larky toilet-trained herself completely at twenty-six months. Three months later, she wasn't trained—after I'd given my best diapers away, too! It took quite a while before I realized that I had been saying, "Only little babies nurse. Big girls don't need to or want to." Then I was praising her for using the potty and being "such a big girl." What a choice I gave her (and I really didn't know it at the time)—to be a baby or to be a big girl. She didn't take long to decide.

Much later it helped to say that it's quite fine to nurse and use the potty. Bill and I tried to forget the extremes and just call her our girl. She took gleeful advantage of the fact that if I was busy I would drop anything when she called, "Potty, Mommy!"

My conclusion about nursing is that the real decision is yours. It depends on what kind of child you have and what you value most. If he or she really needs to nurse, you know it, even though public opinion can really put you through a wringer.

The clinging-vine, late nurser does eventually become very independent one day. I despaired about that ever happening, but now I'm very proud of Larky because I know she weaned herself when she was ready. It wasn't because I pushed her into it, as my best friends advised. I can't help adding that she's more independent now than their three- and four-year-olds. I'm sure late nursing helped.

Now I know that it was worthwhile—and I was able to find the right time for weaning for the two of us. After I decided to stick it out until she was ready to wean, we had our happiest nursing.

We are expecting our second baby in June, and if it's another little addict like Larky, I will nurse into toddlerhood again. It'll be an intimate affair between me and the baby, but if asked outright about it, I'll be delighted to confess. After all, I can point to Larky as the living proof that this practice produces a healthy, independent, responsive child.

Of course, nursing isn't the whole story, but it's tempting to say that late nursers are better for it. I suspect that a family that's willing to let the child's needs come first and not give in to public pressure could do as well with a bottle-fed baby. It would just be harder to keep in such close touch with a bottle-fed baby's needs.

Weaned Too Soon for Me

Barbara Pitre
Quebec
1968

In view of all that has been said and written in the League regarding the desirability of the mother's continuing to nurse her baby as long as they both want, it seems to me that some words of consolation should be offered to those mothers, like myself, whose babies wean themselves "too soon." I'm speaking, of course, of those mothers who have matured to the point where they think of breastfeeding in terms of years, rather than months.

Though I was fully anticipating nursing our daughter for two years or more, she weaned herself quite abruptly at twelve months and two weeks, going from three feedings a day to one a day, within a week's time, and two days later refusing the breast completely.

In this case it is the mother who suffers the shock of an abrupt and early weaning. What should she do? Resent the fact that the baby doesn't appreciate what a wonderful mother she is? Have another baby as soon as possible? Take advantage of her early emancipation by taking up other interests? All these thoughts occurred to me in the first days while I was still trying to accept the fact that she no longer needed me as she had before. I felt lost, bewildered, and resentful. I kept offering the breast for a week afterward. I even took her to the doctor to make sure she wasn't sick. Finally I had to accept the fact that her need was satisfied even though mine apparently was not. And from this understanding came the realization that my "maturity" was not all that perfect.

Maturity for a mother should include the capacity of understanding and responding to her child's needs, whatever they may be at a given time. Though this means, ideally, nursing as long as the baby wants to, it also means stopping when he wants to, and accepting the end of this particular need with as much equanimity as she earlier accepted the existence of this need.

It is true that the special closeness we knew before is changed. But the end of breastfeeding—at whatever age—does not mean the end of mothering. Especially when a baby weans himself early, he still needs a lot of physical cuddling. I hold and cuddle my baby as much as I ever did while she was nursing. I usually rock her to sleep at night. When she wants to be carried around, I carry her—for as long as she wants. And I wouldn't dream of leaving her yet for any length of time, weaned or not, because she still has a strong need to be close to me.

Mothers should cherish every minute they are nursing their babies, for eventually, inevitably, it is over. It is natural that the mother should feel a certain sadness at this time, but this sadness should be for her loss only. She should rejoice in the fact that the particular need of this particular baby for the comfort and security of the breast has been met fully and that in voluntarily giving it up he is taking his first step on the long road to independence. What mother would have it otherwise?

Regrets—and Understanding

Geri Doris Meretsky
New York
1972

So often lately I find myself lamenting having stopped nursing Eric when he was eight months old. When he falls and hurts himself; when he's scared; when he's ill; when he's simply thirsty and I've forgotten to take along something for him to drink—then I ask myself, "What made me stop?"

If I'm to be quite honest with myself, I must admit that what I actually did was to give up. Assorted friends and relatives kept greeting me with "What, are you *still* nursing?" Finally, when Eric had learned to hold his own cup and no longer nursed at mealtimes, I convinced myself that he no longer wanted to nurse at all. From there it was only two steps to weaning him completely. When he woke up I gave him a cup of milk instead of nursing him. I did the same thing again before bed. By the end of the week he seemed to have forgotten about nursing.

The sad thing is that I didn't stop to realize then that his cup doesn't offer any comfort when comfort's what is needed. I wish I could go back and tell all the people who pressured me to wean how I feel about now.

The Art of Letting Go

Penny Corn
Connecticut
1981

For days now my boy-baby has often been "too busy" when my heart calls to him. Oh, he had a nibble at bedtime and with that earache and when the blue crayon broke, watching life beckon out of the corner of his eye. But now he goes to bed with Teddy and colors in the lines and makes do with a quick hug for comfort.

His greatest joy are a bowl of Buc Wheats and his football suit. He jumps from my lap to loves that do not include me.

Yes, I have helped him to his independence. I have been there and been there and been there. And now, I am still there but he comes so briefly. That is what it's all about.

Life will be good—and not so good, but it will be easier for him than some. Because somewhere down deep where he may not even be aware of it will be the knowledge that security lies within himself—available for instant use. It was a natural byproduct of mother's milk given freely.

So there he goes, and I *am* happy. The tears? Why I *always* cry at weanings.

Part Six

Time for Sleep
Bedtime and Beyond

The Family Bed

Carrie Scully
Colorado
1979

It's only a double
And sometimes there's trouble
With covers and kicking about.
But o-o-o-h it's so warm
And it can't do much harm
When you feel all the love in and out.

This morning I woke
And this is no joke . . .
I was holding my little girl's hand.
So who could disgrace
This love that took place
While we dreamed our sweet dreams
hand in hand?

22

Quiet Moments

*"I think for each of us, as for all families, we must find
our own particular solutions to things, and these will not
always be the same. But recognizing that the needs of a
baby and a very young child are important, immediate,
and urgent and being willing to make some adjustments
and sacrifices to satisfy these needs will go a long way
toward raising secure and happy individuals who will
make us proud parents as they grow up."*

   Mary White, LLL Founder, 1975

Rendezvous at 3 AM

   Denise Heidel
   Washington
   1981

It seems every time mothers talk of night feedings, it is with heavy
sighs, a note of exhaustion, and prayers that baby will sleep
through the night.

   Now a new mother myself, I wonder why these women relayed
such negative feelings to me. I find my "3 AM rendezvous" with
Forrest to be one of the most precious hours we spend together.
When I reach for him and snuggle him to my breast, he calms

instantly, searching for my eyes, grasping my fingers tenderly. Our eyes meet, and all is quiet, so full of peace and satisfaction. At no other time of the day are these feelings so pronounced and uninterrupted. It is as if he and I are the only beings in the world; the only important thing is that we need and have each other.

As we sit in stillness with the small lamp glowing, I often reflect on his birth, how much love his father and I felt the first time we saw him. I think of how much we wanted him, and how Forrest has fulfilled our lives in just the short time he's been with us. His eyes meet mine again, full of dependence and happiness, and I think ahead with some sadness, knowing one night much too soon he won't need this early morning nursing.

Confident of My Love

Kathy Simonds
Illinois
1981

I was *so* sleepy after a long and busy day, but you weren't at all. you were content and full from my emptied breasts, oblivious to the clock ticking away in those wee hours. No snuggling off to sleep together that night, you wanted to play. Half-heartedly I complied. I talked, I sang, we did "sit-ups" and "leg stretches." We talked, rocked, bounced, and sat still. Another hour passed by and you were still wide-eyed.

My resentment mounted. I began to rock with a vengeance when you again refused to nurse—my offered breast held no sandman charm that night. You wanted to "talk" and insisted on a two-way conversation. The clock said 3:30 and my eyes were red and itchy. My jaw was tightly clamped and my patience lay in shreds. All I could consider was that you were keeping me up all night. Tomorrow would be another full day with you and your brothers, and I wondered how I'd cope with no sleep.

I held you away from me, all ready to give you an evil eye— when suddenly your eyes crinkled warmly and your mouth turned up into your big, funny, "O" smile and a gleeful squeal delighted the silent night. So confident of my eternal love that you couldn't even *imagine* anything else, your grin continued, with another squeal. I could feel the frustration flow out of my heart and disappear into the hot summer air. And I had to join you, laughing out loud, welling up with love so much greater than the frustration could ever be. I held you close, and joyfully we rocked as you slowly melted into my shoulder. Within minutes you were sound asleep . . . and then, dear little one, I didn't want to put you down.

As the Storm Slipped By

Ellinor Hamilton
Maryland
1978

Nothing relaxes me like nursing Jonathan. Last night I was wound up like a watchspring unable to sleep at all. We were having heavy thunderstorms, and I kept expecting the children to awaken crying in terror (which they didn't). The rain itself was deafening, to say nothing of the thunder. I tossed around for over an hour, and when Jonathan began to request company, I felt even worse: "The last thing I need now is to get up with him!"

We have a mattress on the floor in his room, and feeling my milk let down as I lay with him, I also felt my muscles unwind almost instantly. The next thing I heard was birds singing, and the light was coming from the sun rather than from lightning. How did that storm slip away?

Even at ten months, an hour of unbroken sleep is still a rare thing for Jonathan—but last night he slept several hours. Nursing is still pure joy for both of us. How would Jonathan ever survive nighttime without it? And how would I?

Content at Last

Edwina Moldover
Maryland
1976

My nursling Rachel is busy the whole day long learning to walk and attempting to do everything her nearly three-year-old brother does. The challenges of nursing her are not insignificant! Rarely can she spare more than a few brief moments to nurse before jerking away to be certain the world isn't leaving her behind.

So when bedtime nears, I carry my weary busybody upstairs

and drop into the rocking chair, knowing this is the one time I can count on a leisurely feeding.

She nestles in my arms and nurses to sleep. All day long she works her senses to exhaustion, taking in all the stimuli of her world, busily learning and living. But for this one last lingering nursing, the stimuli are simple, and I have the privilege of providing them all. She tastes sweet milk and watches my face until her eyes close in sleep. She cuddles close as I rock gently and sing to her. And soon she sleeps—blissfully content.

But I rock on and on sometimes, enjoying the stimuli *she* provides for *me:* the feel of her warm, relaxed little body in my arms, her soft cheek against my breast, the pretty sight of a sleeping baby in the dim light, the soft sounds of her rhythmic breathing, and her sweet baby smell.

The greatest pleasure of nursing a baby must surely be the intimacy—not just the physical closeness, but the spiritual closeness. If only I could suspend time and save forever the precious experience of nursing my baby to sleep.

Our Favorite Time

Karen Lew
California
1967

There is a certain sense of protective pleasure a mother feels as she watches her baby fall asleep while nursing. This is nothing new—probably most babies nurse to sleep most of the time during their first few months of life. But the full appreciation of my baby's nursing me to sleep didn't come until our third child was born.

I remember . . .

It is past eleven o'clock. The house is dark and quiet except for the hum of the dryer with its load of diapers. I rouse the cat and send her out for a night of feline wanderings. As a maternal-type night watchman, I make the rounds.

Amazing that Danika, who is a three-year-old tomboy in the daylight, can look so softly feminine in sleep. I marvel at the profusion of dark soft hair as I remove two beads and three plastic plates from beneath her head. And Kent—it is a major job to untangle his four-year-old body from the covers! His incessant questions are stilled by sleep, and I can kiss him without his turning away.

All's well here, so I tiptoe back to my own room to talk quietly with my husband. But he, too, is sleeping! I mark the place in the stock report book he has dropped and turn out the light. My wifely kiss evokes a typical husbandly grunt.

I see by the night light that my little Mark has turned on his back in his sleep. This turning over, such a major accomplishment by day, is now firmly enough learned to occur unconsciously in sleep. So nice to have him here in his portable crib beside me. I can still reach out to touch a tiny hand and feel his fingers curl before I pull my own covers up.

All is well—my house, my pets, my family taken care of for the night. Why then can't I sleep? It's been a long day and I'm tired.

Ah, there it is! Marks stirs and barely whimpers, but I turn immediately and gather him into my bed, snug in my arms. And I close my eyes to the soft, sleepy sucking sounds of my son.

The sequel? Well, Mark is sixteen months old now and has long since moved to the bigger crib in his own room. But that late evening nursing is still the favorite for both of us. He is far past needing the extra sucking or the milk itself. He needs me! I think it is because Mark, unlike his older brother and sister at his age, rarely has an opportunity to nurse and be with me exclusively during the day, and therefore still needs this "evening time" to be alone with me.

Moonlight Magic

Joan Hitzges
New York
1981

When we started camping, I wondered what I would do if Patrick, age fifteen months, would awaken crying and rouse the entire campground. The first summer he was still nursing, so there were no problems, as he was easily quieted if he woke at night. The next summer he was weaned, but I didn't expect any problems as he usually slept through the night.

But one night he unexpectedly woke howling and yelling. Nothing I did would quiet him. Finally, in desperation, I tossed clothes over my pajamas and carried him outside.

We were parked in the woods with a seldom used road a few feet behind us. I stepped out on the road and froze. Patrick was instantly silent. We had stepped into fairyland. It was as light as day as the full moon shone down from almost directly overhead. This world had no colors, only black and white and millions of shades of gray. Even small pebbles were quite visible on the road.

I began walking up the road as it crested a hill. Patrick's eyes shone as he twisted from side to side to see this strange, new world. We could hear a myriad of small insects and animals moving in the dark sinister woods, but we were on a magic road, safe in enchantment.

At the top of the hill we found an old barn and a small farmhouse. As we stood admiring what appeared to be an etching of a country scene, I suddenly felt the presence of someone else. I turned and saw two horses standing behind a fence. When they saw us looking at them they neighed softly. We moved over to them and patted their necks and soft muzzles. Patrick laughed and giggled as his hand touched the friendly horse. After a short time I said, "It's been very nice meeting you but we must go now." I was a little surprised when the horses only neighed in reply; it would have seemed quite right if they had spoken to us. Perhaps I was too old for the magic to work that well.

We went down the hill singing quietly, "I see the moon, the moon sees me . . ." Patrick fell asleep. My husband solved the problem of my finding the right trailer in the black woods by meeting us on the road. He took our sleeping son and we went back to the camper.

Whenever people ask when our children slept through the night, I remember the night Patrick and I had a glimpse of a magic world. Maybe there are some things in life better than sleeping through the night.

Almost Instantly Asleep

Carole Sheron
Kentucky
1974

I had saved putting him to bed until last because he is the hardest. Michael Patrick . . . three years old. His daddy and I call him the blond bombshell. His five brothers and sisters have all been individually Bible-lessoned, storied, prayed, watered, and tucked in. Michael is sitting on his bed, impatiently waiting for me to lie down with him. I look over to where his adopted brother, four months younger, is already asleep, curled into a little brown ball. Raised in a foster home for twenty months, he has always gone to sleep like a model child. I'm tired from a busy day, all I want is a leisurely bath and to go to bed early. Michael is urging me to "hurry up and lie down with me" and I wonder where I went wrong. Why won't this child go to bed by himself?

Michael wants a song. But it's not that simple. He wants me to play my guitar and sing. Two choruses of "I've Been Working on the Railroad" later, I carefully and logically explain that Mommy wants to take a bath and caution Michael that he is to stay in bed until Mommy finishes and then I'll lie down with him again. Blue eyes regard me solemnly and blond hair bobs as he nods his consent, but as I walk out the door he warns me, "A fast bath!"

The water is running into the tub and I'm pinning my hair up when I hear the familiar pitter-patter of hurried footsteps down the hall to my bedroom, a satisfied "thump," and I know he's in my bed. I take a hurried bath (is there any other kind?), dress, retrieve Michael from my bed, and we start all over again.

"I thought you promised Mommy to stay in your bed until I finished my bath?"

"I did Mommy. But then when you were gone, I got a'scared and zoomed to your room."

Pretty soon we're both tucked into Michael's single bed. Very cozy. Nurtured on the closeness of the nursing relationship, Michael is a toucher. His arms are wrapped around my neck, his legs plopped across mine, his silky blond hair snuggled against my cheek. I savor the moment, but also wish he'd hurry and go to sleep. I have things to do and I'm tired.

The silence lasts but a minute, "Mommy . . . Your teeth look pretty and clean."

"Thank you, Michael. I just brushed them."

"Mommy . . . why does teeth get dirty?"

"Because food gets on them." Silence again.

"Mommy. . .how does the water get off your toothbrush after you put it away in the cupboard?" Mentally I discard the word "evaporation" and answer, "Because the air moves around it inside the cupboard and dries it off." Silence again.

"Mommy . . . why don't pigs have hair?" My mind boggles at the sudden change in subject. "Well," I begin gamely. "If pigs had hair like you and me, when they wallowed in the mud, it would get all stuck in their hair and make them messy." Thankfully he's satisfied with my improvised answer.

"Why did Mrs. Centers cut up her pig?" Long ago he spent the day with a friend the day they butchered their hog. I explained that they needed it for food.

"We don't do that, do we? We get our food from the store." We are vegetarians so the idea of killing animals for food was new to him. He seemed a little disturbed by it.

He turns over and snuggles down into his covers. I think the magic moment has arrived, but not yet, "Mommy . . ." And I am entertained with a long and complicated adventure story plucked from the world of "pretend" involving himself and his imaginary horse Trigger. As he talks his eyes get rounder and rounder and his eyebrows disappear under his long, blond bangs as his face becomes more animated. Finally the story is over, he begins to yawn. He turns toward me again, takes my hand in both of his and is almost instantly asleep.

Suddenly I am caught up by those feelings of tenderness and overwhelming good will that a sleeping child bestows. There is something about sleep that transforms children into angels. Tangled lashes lie against cheeks. I gently kiss the soft mouth that in infancy searched eagerly for my breast and the milk that was his sole nourishment for the first six months.

As I slip quietly from his bed, I am suddenly aware of the instinct of children to demand what they need. Busy with five other children and a full day, were it not for his terrible bedtime habits, I might not have found time for this special hour with Michael for cuddling, and just learning to know him. I thank God that he was born healthy and bright and whole, and even the knowledge that he'll probably be back in our bed before midnight can't destroy the peace that I feel at this moment.

Expectations

Judy Thurman
Ohio
1977

It's late at night right now, our two children are asleep, Daddy is away on business, and I have a few quiet moments for reflective thought.

For the past four years I have, with my husband's support, put into practice the ideas and concepts I learned as a new mother. Such things as meeting the needs of newborns by nursing on demand, much touching, and unrestricted contact day and night.

However, for some time now we have found our five-year-old son's reluctance to fall asleep *alone* upsetting. More than that, we've been irritated, angry, and frustrated at our failure to "help" him do something everyone else's five-year-old child can do. Such behavior in a child at "his age" would be embarrassing if others found out! "We obviously have done something wrong—but what could it be?" we asked ourselves time and time again.

Taking everything we knew to be good and true—our rational thoughts and our child's obvious need to be with his parents at sleep time, we made a discovery. Eureka! There is absolutely *nothing* wrong with our child. There was *nothing* wrong with the closeness and total love we shared with him since birth. Being an innocent child, he sees no reason to give up the joy of falling asleep in the company of a loved one. Why am I writing this letter at 12:10 AM? My husband is away, I feel alone without him, and it is very difficult for me to go to sleep when he is not close by. To think we expected more of a five-year-old!

Mid-Night Mothering

Mikell Billoki
Ontario
1984

Last night I was awakened in the middle of the night by a little voice calling me from another room. I quietly slipped out of bed in the dark and found three-year-old Noah standing beside his bed unable to fall back to sleep.

He'd had a rather hard day, getting more than his share of scoldings, and now the nighttime seemed less than friendly to him. "Will you snuggle with me?" he asked, and we both crawled into the double bed that he shares with his five-year-old brother, Benjamin. With only a reassuring hug and a touch, he turned over and slipped back to sleep.

As I lay there with my cheek close to his, I thought of him, not as the little boy who took scissors to his storybook earlier that day, but as a middle child. His older brother just started school, and his younger brother always seems to need his mother's attention.

Maybe he feels a little shortchanged at times.

When I could tell by his breathing that he was soundly asleep, I made my way back to my bed and slipped under the covers just in time to sense six-month-old Abram stirring as a prelude to a nighttime nursing. I gently lifted his warm body into the circle made by my arm and his instincts and months of experience took over as he effortlessly began to nurse.

I realized that these encounters in the dark and peacefulness of the night must be very special to him. He can enjoy the comfort of his mother without any interruptions from telephones, older brothers, or the many tasks that must get done. His contentment is so obvious as his body gradually relaxes, releasing him back to his dreams, and we both fall asleep as quickly as we wakened.

Waking up several times each night is not always a wonderful experience, but last night I realized how important mid-night mothering can be. It gives children a chance to reaffirm the presence of love and busy mothers an extra opportunity to give a little individual attention. In the stillness, thoughts are clearer, and in their sleeping innocence, children always seem more dear.

How often we wish that there was a little more time in each day. Well, if we don't resent having to wake up in the middle of the night, we just might find that this is the extra time we need.

And the next time someone pities me because my baby doesn't "sleep though the night yet," I will feel at least a little bit grateful than even my older children give me that occasional opportunity to feel good about truly meeting their needs while sharing a special mid-night time of love.

Elizabeth Is Seven

Mary White, LLL Founder, 1979

How do you get a baby to sleep? Nurse her, of course. How do you get a toddler to sleep? Nurse her, of course, after her bath and a story and a nice juicy apple to munch on.

But gradually the snack and the story take on more importance, and the nursing is just a nip and a hug . . . and sooner than you think it's just lights out, a hug and a kiss, and she's off to sleep.

Elizabeth is seven. Summer evenings are long and often spent outside with one last bike ride or a chat with a friend. No school schedules to watch. We all lose track of time. But pretty soon it's "Come on, Mom, let's go to bed." "Okay," says I, "run up and take your shower while I knit one more row." (I'm a slow knitter!) Down she comes, long braids dripping, face and feet shiny clean, and skinny nightie in between. I fold up the knitting, and up we go, together as we always have, with Elizabeth leading the way and finding the place in our current book. Tonight, it's *Little Women,* and we both love it. I haven't read it in a long time and Elizabeth has never heard it before. We prop up the pillows, climb into her bed, and I read . . . and read . . . and read . . . (such long chapters!), until I find my eyes won't stay open and the words come out all wrong. Elizabeth gives me a nudge and a funny look. Oh, well, time to stop. Lights out, prayers together, a hug and a kiss. Most nights I stay a few more minutes as she falls asleep. Sometimes I fall asleep, too, and wake up with a jump when a head comes poking around the door, "Mother, telephone."

Later a storm blows up, lots of thunder and lightning and rain gusting in the open window. But Elizabeth sleeps soundly on until morning. Elizabeth is almost eight.

23

Nighttime Needs

Sleep—A Question of Attitude

Pat Yearian
Washington
1972

It seems that whether it's the baby's or the mother's, sleep (or lack of sleep) is a much discussed topic.

We all believe in sleep and certainly enjoy a full night's rest. Who doesn't? But after the birth of our baby we find, also, our sleep is being interrupted, not just once at night but often. Then we try very hard to catch up by napping in the daytime so we will be rested. Sometimes we meet with success, but more often than not we are interrupted again either by the baby, the phone, or a visitor.

How you react to this situation is truly up to you. If you resent it, you will face each day more frustrated and trying harder and harder to fit the baby into your type of sleep pattern—which in the early years is difficult. On the other hand, if you can adjust your mental attitude to one of acceptance of this fact of interrupted sleep, you will find yourself able to enjoy those quiet moments in the night with your baby who needs to be held or nursed. Or with your toddler who is not nursing, maybe, but just wakes up and needs to be with someone. You will also find you are not any sleepier, or at least not noticing it as much. This acceptance doesn't come right away. But when you begin to notice that your sleep can be interrupted many times a night and yet you are still able to face the day with a smile, your attitudes are changing.

As I lie "squished" between my dear husband on one side and either the two- or four-year-old on the other, I often think to myself, "I am such a lucky woman to be so close to two people I love so very much."

Notes from Grandma

Betty Wagner, LLL Founder, 1974

It's just not fair, or it doesn't seem so to me, that a first-time mother could produce a baby that sleeps through the whole night. She smugly tells of nursing her marvelous baby at about 10:00 PM, places him in his darling basket and doesn't hear from him again until 6:00 AM the next morning. She really thinks she knows how to raise babies and wonders why the rest of us don't. I do hope she has at least one or two more so she can see that all babies are different.

These mothers' stories really used to bother me when I would be awakened several times each night by my nursing babies. I wondered when I would ever be able to sleep through the night again.

Well, I finally did with my fourth. Mary slept through the very first night I brought her home from the hospital. I couldn't believe it and woke several times just to check and see if she was still breathing. She never did disturb my night's sleep, and so I could now smugly tell about *my* perfect baby who must have read all those baby books before she was born and knew how to act.

But only so long can we live in that paradise of enjoying a full night's sleep. And I came down with a bang when I had my sixth, Dorothea. She *never* slept. The only catnaps she took were during the times I held her or slept with her. Now this was very nice when she was new and I needed the rest. However, I felt this couldn't go on and devised various ways to keep her sleeping while I slipped away. One of my favorites was accomplished with the use of a couple of large diaper pins. We would lie on the bed and she would nurse to sleep. Then I would pin her clothes to the bedsheet, so she wouldn't fall off when she awoke, and I would slip away. Other times I could gently slip her into bed with another sleeping child and at times she would continue to sleep. Another warm body seemed to keep her happy. A basket of warm diapers, fresh from the dryer, was one of her favorite napping places. Never did she sleep long but I valued every minute she did sleep. And I learned more about babies from each one I had.

A Vote for the Cradle

Mary Jane Hershey
Pennsylvania
1970

When our third son was born, my husband's parents gave us a beautiful old Pennsylvania Dutch cradle, complete with hand-carved hearts on each side. I was delighted with it; my husband and I are tenth- and eleventh-generation Pennsylvania Dutch. I was doubly pleased to find how convenient it was. It was placed right beside our bed, and I could reach over to pat and rock or pick him up without getting out of bed myself.

Now, five years later, we have our four-month-old adopted daughter in it, and I am again impressed with what a practical and useful bed it is for a young infant. The high sides prevent her falling out; it is quite narrow, giving her feelings of security with blankets close on each side; she is protected from cold air in our drafty two-hundred-year-old farmhouse; and she has mother just an arm's length away any time during the night.

A New Arrangement

Sharon Falatovics
Indiana
1971

Our sleeping arrangement for our nursing toddler wasn't due to my own ingenuity but happened quite accidentally. One summer when we had guests for several days, my two children, then about three years and seventeen months, slept on a lightweight mattress on the floor. I did, too, since I had to nurse Michael at bedtime and during the night if he awoke. Long after our company left, the mattress remained on the floor of our bedroom. During the day, I would turn the mattress on edge and slip it behind the dresser or the headboard of the bed. The children liked their new sleeping arrangement. It wasn't just a novelty that wore off, since it lasted for over a year.

A Change in Pattern

Joyce Walker
Maryland
1971

At twenty months of age or thereabouts our toddler was up each night, and even the soundest of sleepers would have been hard-put to sleep with all of his thrashing and kicking—no snuggle-up-and nurse for him. Somehow behavior that seems reasonable in the light of day takes on a different hue at midnight. I really didn't want to nurse Michael grudgingly night after night when all our other nursings were generally pleasant experiences for both of us.

So I no longer took him back to bed with me when he woke up; I sat up and nursed in the dark of his room. No sleep at all for me, of course, but at least his father wasn't awakened. After a while, I didn't automatically offer him the breast but would just sit and rock and sing softly. I never refused to nurse him but waited for him to tell me that nursing was what he wanted. His greatest need seemed to be to know that we were there and would come immediately when he called. Gradually the nursings stopped, and gradually, too, the waking up stopped. Now, at twenty-seven months, on the rare nights when he awakens, I seldom need to do more than go into his room, touch him, and speak to him.

As I look back on it, I think that Michael was growing out of the need to nurse at night, but it took an outward change in our nursing pattern to help him outgrow the habit. After all, he had known no other experience than nursing in our bed when he woke up after dark; no one had offered him a rocking, a glass of water, a soft serenade, or anything else. Perhaps babies need to be presented with alternative solutions just as mothers do.

Variety

Gail Mraz
Minnesota
1971

Just as there is great variety in babies, so there are lots of different mothers and mothering ideas. Some envision for their baby a cozy crib with a patchwork quilt, some a pretty cradle (perhaps handmade), and others a relaxing floor mattress.

I've used all three at various times with my children. It was a real delight to see my Nicholas tucked into a prewarmed rocking cradle after his birth at home (though he usually slept with me). As we have hardwood floors and cold Minnesota winters, a cozy four-poster crib was right at times for two-year-old Jessie. At other times she slept in a bottom bunk with her big sister Gina. Four-year-old Paul really liked his mattress on the floor. (He could jump on it during the day.)

Mothers are all different. Some will give birth at home and some in the hospital; some will bake their own bread and some buy it at the bakery; some will wash their scrub rags and some will throw them out after one use. And so on. One of the things about La Leche League that I most appreciate is their acknowledgement of the many different ways that we can mother our children well.

Following My Heart

Mary Ann Barwick
North Carolina
1977

Christianne, our first, was always a fussy baby. She loved to nurse and nap, nurse and nap. But she still cried almost every night for about two hours straight. Everyone offered suggestions of what should be done. What I did was hold her, walk her, and rock her. At about three months the two-hour period of crying stopped, but Christi started waking up about every hour all night long, and this went on for months with only an occasional break when she'd sleep two or, once in a while, three hours. It was the occasional "long" stretch that sustained me. What did she need? Who knows? All I knew was that she cried and I could stop it by holding, nursing, or cuddling her.

But I was determined not to sleep with her because everyone said that was a terrible habit. So I went back and forth till my poor husband became tired, too, from lack of sleep. Sometimes I'd wake up with her in my arms and realize that we'd slept two or three hours. I'd put her back in the crib, and she'd be crying again in thirty minutes.

Meanwhile, I was vulnerable to critical comments from every direction. But deep down within me, I knew that I was doing as well as anyone could under the circumstances. My housekeeping and cooking were always done with her in my arms, and my husband supported me, though he really didn't know how to help.

At five months, when I complained to the doctor that Christi never slept, he prescribed a strong drug which I was to use for three nights straight. That was supposed to get her in the habit of sleeping well. The first night she slept six hours. The second, four. The third, two. Then I was instructed to put her in her crib and leave her. "Let her cry; it's good for her lungs." Well, my Christi's bound to have great lungs. She'd cry for two hours, fall asleep, sleep two hours, wake up, and start again. This went on all night long. I undoubtedly made it harder on her by looking in from the door (pain on my face) checking her diaper (hoping it would be wet so I'd be justified in picking her up). Nothing was ever harder for me to do, hurt me more, or was more useless. When I realized it wasn't going to work, I discontinued that "therapy" and tried another doctor.

It was during this period that I reached out to La Leche League. The new doctor told me to wean her; this would solve my problem. But I couldn't bear the thought of weaning her. Help came from La Leche League quickly: a kind personal letter with articles on other babies who slept poorly and how mothers coped. I read them all and immediately put into practice the ideas that seemed best to me. I put a mattress on the floor, and after my husband had gone to sleep, I went to bed with Christi. When she woke up crying, I gave her my breast. I finally learned to go back to sleep while she nursed. I determined to follow my heart and my instincts and pay no attention to attitudes of the unsympathetic. I quit trying to change something she couldn't help and accepted her as she was. I gave myself completely, and that's when things began to improve.

I began to feel better. Christi, responding to my being there when she needed me, slowly began sleeping for longer spells—two hours, then three hours. This didn't happen immediately, of course, but I felt better overnight because the struggle was over. She simply needed me there with her.

In the last week of her fifteenth month, she suddenly "outgrew" the breast. She substituted books for nursing; for several nights I had to read to her off and on all night long. But she was through with the breast. If I offered it, she refused it.

The sleeping gradually improved, and now she sleeps all night three or four times a week. You see, weaning wasn't the magic solution to her sleep problem.

I'd like to encourage mothers everywhere to follow their hearts and instincts with their children. You'll be doing yourself, your child, and your family a favor.

In the Darkness

Ellinor Hamilton
Maryland
1979

I remember with fondness nursing my son Jonathan during the night when he was a baby, but Jonathan is now twenty-two months old and still crying for me three, four, or five times a night. I'm often tempted to yell (and sometimes do), "No, no! This has gone on long enough! You are almost two years old; you are not a baby; you do not have to nurse all night!"

Recently I've been recalling something I studied a hundred moons ago . . . a theory called "needs-regression." It suggests that when humans are in a basic state such as sadness, illness, or sleep, our needs are not the same as when we are alert and in control of ourselves. Instead, they are the needs we experienced as a young child or baby—to be held close, wrapped warmly, reassured by the physical presence of a person we can depend on for comfort. We can all picture ourselves in need of these comforts: snuggling in bed under a blanket; nestling against our spouses; even weeping in misery. They are all basic human responses.

Maybe Jonathan really is still ten months old in the quiet darkness. Maybe even less. The desire to pass the night curled against mother's breast is an appropriate one for an infant. I'm not really comforting Jonathan, the two-year-old; I'm comforting Jonathan, the baby. He still needs me.

Nothing, they tell me, lasts forever. It seems like a long time. I often feel resentment and doubts. But I also feel love and softness for this growing-up little boy who is still my baby.

24

The Family Bed

"Allowing a baby in bed with you in the League's early days was considered something just short of immoral. So powerful were the warnings and threats of what could happen that it was only a few months ago that my mother revealed that I (lucky baby) had spent most of my first year sharing my parents' bed. Maybe she was waiting to see how I would turn out!"

Marian Tompson, LLL Founder, 1981

In Their Own Time

Anne Scheidler
Indiana
1981

What began out of sheer exhaustion coupled with loving concern for our little baby years ago, has become for us a most important and essential way to met the nighttime needs of our children.

Like the majority of new parents today, we were well indoctrinated by our culture in its adult-oriented childcare practices. We accepted many of these as the norm, including baby's sleeping through the night in his own crib. When we discovered that I was pregnant, we set about acquiring all the necessary equipment for

215

childrearing. This, of course, included the baby's crib to be placed in the baby's very own beautifully decorated nursery. Well-meaning friends and relatives advised us with regard to the need for schedules, the dangers of "spoiling" by rocking and nursing to sleep, and the importance of the baby "learning" to sleep by himself.

By the time our first child, Christopher, was two months old, he was beginning to show his deep-seated need for closeness and security by very frequent (it seemed almost constant) nursing. He only slept for short intervals during the day and generally this occurred in Mommy's arms after nursing to sleep. We wondered why our child required so much nursing and holding. We were grateful to La Leche League for supporting our natural instincts to caress, hold, nurse, and cuddle our baby frequently and not to "let him cry it out" as so many encouraged.

For some reason it was easier to handle his need for constant nursing during the daytime hours, but late evening and night-times were quite difficult. Our nighttime ritual became longer and longer in a desperate attempt to get him to sleep in his crib. The evenings started like this: after much nursing, rocking, walking, he would fall asleep in my arms. I would ever so quietly take him into his room and gently lay him in his crib. But as soon as his head touched the sheets, he'd awaken. Then tiredly, we'd return to the rocking chair to nurse him back to sleep. I spent many sleepless hours trying to accomplish what seemed so impossible then and seems so unnecessary now: getting him to sleep alone in his crib. Of course, Chris would eventually be so tired from repeated "rude" awakenings during attempts to lay him down that he would finally stay asleep. And he would generally sleep through the night as well, what was left of it anyway.

When he was nearing five months of age, he began awakening several times at night. We figured that teething discomfort accounted for some of his nighttime wakefulness, although his first tooth didn't erupt for two and a half months. But no matter the reason, I was so exhausted from traipsing into his room to nurse him back to sleep that I didn't think I could take it much longer.

After a couple of these tough nights, Dan suggested that we bring Chris to bed with us at his naturally sleepy time. I think I was too fatigued to discuss the idea, so we just decided to try it. The first night was pretty scary with worries that we might smash him or that he might roll off of the bed. Pushing the bed against the wall on one side took care of some of the concern.

After the first weeks of adjusting to a "little body" in bed with us, we finally relaxed and soon were enjoying sleeping with Chris. It was so easy during the night to roll over and nurse him when he stirred that he never really awakened. I wondered why we hadn't tried this sooner. The benefits of more sleep for the entire family were great, but seeing his smiling face first thing in the morning was the real reward. This started each day on a cheery note, and no longer did we dread the nighttime ritual. Instead, we all enjoyed lying down together and watching Chris drift peacefully off to sleep snuggled between us.

In the beginning, our queen-size bed was big enough for the three of us. But by the time Chris was eight months old, we felt the need for more space, so we added a portacrib with one side down on the same level as our bed.

When Chris was two and a half and still needing nighttime nursings, we enlarged our bed again by adding a twin bed to one side. That made one "big bed," which is the name we eventually came to call it. We realized that we could possibly get Chris to fall asleep in another room, but we sensed that very soon he would want to join us in our bed anyway. Besides, we really had grown to prefer having him near us at night. He was safe between us, and it was very comforting to know that in the event of fire or other danger, all we needed to do was scoop him up and take him with us. We also benefited by increased sleep, as we never had to get up to check on him. All we had to do was open our eyes and he was always within arm's reach to quickly cover him up or just to make sure he was all right.

A year and a half ago our second child, Nicholas, was born. When he was five hours old, we came home from the hospital to rest in our "big bed." We all began to get to know Nicholas that day lying together in our bed. We have not had to suffer the trials and tribulations of our former "nighttime ritual" as we did with Chris. Nicholas benefited (as did we all) from the knowledge we gained during the growth of our first child. We had learned the beauty of the family bed for meeting the needs of nighttime closeness and security of our children.

We have been told by many that we will never get them out of our bed. We realize that "this too shall pass" and are willing to let them grow out of this need in their own time. We are just hopeful that when they grow out of the need for nighttime closeness, that we are ready, too.

Valerie's Dollhouse

Noreen Humes
Iowa
1981

Six-year-old Valerie was very puzzled by her new dollhouse. She could not figure out why the baby's bedroom was located on the third floor and the parents' bedroom was on the second floor. She had commented several times about this arrangement. One night, as I was putting toys away, I noticed that Valerie had solved the problem herself. The whole third floor had been turned into the family bedroom. The cradle was sitting next to the parents' bed and the baby was tucked cozily between the mommy and daddy dolls.

Animal Lovers

Linda Back
Pennsylvania
1982

My hobbies include breeding Great Danes and obedience training. In pursuing these hobbies, I made contact with many dog owners. They all have one thing in common—they love their dogs. Talking with them, I have found most of them feel sorry for their pets at night. They feel the dogs are lonely if they are left outside or kept apart from the family. Many of these dogs are allowed to sleep in their master's bedroom and at times even on the bed.

It made me stop to question why we feel such compassion for our beloved pets, yet feel we will "spoil" our children if we answer to their loneliness and nighttime needs.

The Three Bears—Revisited

Brenda Sheets
West Virginia
1983

One evening while reading "Goldilocks and the Three Bears" I noticed that my two-year-old son, David, was deeply interested in the pictures. We had reached the end of the story and were reading about the lumpy bed, the hard bed, and the little one that was just right, when David interrupted me to ask, "Why do they have so many beds, Mommy?" I replied that I didn't really know. He looked at the pictures of the three beds once more and said, "But Mommy, they can't hug each other."

Perhaps the family bed isn't for everyone, but it certainly is for us. After finishing our story David decided that the bears should push all their beds together . . . now, haven't I heard of that somewhere before?

A Radical Approach

Nikii Frank
Virginia
1983

All went well after my son's birth except for Matthew's sleeping habits. He never slept more than ten hours a day, including naps, and woke frequently at night. Matthew's bassinet was kept next to our bed and when he woke I would nurse him sitting up on a sofa we kept in our bedroom. When he fell asleep I'd try and get him back into his bassinet without waking him. This was not always successful. All of my attempts to help him sleep longer stretches failed and I resigned myself to the situation, patiently waiting for the magical day the baby books talked about when Matthew would sleep through the night. Bob, my husband, would often wake up to find me asleep, sitting up on the sofa with Matthew in my arms.

Matthew's great-grandmother, Mother Veta, had visited us when Matthew was a month old and said that her mother (Matthew's great-great-grandmother) never had to get out of bed at night with her babies. They lived on a farm and the newest baby just slept with his parents until the next baby came along. The older baby then went to sleep with his siblings. Mother Veta said she was convinced her mother had nursed her babies in her sleep. I had dismissed this "strange" idea because I was afraid of starting a "bad habit."

When Matthew was five months old, my resentment of the situation mounted due to my exhaustion. I tried calling various mother help groups for advice and checked out childcare books at the library. They all advocated letting the child cry it out. My own motherly instincts wisely kept me from following this course of action. I knew Matthew was waking for a reason—hunger, wet-ness, loneliness, fear, or whatever—and ignoring his cry would not take care of his needs. It would tell him that no one cared about his needs. When I called my local La Leche League Leader, she said she had no magic formula for making Matthew sleep through the night but that it was a common occurrence for ba-bies to awaken frequently. She then went on to explain the fam-ily bed concept.

With Bob's urging, I tried this "radical" approach. Matthew loved it from the start, waking only long enough to nurse and fall eas-ily back to sleep. After a week I realized he wasn't going to be smothered and I, too, relaxed. When a blanket would get close to his face, his arms and legs would thrash about, throwing off the blanket or awakening us. Even though he still nursed often during the night, I awoke in the morning feeling well-rested be-cause I never had to awaken myself sufficiently to pick up Mat-thew and walk with him to our nursing spot as I used to do. Now I just laid quietly in bed, nursing, and both of us would drift back to sleep. Now the only time I'm out of bed is when I have to go to the bathroom!

We retired our double bed and are enjoying a new king-size bed. Matthew likes to sleep with his feet towards his dad and his mouth towards me. When he is ready to nurse he just rolls over to me. He doesn't cry and never fully awakens at night anymore. In the mornings, we are greeted with big smiles and it is a special time for his daddy and him to play together.

At Our House

Beverly M.   Kirk
Alaska
1983

The family bed has much to recommend it, and in our case, it may have saved our son's life.

All of our children (including some foster children and our adopted daughter) have slept with us, weaning themselves from our bed as gradually as they weaned themselves from the breast. Our youngest, James, now six and a half, has been the slowest "weaner" in most regards and is still not ready for regular nights in his own bed.

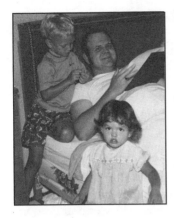

Bev Kirk and her family were featured several times in LLL NEWS with stories and poems. Photo above shows Bev nursing Kirsten in 1972; photo at top left shows Bud Kirk with Frankie and Cricket; on the left, Jamey at age 4 playing the violin; below, the Kirk family in 1986.

The month after Jamey's fourth birthday he awakened me one night with an isolated incident of what seemed to be intense shivering. He is normally a very warm sleeper, but I pulled him gently to me and nestled the covers back around us. It was a full year before this happened again, and then obvious "grand mal" seizures began in earnest—always during Jamey's sleep. I lost no time in getting him to our pediatrician. He was started on medication to control the seizures and the doctor ordered further tests.

A bright, alert, happy child of five, Jamey was certainly of the age when normally a mother might run a shallow bath and allow her child to play in it for awhile as she carried on a running conversation with him from an adjoining room, but Jamey has always been more comfortable with me in sight. Thus one afternoon when I was helping him finish up his bath I was right there with him when he had his first seizure while fully awake. I have had foster children who have had seizures in the bathtub, so my body mechanically took over and took care of Jamey while my mind flip-flopped in and out of horror stories.

Since then James has been diagnosed as having epilepsy and is under good control with medication. His neurologist has cautioned us against allowing him to bathe alone and has also stressed that he must be carefully watched whenever swimming or boating.

In the meantime I have been so thankful for the sensitivity that breastfeeding has enabled me to develop toward each of my children. Without nursing my children, I probably would never have considered allowing them to sleep with us. For over a year, Jamey's seizures occurred exclusively during deep sleep. Had we sent him off to his own bed years ago, it is possible that the first we would have been aware of them could have been finding him in the bathtub that day!

Night Visitors

Mary Ann Gebhardt
Michigan
1975

Our children have always had their own beds, but were always welcome in our bed. This simply means that they start out in their own beds. When Mama and Daddy go to bed, we have at least one hour, sometimes two, alone. We are then joined by nine-month-old Matthew. His bed is next to ours. He usually wakes to nurse about three times a night and when he is finished, if I'm awake, I return him to his bed. He seems to sleep more soundly in his own bed. Four-year-old Kim still comes in every night. I'm not sure when, as I never hear her, but she is always there in the morning and I suspect she has been there for a while. In the wee hours of the morning six-year-old Tami usually finds her way in, and once in a great while eight-year-old Teresa joins us for the last hour of the morning. Two years ago she also was a nightly visitor.

This is a pattern all of our children have followed and as you can see, as they get older, their need to be near us diminishes. When I'm asked if our children sleep with us, I always answer, "Not really." After all, they all do have their own beds and start the night there. Upon rare occasions they even stay there! Mama and Daddy have all the time alone together we want and from there we welcome lonely, cold wanderers of the night. Whether you consider that "sleeping in the family bed" or not depends on your attitude on the subject.

Isn't it funny how one's attitude determines whether something is a problem or not? Recently a mother told me, "I'm so lucky! My baby sleeps all night from 11 to 5." Another time a mother complained, "My baby is driving me crazy. Will he ever sleep through the night? He only sleeps from 11 to 5."

A Real-Life Education

Michele Smolek-Houghton
Michigan
1983

I hope my students at Central Michigan University, the various parent groups I have spoken to, and the families I have counseled, will all read this statement: "Don and I and our three-year-old son sleep together, and we know the experience is healthy and right!"

During my four years on staff at the university, one of my lectures was entitled "Twenty Ways to Destroy Your Child." Sleeping with him was on the top of the list. I quoted research and told of counseling incidents that proved this to be true. I did not have a child at the time. I retired from teaching when I was seven months pregnant.

When John was four months old, Don and I vacationed to South America with him. He loved the closeness of our ship's cabin facilities so much that after two weeks on the ship John wanted our nighttime closeness at home, too.

Of course, I'd never agree to that. I lectured for four years against it! I had "research" to show it supposedly wasn't good.

Don and I have never believed in letting our son "cry it out," so we spent an exhausting week running to his crib to hold him. He would fall right back to sleep, then awaken again when we left him alone. All John wanted was our closeness.

When some dear friends heard about our sleepless nights they gave us the book *The Family Bed.*

"Take John to bed with you . . . you need the rest," was our family doctor's advice. He gave us names of several of our friends, including his own family, who sleep with their children. We talked with them, prayed about it, and could see only family closeness coming from it . . . with restful nights.

So, John has been sleeping with us since he was five months old. Unless you have slept with your children, you probably won't understand. If you have slept with your child, I needn't explain. You will already be smiling and saying, "I know how beautiful it is." Don and I know in our hearts it is the right thing for our family to do. I can't even put into words the family love the three of us share together, the security of the child (our son, John, actually sleeps with a smile on his face), the rest we all get (John has no sleeping problems as so many other children have, no bad dreams keep him awake, no storms scare him), and the fact that he enjoys bedtime. After we read the Bible and say our prayers, he's asleep within minutes.

Don and I feel very good about our parenting. We have a loving son to show for it. May I ask forgiveness from those I tried to teach during my "inexperienced years," and thank La Leche League for my "education" into *really* loving my child.

Part Seven

Working Together

The Family and the Medical Community

Krista

Susie Bartz
California
1978

Flesh of my flesh, blood of my blood,
formed, fed, born by my body.
Together we grew, unfolded, strained,
  and grasped
in that primal knowledge that one had
  become two

We reached out and found each other
and we were one again.

And the sweet goodness of my milk
flowed into the fragile perfection of
  your body
still curled and cradled by my own.

As much as I nourished you,
touched, stroked, and fondled you,
so you nourished me.

Tremblingly, tenderly we knew each
  other
in this instant that became forever.

25

The Doctor and
the Nursing Mother

"I have found a very effective way of talking to the doctor is to use the words I feel. If you think or insist, he won't like it. But if you feel you would like to do or not do something, this is a very gentle way to open the discussion, because nobody is going to step on your feelings."

   Viola Lennon, LLL Founder, 1968

Memos from Marian

   Marian Tompson, LLL Founder, 1964

What do you do when your doctor doesn't agree with LLL . . . and you? When, for example, he insists on solids at four weeks while you would like to wait several months longer?

   Should you reluctantly go along with him ("after all, we are paying for his advice"); should you lie and just pretend you're feeding the baby other foods; or should you sit down and quietly talk it over with him, listening to his reasons as well as giving him your own?

Discussing this at a board meeting, Herbert Ratner, MD, LLL medical advisor, gave the last suggestion as the sensible one. For mothers not only have a right to be heard, they have an obligation to speak up if they expect to receive the help they need from the medical profession. As Dr. Ratner pointed out, this dialogue between doctor and patient is essential. Finding yourself up against a doctor whose rigid thinking forbids discussion, disagreement, or any questioning whatever, might well make you consider changing doctors.

The nursing mother must be understood if she is to be helped. This means doctors should be familiar with the psychological implications of breastfeeding as well as the practical aspects. There is a lot of talking to be done.

Selecting Your Child's Doctor

Suzanne Ballard
Montana
1976

It wasn't until my daughter Tamsen's birth last year that I realized fully the importance of selecting her doctor well, and in advance. During my few days in the hospital after Tami's birth, I requested that she be brought to me on demand and that no supplemental feedings be given her, so that she could be entirely breastfed from the beginning. The response was, "Who's your pediatrician?" Luckily, Tami's pediatrician was well known in the hospital for her pro-breastfeeding ways. As soon as her name was mentioned, there was no problem.

My roommate did not fare so well. She wanted to breastfeed Jennifer, her first child, but was apprehensive and unsure of herself. Following my lead, she also requested demand feeding and no supplements, but unfortunately *her* doctor had laid down ground rules that any child under his care could not be brought out of the nursery any more often than every four hours and that if breastfed, must be supplemented until it received over one-and-one-half ounces at each feeding. No matter what Janet wanted or said, the answer was the same, "Oh, Dr. So-and-So doesn't allow that with *his* children!"

While at the hospital, I talked to some other breastfeeding mothers. One had a doctor who insisted that the baby not be brought to his mother until twenty-four hours had passed. Her baby weighed over eight pounds at birth and had no apparent physical problem—it was just this doctor's policy with *every* baby. The mother was frantic because she wanted her baby sooner.

A nurse at the hospital told me that the first day I was in there were thirteen babies in the nursery and twelve were breastfed. I was happy about all these breastfed babies but sad to see all the poor screaming little ones in the nursery and realize that only a few of them were being brought to their mothers on demand.

The nurses, of course, have to follow the doctors' orders, so I'm not blaming them. I *am* a little upset with doctors who refuse to pay any attention to the mother's wishes about feeding her child.

So I am advising mothers to be sure they and their physicians are on the same wavelength about breastfeeding—not only approving in general, which most doctors do, but giving the hospital nurses the kind of instructions about the care of the babies that will enable breastfeeding to get off to a good start.

Product of Our Culture

A Wisconsin Mother
1971

I'm an "old lady" of thirty-nine with my third breastfed baby nearly three months old now, and I ordered your book more out of a sense of comradeship than stark need. I went through my stark need phase in 1953 with my first baby, and I succeeded at breastfeeding more out of sheer stubbornness than anything else. I thought many times that there was a need for something like La Leche League. You hear a hundred clever ways to dry up the breasts and not one word of help to preserve lactation.

I remember telling everyone lightly, "Oh certainly the baby eats every four hours!"—and like a guilty conspirator feeding him every two hours or three or whatever. I think my experiences of that year fitted me for a career in the secret service! Looking back, I don't know why or how I did it. I worried constantly. I knew no one else who was breastfeeding. I seldom consulted the pediatrician for fear I'd be advised to stop nursing. That baby is now six foot two, a hundred and ninety pounds, and is end on the high-school football team, center on his basketball team, and about to become an Eagle Scout.

But things really haven't changed much in seventeen years. I still lie. With this baby each month I confront the pediatrician and he asks with steely, suspicious eyes, "How many times a day do you nurse the baby?" And I tell him whatever I think he wants to hear, varying it a little from month to month to lend dramatic interest. (He is such a nice man in every other way, has pulled our kids through a number of scrapes, and after all, is a product of our culture like everyone else.) In his first month, this baby gained three pounds. The doctor, reading the weight the nurse had recorded, said, "Some little kid has been playing with this scale. We'll weigh him again." But he saw for himself that the scale was correct. I thought that finally he might become curious enough to ask how I had performed this "miracle," which he's practically certain can't be done, but he didn't.

If anyone is curious, shows signs of having an open mind, or asks for help, I talk breastfeeding. Otherwise I keep my peace.

Honesty

Marty Blankenship
Kansas
1972

I disagree with that Wisconsin mother. I picked my pediatrician with some care, partly because he encourages breastfeeding, and I listened when he said, "When I prescribe or suggest, I need to know whether you followed that advice in order to properly evaluate the apparent results. I have had mothers lie to me, and I want you to know that if you ever lie to me about this baby, you will be out one pediatrician."

So if I disagree with him about something, I don't lie; I tell him that I disagree and why. We betray our own intelligence and confidence when we deny that we too have some knowledge that is worth consideration. Perhaps more openness on our part, more willingness to share our own knowledge and experience with the confidence it deserves, would further our cause. Why not respond to the doctor's comments and queries with, "What do you think of what Niles Newton has to say on that subject? Look, she says . . . ." Surely this type of response will do more to encourage doc-

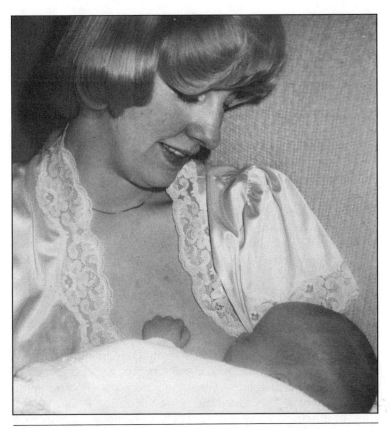

The strong bond between a nursing mother and her child must be understood and respected by doctors and other health professionals.

tors to do more research in this area than "telling him what we think he wants to hear." How is he ever going to change his mind without more input? I expect my doctor to be honest with me, and I must in turn be honest with him.

Mothering at the Breast

Betsy Razza
Georgia
1982

Choosing a pediatrician is an important decision, so before my son, Jonathan, was born I interviewed several doctors. I was pleased with the answers one doctor, in particular, gave me about breastfeeding and felt I had made a good choice.

Jonathan had a slight breathing problem at birth and had to re-main in the hospital nursery under observation for a few days. A variety of pacifiers and bottles were offered, and he developed nipple confusion. This problem was quickly overcome at home, however. For a while we also had problems with colic. Finally at four months the worst seemed behind us. Jonathan had grown like a weed, and he smiled all the time. I was very proud of my baby when we went for his four month checkup.

I was very surprised when my pediatrician informed me that although my baby was growing well, he was not developing properly, as Jonathan did not roll over yet. The doctor believed this was because I did not leave him alone in a crib or playpen. He said that Jonathan had not experienced enough frustration in his life to "develop properly."

I came home from this scolding feeling very depressed. I talked with my husband and a La Leche League Leader. I realized that a pediatrician who advocated breastfeeding might not necessar-ily support mothering at the breast. So I began to look for a new doctor. I asked the usual questions about delayed solids, vitamin and fluoride supplements, and bottles, but this time I asked doc-tors about their philosophy of mothering and "spoiling" as well. I found a new pediatrician who is supportive of my wish to mother my baby at the breast. I discovered from this experience that some doctors advocate breast**feeding**—a way of eating—while others support **nursing**—a relationship. There is an important difference between these two.

By the way Jonathan is six months old and rolls all over the place!

Is Your Baby Too Fat?

Janice F. Nixon
Florida
1979

Being a first-time mother and probably a bit over-anxious about doing everything just right, I may have overreacted when the doc-tor told me my beautiful, three-month-old, totally breastfed baby was fat. But when he went on to tell me that I was doing her harm by letting her develop excess fat cells in infancy that would cause her problems later on and that I should put her on a diet, well, what mother wouldn't be upset at that!

Fortunately, the doctor we had just seen was not Alena's regular doctor. Knowing, however, that many doctors today feel this way, I wanted to be prepared for whatever her regular doctor would say at our next visit.

After all, I really was just a novice at the art of breastfeeding. I had no close examples to follow, either friend or family. In fact, my mother told me she had tried to breastfeed both of her children and had been advised to give it up because she "didn't have enough milk." Could I have been trying to overcompensate by feeding my baby too often or too long?

I thought back over all I had heard at LLL meetings and read. Was Alena happy and alert most of the time? Yes. Did she spit up a lot? No. Was she developing well in all other respects? Yes. Then on what grounds were the doctors basing their assumption that she was overweight?

They based it on charts and percentiles. Alena's weight gain had been plotted since birth on a graph and compared with all other babies studied—most of whom were probably bottle fed. At three and a half months she weighed almost eighteen pounds and was above the ninety-seventh percentile on the growth chart.

Then I remembered my mother had told me that I had been a very large baby. A picture of mother when she was a baby also showed her to be extremely chubby, and she was completely breastfed. Yet, neither of us have had a weight problem as an adult.

I took these pictures of the three generations with me and waited for the weigh-in and lecture at the next checkup.

Sure enough, at four months she weighed almost nineteen pounds and was twenty-five inches long—way above the norm. But when her doctor saw the pictures, he was so impressed that he called in another doctor to look at them. They talked about the loopholes in the "fat-cell" theory, and the obvious fact that fat babies do not always become fat adults. It had been their observation that breastfed fat was indeed different from formula-fed fat and the difference could even be felt in the silky, smooth skin of the breastfed infant. They both agreed that there was no reason for me to alter Alena's present care in any way. Absolutely no diet!

A Fantasy

Melanie Axel-Lute
New Jersey
1978

Time: The not-too-distant future

Scene: A Doctor's office

Doctor: Yes, Judy, the test is positive—you are going to have a baby. Now I'll just give you instructions for the artificial womb.

Judy: Well, doctor, I have been planning to be pregnant.

Doctor: (surprised) Oh! I do have a few patients who say they'd like to try that. It's very difficult nowadays, though, so many pressures on the modern woman. Of course, I'm all for it. It is the best thing for the fetus, though the new artificial wombs are very good. Now—have you done any preparatory exercises?

Judy: I didn't know about that.

Doctor: You'll find it very hard then, especially at first. I usually have my patients do several months of sit-ups and leg-lifts.

Many women say they'd like to try being pregnant but they have to give up in a few weeks. They have morning sickness and are very tired. I always recommend that anyone with nausea switch to the artificial womb.

Being pregnant takes a lot out of a woman. You'll need your strength for the baby. And you don't seem to be very big through the pelvis. You may not be big enough to be pregnant. I'll have to test your amniotic fluid to see if it's adequate.

It's very hard to judge the weight of the fetus when it's in a human womb, too. Some women worry whether it's gaining enough weight. I always like to start intrauterine feedings at about two months.

Now, how long had you planned to be pregnant?

Judy: I planned on letting the baby be born naturally.

Doctor: (shocked) Oh, my! That's really not necessary, you know. Most of my patients go for three months—that's the critical period—although a few stick it out for six. More than that is definitely unnecessary.

Have you thought about what people will say? Most people don't mind seeing a woman pregnant with a tiny fetus, but when it gets to be more than six months—well! It's just very unusual.

Besides, have you thought about how tied down you'll be? You'll have to take that fetus everywhere. Women really need to get out alone once in a while, you know. I feel that most women who prolong pregnancy like that do so for very selfish reasons.

Judy: I want to go ahead with it anyway.

Doctor: (patronizing) Well, I guess I'll just have to let you try it for a while and see how it goes. . . .

26

A Child in Need

Nothing is more distressing than a child in a medical crisis. Health problems bring anguish to all concerned and upset the delicate balance of family life.

When a child must be hospitalized, the disruption to the family is even greater. Although hospitals are becoming more accommodating, parents find they still need to draw on their ingenuity, assertiveness, and tact when acting as their child's advocate and source of comfort during a hospital stay.

Not At All Traumatic

Colleen Quinn
Massachusetts
1983

While visiting Grandma and Grandpa last summer, seventeen-month-old Kevin fell and cut the bridge of his nose. It was an upsetting accident, however, we all calmed down by the time we reached the doctor's waiting room. I began to realize that the worst might yet be coming; how was my baby going to take novocain shots and stitches? Would he scream and call out for me to help him? Would the nurse take him from me and wrap him in a papoose so he couldn't move? I began to feel sick and considered leaving—hoping the cut would heal on its own.

At the office door the nurse offered to take Kevin, saying I could wait in the waiting room. I told her no, I would stay and hold him. If someone was going to put stitches in my face, I would want some moral support from someone I loved!

The doctor on duty happened to be a young surgeon. He said Kevin definitely needed three stitches, and what he usually did was give the novocain shots then leave the room, letting the baby and doctor calm down and regain their composure. Kevin was able to handle the shots with a few whimpers. The doctor didn't have to leave the room! When he was busy getting his equipment ready, I started to nurse the baby. The nurse's reaction was, "What are you doing?" I told her and she said, "Well you'll have to stop when the doctor is ready!" Much to her amazement, I asked the doctor if he could do his job while I nursed. The doctor said he would try, and while my baby nursed, he tied three neat stitches on his nose. There were many exclamations of, "This is wonderful, look at him, he is falling asleep, usually we have a screaming baby at this point!" and "I wish all my patients were this cooperative."

When I left the office I thought for a moment how different things could have been—how upsetting and traumatic for everyone. I was so thankful for being a nursing mother; it felt so good to be able to comfort and protect my baby.

The bad thing that happened to Kevin that day was that he fell; going to the doctor's office was only another place to take a nap.

Weathering the Storm

Patti Farough
Illinois
1982

As I write this, my husband John is lying on the floor while Chris, our fourteen-month-old daughter sits on his stomach happily eating lunch. Less than two hours ago, Chris was undergoing several x-ray tests involving a urinary catheter, and IV, and four hours (off and on) of lying still on a hard table with strange machinery and strange people positioning her this way and that. It is not a pleasant experience for an adult; for a child it is terrifying.

With six years of pediatric nursing experience behind me, I knew in advance what Chris would have in store for her.

The doctors were afraid of a kidney problem that might mean surgery would be necessary. During my experience as a nurse I had taken care of many little girls with the same problem so my mind replayed the scenes—only this time it was my precious baby who was the patient.

During the six-week wait for the tests, I went over and over in my mind what was to come. I was as worried about how Chris would react to the tests emotionally as I was about what they might show. She has always been a very sensitive, timid baby and has had quite a bad time with separation anxiety and feeling "strange" around adults other than her daddy and me. Because of this, we decided to help her "weather the storm" by only being separated from her when *absolutely* necessary.

When the day for the tests arrived, I was emotionally prepared for them, and I knew that the three of us could come through anything. The x-ray technician came into the waiting room and reached out her arms to take Chris from me. I quietly explained that I had seen these procedures before and that I was going to stay with Chris during her tests. The technician became upset and pointed out a sign that read, "No parents allowed in x-ray rooms." But I was insistent and she relented.

I can't say that the next few hours were easy, but I know that standing near Chris, patting her head, and talking quietly with her, made them bearable. The technicians even began treating me as a helper rather than an intruder.

In between tests, we went back to John in the waiting area where Chris would nurse for about two minutes and then jump down to play with the other children. The clinging, frightened baby I had imagined in my dreams was nowhere to be seen. Most children this age exhibit tremendous anger toward their parents when they are made to go through such procedures or hospitalization. Chris showed none and I attribute this to being with her during the tests as well as our close nursing relationship.

I hope that more parents will follow their instincts and ask to be with their children during medical procedures whenever possible. Doctors and technicians would soon find that when procedures are adequately explained ahead of time to parents (and children), it is a help—not a hindrance—to have a parent present to comfort the child.

Fortunately, Chris' test were negative and we have a healthy, *happy* little girl. I can go back to dreaming happy dreams and hoping they *will come true.*

Relaxed and Secure

Elizabeth Hormann
Massachusetts
1972

When our four-year-old Charlie's chronic "glue ear" and large adenoids caused a significant hearing loss, surgery was inevitable. In a major medical center this should pose no special problem, but we wanted to safeguard his emotional well-being too—and therein lay the snag.

To minimize the upheaval in his life and ours, we chose to bring him in early the morning of surgery rather than the day before. The hospital encouraged parents to stay with their children, but like most hospitals, it separated them at a very crucial time—while the child was in the recovery room, drifting in and out of sleep. We felt strongly that a child so disoriented needs a familiar face then more than at any other time. Hesitantly, the hospital agreed to that, too. A date was set, but at the last minute the chief of anesthesia said he would refuse anesthesia unless Charlie was admitted a day in advance. Our surgeon couldn't move him, and reluctantly we cancelled the operation.

Continuing his support, our surgeon recommended another doctor at Children's Hospital in Boston, and we went to see him. Once Charlie asked me, a little plaintively, "How many doctors do I have *now*, Mommy?" and I nearly lost heart, but I soon regained my perspective. Everything was easily arranged at Children's . . . except for the parents in the recovery room. That was the province of the chief of anesthesia, and he had refused every request for it. Undaunted (well, not *really*), I called him and, to my amazement, he was persuaded to let me in.

Once in the ward Charlie was uneasy, and I was glad more than once that I had stayed: when he had to put on the gown and get into the hospital crib; when he saw other children being medicated and heard them crying; when his surgery was delayed three hours. Each time he fought tears and held on to me.

Then the waiting was over. Charlie was in the operating room and forty-five minutes later in the recovery room with me. Each time he woke I was there to hold his hand and reassure him, and he drifted off again. The nurses were amazed to see him so peaceful. "They *always* wake up irritable like this one," said one nurse as she struggled with a two-year-old thrashing about shouting for his mother. Charlie dozed on and off, relaxed and quiet.

It was a couple of hours before he was fully awake, and once he was awake he was quite sick a number of times. But not once did he cry, and for this I should credit his good nature at least as much as my presence. Many times the nurses commented on how relaxed and secure he seemed. Late that night Karl came to take us home, and Charlie slept peacefully in his own bed.

By noon the next day he was himself again, and, except for the mighty silence when he breathes, we've seen no change in him at all—no fuss, no nightmares, no regressive behavior. This was clearly not his favorite experience, but he has taken it right in stride. We're so glad we made the effort to be there with him. By minimizing the disruption, we were able to put this experience in proper perspective as a tedious but necessary medical procedure.

A Caring Family

Cindy Comer
Oklahoma
1981

It was with great relief that I saw my mother-in-law arriving just ahead of the ambulance. She may not agree with all aspects of my mothering, but nevertheless she has always been very supportive and understanding of me and my belief in breastfeeding. In this emergency I could turn my nursing baby, Miles, over to her temporarily and devote my full attention to our older son, two-year-old Cy.

Miles was only one month old when we found Cy lying in the road crying and in shock. He had obviously been hit by a car. We all agreed that my father-in-law and mother-in-law should follow with Miles as the ambulance took us to the nearest hospital emergency center one hundred miles away. I later learned that two or three well-intentioned women insisted that my mother-in-law leave the baby with them. "Why, they could fix up a formula and bottle that would satisfy him," and besides, "The emergency situation was no place for a baby." How grateful I am that she graciously declined the help. She knew I wouldn't want Miles to be fed anything but my breast milk.

Once at the hospital, we learned Cy had suffered a skull fracture, a tendon-related leg injury, and skin abrasions. The nurse in intensive care was very firm in letting us know we could *not* keep Miles with us in the ICU waiting room, regardless of the fact that he was completely breastfed. She said that actually there was no place in the entire hospital where we could go with Miles while my husband and I took turns being with Cy. My sister quietly took Miles to the main lobby where she sat up all night with him and brought him to me whenever he got hungry.

During the four-day hospital stay, my mother and mother-in-law camped out in the lobby with Miles where they could phone me in Cy's room whenever Miles was hungry or needed me. They took turns sitting up nights with him while he slept in a lounge chair. My husband and I were both able to stay in the hospital room with Cy.

How indebted I am to my family and all the many people who helped us. I could have been so torn between meeting the needs of both my sons—wanting to be with Cy throughout the painful and traumatic hospital ordeal and yet knowing that giving formula to Miles could be asking for real trouble, possibly colic or an allergic reaction. And being separated from him would mean an interruption of our bonding and attachment. I was already under a great deal of emotional strain and the added anxiety of separation from Miles would have been almost unbearable along with overfull breasts, the bother of frequent pumping, and possibly a breast infection to top it all off!

As it turned out, I had so much more peace of mind and was very proud of the way both boys came through it all. Miles cooed and smiled at all the passers-by in the lobby. Everyone marveled at such a "good baby." The pediatric nurses were incredulous that Cy had no special blanket or toy.

After we all came home, Cy couldn't walk for six weeks. He was weak, depressed, insecure, clinging, and jealous of my attention to and care of Miles. I had two babies then, and one was very sick with some very demanding needs. Meeting all those needs during that time was one of the hardest things I've ever done. Where would I have been if I had weaned Miles and he was perhaps not tolerating formula and maybe crying a lot? But Miles still cooed and laughed and was so easily satisfied by nursing.

Now over a year later, I can watch both boys running and playing happily. It's evident Cy has completely recovered physically and has overcome the insecurity and jealousy, also. We have since discovered that Miles *does* have an allergy to cow's milk.

I am so grateful that my family was already aware of my priorities so that we were better prepared to deal with the situation. While we were waiting for the ambulance or waiting in intensive care, it would have been the wrong time to put my foot down or make demands of my family. They may have thought I was just being unreasonable. In my anxious emotional state I may have given in to pressures to do things differently. But none of that happened. My family gave me a firm foundation of support, cooperation, and understanding.

Real Life Drama

Kathy and Dennis Shelling
Florida
1980

Our family recently went through a most terrifying experience— out two-year-old son, D.J., drank approximately one-and-a-half ounces of gasoline. He reeled backwards, caught his breath, and started choking and crying. By the time we rushed him to the nearest hospital, he was vomiting and passing out. He was color- less and breathing erratically. The emergency x-rays showed chem- ical pneumonia.

Needless to say my husband and I were feeling inner panic and desperation and I found myself praying out loud through my tears.

To add to our misery we were totally dissatisfied with the atti- tude of the emergency room doctor. We contacted our own pedi- atrician who advised us to rush D.J. to another hospital where he could be admitted under his own care. This we did, as D.J. grew weaker and sleepier. We were so much more satisfied to have our own pediatrician check him thoroughly and explain the risks and possible complications. D.J. was put into a vaporized oxygen tent and slept for a while. The doctor told us to expect a bad night with a state of depression. If he began to show improvement the next day, the doctor thought he might only have to be hospital- ized for two or three days.

During this confusion, I telephoned my LLL Leader. Her ad- vice and encouragement were most comforting. She suggested that I climb into the oxygen tent to nurse D.J. if he woke and wanted to nurse. I was so glad she told me this, as shortly after I talked to her, D.J. did wake up, and with what little strength he had left he crawled out of the tent calling for me. I asked the nurse if it would be all right to climb into the tent with him, and she said, "I guess so," and I quickly climbed in with my little boy. I must admit I felt a bit awkward and cramped, but the rewards were well worth it. His weak little cries for "Mommy" would have torn me up if I couldn't have held and comforted him. It didn't take long before word got out that there was a mother in a crib with her baby! Now and then someone would come to the observation window to view this scene. I cheerfully responded to all staff comments that we believed in a philosophy of living and loving freely. The results were to prove themselves.

D.J. started nursing soon after I joined him. Penicillin shots every six hours, along with a blood test, urine test, temperature and pulse recordings, all were traumatic experiences for him and he nursed steadily each time. There is no way to explain the good feelings I had being able to relieve his pain in some way.

Daddy was the first to get a smile out of him—and a playful kick through the tent. Sometimes when he'd fall asleep, I'd slip out to stretch and Daddy assumed watch. There was a twin bed near the crib, so both of us stayed and helped our small fellow through this ordeal. At midnight the doctor returned and was amazed at how well he was progressing. By morning he was feeling like himself and eager to play. Now and then he'd be a little grouchy, but with his Daddy there willing to play with him, he couldn't stay grouchy for long.

It was no surprise to us that D.J. did not experience the depression because we were there. Nighttimes are dark, scary times for babies and children and it's no wonder that they often suffer depression and usually "get worse" during the night. Little ones who do not talk well or not at all cannot express their terrors except by crying and this is commonly ignored. No wonder they despair over their abandonment—certainly not a healthy antidote for anyone who is sick. Since D.J. responded so well, we were able to persuade the doctor to let us go home that same day, and return to his office for follow-up tests and checkups. These special people gave us the courage to preserve our rights to stay with our child and give him the emotional treatment that was as necessary as the medical.

He Needed Me

Gail Warta
Illinois
1977

With my husband, Gary, in attendance, our twin sons, Matthew and Michael, were born. We were pleased that each baby weighed six pounds ten ounces.

The birth of the boys balanced our family; we already had two little girls—Christine and Jennifer, whom I hadn't been able to breastfeed. This time I was determined to nurse. Breastfeeding twins presented numerous problems, but my close association with La Leche League over the preceding months gave me the knowledge and courage to continue.

The boys grew by leaps and bounds. We were especially thrilled that Matthew was keeping pace with his brother, because he had been born with a heart murmur that the hospital heart specialist said was caused by a ventricular septal defect. We had been told that it was mild and should cause no problem, but that we should watch for any failure to thrive and grow normally. At three-and-a-half months we were told by the pediatrician who had been following Matthew's progress that all was well and that we need not consult the heart specialist again.

We felt relieved that our worries were over. Since we felt secure in our baby's progress, we had the records transferred to our own pediatrician, Dr. D'Sousa. He first examined the babies for a routine check at four-and-a-half months. At that time he requested an EKG and x-ray for Matthew, since none had been done since his birth.

The following Saturday Dr. D'Sousa called me. He had shown the test results to a pediatric cardiologist. I can still remember his exact words to me. "Dr. Sinha feels the baby should be seen immediately." I asked when I should make the appointment, and his reply was "Wake the baby and bring him now. We will wait for you." My eyes filled with tears and my hands trembled as I awakened my precious child.

Dr. Sinha told me that he felt Matthew had a pulmonary stenosis and it was not mild. He scheduled his admission to Loyola University Hospital for a heart catherization for the next week. My head was spinning with the confusion and concern. Of course I would stay with Matthew, but what about Michael? Both babies were totally breastfed except for a little cereal and banana.

One evening a few days later, Matthew awoke at 11 PM and was nursing. I was looking at his sweet face snuggled against my breast, trying to understand how so lovely a baby could have anything wrong with him. His nursing stopped—his mouth opened, his head fell back, and he went limp. He had stopped breathing! Frantically I shook him and called his name. There was no response. Still holding him, I began pushing on his chest and began mouth-to-mouth resuscitation in a clumsy, panicky way. Then I heard the most beautiful sound—a gasp for air. I grabbed him and raced to find Gary. We stuffed a suitcase and left for Loyola. Matthew was admitted, and immediately put on a machine that would sound an alarm if his breathing became irregular or if his heart slowed too much. That first night, the buzzer rang a dozen times. I sat in a chair with him cradled in my arms, afraid to put him down.

The heart catherization was done, and it revealed that he had a severe pulmonary stenosis but not ventricular septal defect. The condition had been misdiagnosed at birth. The doctors tried to be encouraging, but all agreed that his condition was critical. He was in severe stress, and his chances of surviving the trauma of open heart surgery were slim.

I couldn't bear the thought of losing him. My first baby had died at birth, and I had barely been able to cope with that loss. To have and hold and love a baby and then to think that he too might die was nearly too much for me to handle. What kept me fighting was the thought that he needed me there in one piece to help him through that painful and terrifying experience. I had to cope. From somewhere the strength came.

Matthew needed immediate open heart surgery. While the preparations were being made we remained in the hospital. The one thing in his favor was his good state of nutrition, thanks to breast milk. Nursing a nearly five-month-old was a topic of conversation among the nurses. It brought many questions and a few raised eyebrows.

Only three weeks after first seeing Dr. Sinha I nursed my baby for what I feared might be the last time. It didn't seem possible that so much had happened in so short a time. At 6 AM we took our unsuspecting cherub to the doors of surgery and he smiled a goodbye as they wheeled him away from us. Terror was in my heart, for I had seen his lips turn blue that morning.

For six hours we waited before the news came that he was still alive. We raced to the intensive care unit. Matthew was a pathetically beautiful sight to behold. We could barely find his little body beneath all the tubes, wires, and tape. We were cautioned that he would be in critical condition for three more days; but deep down I knew that he would make it. For the first time I was not allowed to sleep in the room with him. But nothing was said to me as I camped in the corridor to be within easy reach of him. Understanding nurses let me be with him often, and it was easier on me to see that he was all right. Twenty-four hours later he was transferred to the pediatric intensive care unit, where I could be with him all the time. I talked to him when he was awake and stroked the few uncovered places on his body. I wanted him to know that he was not alone and, in spite of the pain, I was always there.

Four days after surgery I could give him one-half ounce of my milk mixed with water. He kept it down and I was allowed to again hold and nurse my tired, sick baby. I was told that his recovery was the fastest of any baby they had seen (the only breastfed one, I was informed). I can't help feeling the answer was lots of mother and mother's milk.

I stayed with Matthew constantly for the month he was hospitalized. I bathed him, dressed him, slept with him, and carried him to and from his tests. I held him during all procedures and nursed through many EKGs.

You may have been wondering, "How about Michael? Where was he all this time?" My mother came in from Arkansas to take over his care, and his sisters helped all they could. Jennifer and Christine were wonderfully understanding about this family crisis, and in their own way did many little things to ease it, mainly by being there. But when I took Matthew to the hospital, I was also taking Michael's mother and his total food supply.

At first he refused the bottle my mother offered. All day she tried to give him formula, but to no avail. Then a loving friend brought over some of her frozen milk, and Michael eagerly downed it. Over a period of a few days he began to tolerate the bottle. In order to keep him used to accepting the breast and to know that his mother still existed and still loved him, Gary drove him the 120-mile-round trip to the hospital each day, so I could cuddle and nurse him for a couple of hours. Since Michael could no longer nurse to sleep, he developed a loving relationship with his blanket that still persists. Today, the boys and I and Michael's blanket have an exceptional relationship, with many of our nursings including all of us.

This past January, Matthew and I returned to Loyola Hospital for another heart catherization. (We must keep close tabs on his condition.) An active toddler is a real handful to keep pace with.

How sad it was to hear so many little ones in other rooms, sobbing, alone, each night. My little guy needed me during each exam and test. I was the only constant in his new strange world of doctors and nurses. How glad I was that the boys still nursed. Nursing calmed Matt when he was hurting and afraid, and it relaxed him when he was overtired. The entire afternoon following the unpleasant catherization he nursed his misery and confusion away. It was satisfying to see how much the nursings meant to him.

Poor little Michael! He was bewildered at being without mother and brother. When I returned home after the four days, he wouldn't let me hold or touch him. Fortunately, his resentment was short-lived, and he climbed onto my lap and eagerly nursed. We three were again as one, with yet another growing experience behind us.

Matthew's correction is holding well, and we have hopes that a couple more years will pass before he must return to the hospital.

We are forever grateful to a handful of fast-acting, talented doctors and nurses for saving our baby's life and to a hospital that understands the close inseparable tie between mother and child.

All Too Brief a Life

Mary Rowan
Ontario
1982

I am writing you because you helped us to prepare for our daughter's birth—no one could help us prepare for her death. My husband Mark de Jong was completing a PhD in nuclear physics and I was finishing up in city planning when Maaike was born. She was perfect—nine pounds four ounces with dark hair.

Everything was falling into place—we had a beautiful outgoing little girl, we finished our studies, and Mark got a good job (at last). I was a full-time mother and housewife and loved it. I joined the League here and decided to let Maaike wean herself. Life was great.

In February of this year Maaike and I visited the grandparents and I took a lot of flack because I was still nursing and spoiling my baby. "Babies need to cry" they said. Maaike didn't have to cry—I gave her what she wanted when she wanted it.

When we returned home from Winnipeg on February 14, Maaike had a cold—or so I thought for the next three weeks. She was tired—but Mark and I both had the flu and she was getting her eye teeth so I didn't worry. I took her to our local doctor on March 5 for her shots. He examined her and thought she might have mono because her liver and spleen seemed to be enlarged. He sent us to Pembroke. They thought it was a liver storage disease. On March 17 at Children's Memorial in Ottawa it was diagnosed as cancer of the liver. It had already spread to her lungs. Compared to the other babies there Maaike didn't even look sick.

Mark and I decided not to let the doctors treat her, as any form of treatment was an experiment because they had never seen this form of cancer in a child so young. They could only tell us what we could expect but could not give us any estimate of how long she might live. After a total of seven days in the hospital in Pembroke and Ottawa, we just brought Maaike home to die.

I nursed her through everything—all the tests and all the examinations. Mark was with her for the bone marrow test and liver biopsy. Only once did I make a mistake. In Pembroke there were no sleeping accommodations for parents so the nurses told me to sleep in the lounge down the hall and they would wake me when Maaike called. They didn't wake me though—they thought they were being kind. They let Maaike cry—something she had never done before.

Maaike died at home in our arms on March 31. She had lost fifteen pounds and her little body was deformed from the horrible growth in her abdomen, but her face was peaceful and beautiful. There were no IVs or bright lights and she didn't suffer very much. Maaike's body was donated to science so they could learn more about this type of cancer. That may help someone else.

We did everything we could to make her happy while she was alive. We took every precaution to keep her safe. She was healthy and beautiful. At birth you consider the possibility of death or deformity perhaps, but after a year you think you are home free.

You taught us about bonding and love and nursing our baby. I think we did a good job. No one wants to think about death especially when they are preparing for a birth—and our baby was a very rare case. But it could happen to someone else. If knowing about her will help anyone else prepare for their baby's death I will be happy.

Miracle

Kathy Eickmann
Ohio
1979

In 1947 in postwar West Germany, my mother-in-law gave birth to a daughter. The family had fled East Germany two years earlier and were living a desperately poor existence as refugees. My mother-in-law sacrificed much of her own food so that my husband, then three years old, would have enough. Consequently the baby girl, although born close to term, weighed about two-and-a-half pounds. There was no special life-saving equipment at the hospital for this tiny bit of humanity; my mother-in-law had nothing but an eye-dropper with which she fed the baby her own breast milk around the clock.

At six weeks, little Jutta developed serious pneumonia, and a doctor was called. Shaking his head, he told my mother-in-law to put the baby in a cigar box and bury her in the garden—she was as good as dead anyway. Shocked and angry, my mother-in-law threw the the doctor out and called in the local midwife. Together they worked to save the baby.

A year later, my mother-in-law met the same doctor out walking in the village. He was amazed to see a little girl toddling along at her feet. "How did you have another baby so soon?" he asked. "This is the same baby you told me to bury in the garden last year," she replied, and left him there gasping over this incredible miracle. Today Jutta is a healthy, happy woman with two fine children of her own.

I sometimes feel that many people in the medical world have forgotten the miracles the human spirit is capable of—especially in the mother-child relationship—and want us to rely completely on modern technology. Somehow we must learn again to rely on the miracles of the human spirit, with aid from the miracles of modern science only when necessary and never as substitutes.

27

When Mother's Need
Is Greatest

For most nursing mothers, the physical nourishment their babies get from breastfeeding is only part of the story. Even more important, nursing is a way of giving and receiving love. It is no wonder, then, that when a breastfeeding mother is injured or ill, her immediate concern may not be for herself, but for her nursing relationship with her baby.

A Family Hospital Stay

Nancy Sherwood
Thailand
1982

Last week I felt a lump in my groin that was diagnosed as a femoral hernia. My husband and I decided that it would be best to have it repaired before it became a medical emergency. My main concern was being separated from eleven-month-old Morgan and four-year-old Courtney. We are living in Chiang Mai, Thailand. Since my daughter was born in Bangkok four years ago we were aware of the family-oriented hospital care here. Family members of all ages are expected to stay with the patient.

I spoke to my doctor to tell him that I wanted an epidural so I would be able to nurse Morgan as soon as possible. There was never any suggestion from the doctor that I wean him. He understood my concern about being separated from my family.

When I checked into the hospital my husband, Nick, and baby, Morgan, came with me. (Courtney decided she'd rather play with her friends.) While Morgan played in my room, I could hear the sounds of other small children—presumably staying with their mothers or fathers, too. Morgan nursed himself to sleep about an hour before my surgery. Nick took him home and returned to wait. I was awake for the whole two hours of my surgery, and found it fascinating. I never went through the drowsiness or nausea that often go along with being anesthetized.

After making sure I was okay, Nick went home, fed the kids, and returned with Courtney and Morgan. One of the nurses made up the couch in my room into a twin-sized bed. After playing for a while, Courtney fell asleep on the couch. We put up the side rails on my bed, and Morgan nursed himself to sleep and slept in my arms all night. Nick shared the couch with Courtney. I had some discomfort during the night from the surgery, but Morgan slept, nursing on and off through it all. I'm sure if I hadn't been able to have Morgan with me I would not only have had a sore tummy, but sore breasts as well!

When the doctor came in to see me in the morning he wasn't at all surprised to see Morgan in my bed (after all Thai children sleep with their parents.) His main concern was not to wake Morgan while examining me!

I am happy that we were living in Thailand when this happened. We really appreciated the attitudes about family-oriented health care.

Breast Surgery While Nursing

Diana Weisenbach
Ohio
1982

Recently I noticed a small lump in my breast. My initial reaction was one of intense fear, partially due to the fact that my aunt had undergone a mastectomy several years ago. I decided to consult a surgeon. The thought of losing my breast terrified me, especially because I am nursing my baby, Sara, now nineteen months old. Although the doctor assured me that the lump would most likely be benign, my fear escalated until the final lab test was in.

The doctor suggested that I stop nursing Sara so he could watch the lump over a period of a few months. He was reasonably sure that it would disappear if I discontinued nursing. Being a strong advocate of baby-led weaning, I could not accept this procedure. I politely, but firmly, expressed my viewpoint, and asked for an alternative method of treatment. My doctor patiently explained that surgery was the only other option. He was almost certain that the lump was benign, but he wanted to be positive.

My next problem came when I was told that the procedure would require a general anesthetic, which in this area usually means an overnight stay in the hospital. Again, I expressed my feelings that I didn't want to be separated from my baby for even one night. She has always been a restless sleeper, and still wakes often during the night. Nursing always calms her back to sleep again. I asked if it would be possible to be discharged on the same day I would be admitted. Surprisingly, my doctor agreed to this arrangement.

My surgery was scheduled to take place on Friday of the next week. On Wednesday morning I had my blood work done. This is mandatory for anyone undergoing surgery. Friday morning I was admitted to the hospital at six AM. By seven-thirty I was gowned and had had my pre-op shots. By this time Sara was barely aware that I had left. I was wheeled to surgery at eight-thirty promptly. The next thing I remember was waking in the recovery room one hour later. I was told immediately that my lump was benign as expected. My relief was unsurmountable! After being taken back to my room, I ate lunch and consulted with my doctor. He discharged me at one o'clock in the afternoon. I was hospitalized for a total of seven hours! My baby, who stayed with her grandmother during my hospital stay, hardly seemed to have missed me at all. Of course, I rested for the remainder of that day, but I was at home with my family around me.

I am hoping this account will make other nursing mothers aware that there *are* other alternatives than those of weaning and separation in the case of some surgical procedures. You, as the patient, have the right to explore every alternative. I feel that if the patient handles the situation in a kind but firm way, she will most likely get the cooperation of her doctor.

As a footnote, the breast that was operated on is once again producing as much milk as before, and Sara and I are still a happily nursing couple.

A Frustrating Episode

Gayle Earle
Arizona
1982

We were looking forward to our trip to California for my sister's wedding with great excitement. My nine-month-old daughter, Jennifer, and I arrived in California on Tuesday with plenty of time to prepare for the wedding on Saturday. Since I was to be Matron of Honor, I was worried about not being able to meet my daughter's needs during the service. While the church filled up I nursed Jennifer to sleep. She slept through the entire service in her daddy's arms. Things couldn't have worked out better! I was very relieved and we looked forward to going home. Our plane was to leave Sunday morning.

Throughout the week I had been feeling pain in my chest when I would breathe. I attributed it to smog although no one else seemed to mind it. Saturday night the chest pain became so severe I could not sleep. The pain got progressively worse and I developed shortness of breath. We were staying in a hotel with my mother, so I asked her to take me to an emergency room. I was hoping I could get something for the pain and be able to make it home to see my own doctor.

Although Jennifer was sleeping, I woke my husband so he could bring her along in case she would wake and want to nurse. At the hospital, a doctor examined me and suspected I had pneumonia. I was given oxygen, and the doctor wanted to admit me to the hospital immediately. I told him I wanted Jennifer to be with me. At first he said it was impossible, it had never been done in that hospital before. Through information from La Leche League, I knew it had been done in other hospitals. I insisted it was the only way I would stay, so they gave me a private room and said that someone should be with me at all times to be responsible for Jennifer. Things were working out well so far.

My room had an extra bed for my husband and they even brought in a crib for Jennifer. Throughout the day the nurses came in to see Jennifer. They couldn't believe she had been allowed to stay with me, but they seemed happy about it. They were making us so comfortable. I was feeling better and nursing Jennifer as she wanted. My mother and husband took turns going out for something to eat and playing with Jennifer, although she was most happy sitting in bed with me.

The doctor assigned to me (a pulmonary specialist) was surprised to hear I was "still" breastfeeding. He also said, "I know you love your baby but she should not be with you." I explained why I wanted her with me. At that point, there seemed to be no strong objection on his part.

On Sunday evening, the new shift of nurses did *not* like our set up. Without warning, at 8:00 PM they came in and told me Jennifer had to leave. I objected. The specialist then called and told me I was putting Jennifer in danger because I was contagious. I explained that Jennifer is totally breastfed, she refuses a bottle, and most of all I didn't want to be separated from her. The doctor then proceeded to tell me it was medically advisable that a child her age (nine months) should have already been weaned. We argued back and forth unable to reach an agreement.

Thanks to my involvement in La Leche League, I had contacted a nearby League Leader earlier that day. I told her about my situation. After the argument with my doctor I called her again and she helped me get in touch with a pediatrician who supports the same mothering ideas La Leche League has. I spoke with him and he assured me Jennifer was not in danger from being with me. He said breastfeeding was the best thing for her and the antibodies in my milk would help her fight off my infection. Since Jennifer had been with me up till now, he said she was already exposed. He even spoke with the nurse in charge, explaining it was best for Jennifer to be with me and suggested I be allowed to sign a form releasing them from all responsibility for Jennifer. The nurse was very nasty to him and told him it was impossible. The pediatrician was very kind and understanding, but explained his hands were tied because he was not my doctor. (I later found out that twelve hours after I received my first dosage of medication I was no longer contagious; this was sixteen hours later that they were taking her away.)

The doctor assigned to me and the nurses did not agree with any of our arguments. Two nurses came in and said very sternly, "You are pumping your breasts and your baby is leaving." I was horrified; I said, "Pumping milk is not that easy and I have none to give them to use tonight. Jennifer nurses through the night and we've never been separated." At this point my mother and husband grabbed Jennifer and all their things and began leaving. They were afraid Jennifer was really in danger, so they thought it was best to leave. I told them it would be difficult for them, too. Little did they know what they were in for! I was frantic. No one believed me or the pediatrician. I felt as if I were in a cage and couldn't get to my daughter. I felt out of control and so helpless. I was furious with everyone.

I called the League Leader I had spoken with earlier. Sobbing, I told her, "They've taken my baby!" She was very sympathetic and reassuring, telling me my baby would be all right although she knew how helpless I must have felt. I felt as if Jenny was gone forever at that moment.

I got myself somewhat together, now only filled with rage toward the nurses who did this. I knew I had to get some milk for my baby. If she couldn't have me I wanted her to have my milk. It took quite a lot of nagging to find a pump but the nurses finally came up with a cylinder-type hand pump. Now to get some milk. I began pumping, with tears rolling down my face, but was only able to get about half an ounce. I kept trying to relax so I could get milk but was unable to. I had no will to get better. Finally I got a little sleep.

At 3:00 AM, much to my surprise, I pumped nine ounces of milk at one time. I called my mother to come and get it for Jennifer. She came right away. She told me they had bought some goat's milk but Jennifer had refused it from bottle, spoon, and cup. They had to take her for a ride in the car to stop her crying and put her to sleep. She kept waking up crying. My husband slept with her right against his chest so she would go back to sleep. My heart ached. I hoped this milk would help.

When the doctor examined me on Monday morning he said Jennifer could *visit* me and would be allowed to nurse but must then leave. He also said I would be released on Wednesday. Now it was 9:30 Monday morning. I was all excited as I called my husband and told him to bring my baby. Both my mother and husband were much relieved. Jennifer had also refused my breast milk. She wanted me as much as I wanted her. My poor baby had gone fifteen hours without food.

When they brought Jennifer to me she didn't smile at me as she usually does. She wouldn't even look at me. She looked weak and her tummy was so flat. She latched onto my breast immediately. It felt so good to hold her in my arms again. When she stopped nursing I didn't want to let her go, but they left. I knew then I couldn't stand to be separated from my daughter this way for two more days.

I got in touch with my doctor in Phoenix. He told me it would be safe to fly home but I must go directly to see him. I had to sign a release form to discharge myself. I saw my doctor that evening and he sent me home with an antibiotic in pill form. That night was wonderful. Jennifer and my husband and I all slept soundly and peacefully together.

Two days after we were home, I began feeling sick again. I had a high fever, but by working very closely with my doctor, I was able to stay home and not return to the hospital. It took a couple of weeks before I was back to normal, but I was able to be with Jennifer and nurse any time. Jennifer was "clingy" for a while but I felt "clingy" toward her, too!

I feel so fortunate that I had the knowledge to know I can nurse through almost anything. I hope that by sharing my story I can help someone else to feel confident that she can nurse through an illness. Nursing brings such a close relationship between a mother and her baby, it would be so sad to terminate it for an illness that lasts just a short time.

The Benefits of Love

Mary E. McQueen
Oregon
1972

A few years ago we had an experience which I have been waiting for time to put into proper perspective.

Eight years ago I sustained a serious and permanent injury to my neck and back in an auto accident. The following years have been filled with varying degrees of pain, and I have undergone all kinds of treatment to keep it at livable levels. During this time I have given birth to and nursed our three daughters.

Three years ago I fell and reinjured my neck, also causing injuries to the lower spine. Caralyn, our youngest child was still nursing frequently. Thanks to the efforts of LLL mothers, Leaders, and friends, my housework and cooking were kept fairly current. My husband, then studying for his Master's degree, dropped school and devoted most of the following six months to his family.

I spent most of the time until mid-October on a heating pad in bed, heavily medicated. My orthopedic surgeon closely watched the medications, for he realized how important it was for me to continue nursing. Caralyn continued nursing and remained a happy, growing baby. Having taken her first step at eight months, she was busy but seemed to thrive on the extra time I now had for her.

Despite our many efforts the symptoms became so acute that the doctor insisted on my entering the hospital for therapy, testing, and possible surgery. We talked to several hospital administrators to determine which hospital's policy was most family-centered. Two days later I was admitted, panicked and depressed, and feeling rather worthless. Bills were piling up, and now thousands of dollars of hospital expenses loomed ahead. My precious moments of holding cuddly Caralyn, seeing the trust in her eyes and feeling the need we had for each other provided a strong solace for me. None of the medications stilled the discomfort as much as a few moments with her.

I spent the next two weeks in total pelvic and cervical traction. Caralyn and Ken came to see me twice a day. She didn't always nurse—sometimes she only cuddled or teased with me; but she always insisted that my attention remain only to her. If I even spoke to Ken she was displeased. Later, Ken told me that at home Caralyn had often stood calling into my room for "Mama." The other girls, too, retreated into bedwetting and other infantile habits. Ken spent many hours talking to them and reassuring them that Mama *was* coming home. This was the reason we had decided that he should be the one to stay at home with them. Even though at times he commented on how hard this constant "mothering" was, it was because of the continuity that only he could provide for the girls that they were able to cope well with their fears.

The story did not end when I came home from the hospital. What the doctors had hoped to accomplish by the traction did not come to pass, but surgery was contraindicated for now. (Some day it will be done.)

So home I went with the words, "You must learn to live with it," and then the word "impossible," alternating in my head. It was my nursling who came to my rescue again with her happiness and joy at my return. She came to me again and again to nurse and cuddle those first few days—and in her baby gurgling of "Mama, Mama" she conveyed to me the very thing I needed most to bring life back into perspective. She was saying "I need you, Mama." And in giving and loving my depression receded.

Now that we look back upon the experience, I am thankful for the love and helpfulness that surrounded me. Financially our decision for Ken to remain at home was a catastrophe; it will take years to recover the time he lost from work and school. But when he was needed, he was there. We received very little encouragement in that decision at the time; even our families thought it was too much to ask of him. But real men do not hesitate to find a way to do the really important things in life.

Caralyn continued to nurse until about fifteen months of age, when she weaned herself. At no time before, during, or after the hospital experience did my milk supply falter. She is a lovely, happy child now, and we cannot help but be thankful that she was able to continue nursing during those dark weeks. It takes time to realize all the benefits of love . . . but they are truly there.

A Second Opinion

Paula Bermingham
California
1984

When our daughter, Nadine, was five years old and our son, Paul, was eighteen months of age, my husband noticed a change in the size and color of a mole on my back. The doctor I consulted recommended complete removal of the mole. I verbally agreed. The doctor then said I would be required to sign a form allowing for my admission to the hospital for a stay of seven to ten days if the incision proved too large to close without skin grafts.

Neither of our children had been away from me overnight. This is what my husband and I feel is best for our family. I explained this to the doctor and he agreed to take only a small sample of the mole for a biopsy, because there would be no risk of a separation from my family with this procedure.

Unfortunately, the diagnosis was cancer. That meant we were again facing a possible hospital stay, plus the doctor said I wouldn't be able to lift my son for two weeks following the surgery. Paul had just begun climbing and usually needed assistance in getting back down. My husband and I felt that with a little time—a few months perhaps—the situation might be easier on Paul.

When I told my doctor that we wanted to wait a few months for the surgery for our son's sake, his startling response was, "You do want to see your son grow up, don't you?

After this remark, we reconsidered. My mother agreed to stay at our home to help with Paul. Paul was certainly able to climb onto my lap on his own to nurse. Before we finished working out the details, I was referred to another doctor. The first doctor felt his schedule didn't allow him to remove the mole as soon as he felt it should be done.

On the way to the second doctor's office, I role-played aloud my concerns about a hospital stay and our preference for surgery on an out-patient basis. This doctor said the incision required would only be half the size of any that would require hospitalization. He had a small grin when he asked if I had any other concerns. I told him how difficult it would be not to be able to lift Paul. He assured me he could stabilize the stitches sufficiently to allow for some stress on them.

I quickly agreed to have this doctor do the surgery. Paul was only away from me for about an hour. My mother stayed a few days to help, which I appreciated.

The value of the second opinion I received wasn't in its new diagnosis or alternative treatment, but in its different outlook. Everyone brings their own perspective to each situation; medical matters are no exception. I hope anyone facing a similar situation will be able to find a supportive doctor, as I did, to help minimize any trauma to their family.

A Painful Weaning

Bernice Maygothling
New York
1984

Matthew, now four-and-a-half years old, was a most welcome addition to our life. We'd tried for four years to conceive a child and when the pregnancy test came back positive, Tim and I were thrilled beyond description.

Matt was a good nurser right from the beginning. Seeing and feeling him latch on and begin to nurse was such a pleasure after the disappointment of labor and delivery complications which resulted in a cesarean birth.

Nursing was a joy; however, Matt decided to wean himself by nine months. It was his decision, though, and he made his desires known in no uncertain terms.

Gillian, Matthew's sister, is now almost two years old. She, too, was born by cesarean. She was a sleepy baby at the beginning, and therefore was not very interested in nursing. When she finally began to wake up, she fumbled around at first and seemed to be nursing for the practice more than to satisfy any hunger.

It wasn't long before she was the "world's expert" at nursing. I was thrilled when she passed her ninth month because I was glad she intended to nurse longer than her brother had. I enjoyed the nursing experience so much; I wanted it to go on indefinitely.

Well, six months ago I was diagnosed as having leukemia—acute lymphoblastic leukemia, to be exact. Needless to say, it came as quite a shock especially since there was no known history of cancer in my family. Although my family doctor and my oncologist (cancer specialist) were both very much in favor of nursing, I was told that I would have to wean Gilli (then sixteen months old). Apparently the drugs that would be used for chemotherapy would be retarding the growth of cells. According to my oncologist, sufficient research had not been done on what effect the drugs might have on the baby's development.

My dreams were shattered! I was diagnosed on Wednesday and would start chemotherapy on Friday. Tim had been bringing in Matt and Gilli to see me at the hospital and Gilli would nurse happily and contentedly. She had no idea what the future held. Thursday at 4:00 PM was the last time Gilli nursed.

She didn't seem to miss the one or two daytime nursings or the bedtime nursing while I was in the hospital. Tim would rock her and when she was ready she'd point to her crib. Tim would put her down, she'd put her head on her pillow, and off to slumber land she'd go. At her 3:00 AM wake-up time, she was satisfied with Papa rocking her and then she'd go back to sleep.

When I returned home and was settled in bed, Tim brought Matt and Gilli in to see me. Matt gave me a big welcome home kiss and a hug and laid on the bed next to me. Gilli first put her head down on my shoulder and after a while tapped my chest which was her way of asking to nurse. I gently told her there was no more milk and offered her a hug and an alternative to drink. Her reaction was one of confusion and frustration and maybe even a little anger.

It took some time for Gilli and me to work things out, but before the end of three weeks she was allowing me to rock her to sleep again. Those were the longest three weeks I've ever been through.

In addition to Tim's support, we also had grandparents and friends who helped out in our difficult time. At last, though, I have my little girl "back" with her bright smile and playful, happy eyes. She and her brother have increased their requests to sit on my lap (one knee per person, please!), and they bring their books to me more often than before. I welcome them both with open arms.

It's been six months since the leukemia was diagnosed. I was in remission by my sixth week of chemotherapy but I'm still taking medication for maintenance and will continue for the next two to three years. I still feel sick most mornings but I do have days when I feel great. I'm glad children are so resilient and loving— it's just what I need. Tim, Matt, and Gilli give me the needed strength and desire to fight this disease.

A Joyous Miracle

Lee Ann Adams
Indiana
1983

John was nursing placidly in my arms, totally unaware of the turmoil surging inside of me. I watched the small face I had grown to love so passionately since his birth five months ago and anguished, "How can I bear to be away from you?"

My sister, Karen, needed a kidney transplant and I was the most suitable donor. I grieved for my sister, who spent twelve hours a week hooked up to a machine; after seven years on dialysis, she deserved a better, healthier life. But I also grieved for the loss of the unique bond that I shared with my son. Having so carefully nurtured our special relationship, I felt that six or seven days of separation while I was in the hospital would be unthinkable. I was sure that I would mourn the loss of the nursing relationship far more than the loss of the kidney. The decision to give the kidney was an easy one; the decision to be separated from my baby was not.

At times I felt very lonely because few people understood my single-minded determination. Well-meaning friends and family members often tried to comfort me by saying, "The surgery won't take place for almost three months. You'll have plenty of time to wean John." Every time someone said that to me, I fled tearfully to my husband, Charlie, for his reassurance that I wasn't insane just because I didn't want to consider weaning as an option. We both shared the deep conviction that babies and mothers belong together, so we began to search for alternatives.

La Leche League friends filled us with elation when they expressed certainty that giving a kidney did not have to be the end of nursing. Because of their faith, convictions, and prayers, I had the courage and the persistence to insist that the hospital consider my request to allow John to stay with me. I was reminded of the necessity to stay positive, calm, and firm in dealing with the physicians and the hospital administration. I'm sure that it was this polite refusal to reconsider that finally convinced the hospital that I was not a crazy lady, but a mother with a deep need to be with her baby.

Because of the liability, the hospital was unwilling to allow John in my room, but after several letters and telephone calls they did finally consent to let John be brought into a family waiting room where we could see each other. It was better than nothing, and we felt it was a softening of their position. In a final attempt, I wrote a letter and tried to speak to all of the concerns that they had expressed. I wrote that I would always have someone with me to take the baby in case I was unable to handle him, that we would not place any extra burdens on the nurses or inconvenience them in any way, and that we would not require a baby bed or any other equipment for John. (He was so used to our "family bed.")

I must have written the right words, because about two weeks before we left for San Diego for the transplant, we received the news we had prayed for: We had permission to keep John with me all the time I was hospitalized. From that point on, I knew that I could cope with anything. The disruption of John's world would be minimal; his security was assured.

While we were in the hospital, everyone was very accepting of John's presence, the nurses often asking, "Where's your baby?" They were unaware that he was with me all the time since they didn't ever hear him cry. As long as he was with his mother, everything was fine with him! People from all over the hospital came to see the baby, and we felt like celebrities. I felt a little like a pioneer and I came out of this very positive experience hoping that the next nursing mother would have an easier time securing the hospital's permission to keep her baby with her. In fact, I hope in time that hospital policy will change so that mothers and babies can routinely be admitted as a team.

John, now twenty-two months old and happily nursing, is unaware of the debt he owes to La Leche League. Without their unflagging support and loving guidance, our nursing relationship would have ended prematurely fourteen months ago.

My sister Karen is in excellent health following a successful transplant and is expecting her own baby in November after twelve years of infertility. What a joyous miracle.

Mountains Are to Climb

Gail Stutler
Colorado
1972

December found my husband, Doug, daughter, Heila, and myself heading for Christmas at home in Colorado. Doug had completed a stimulating and successful quarter of sabbatical leave at Oregon State University in Corvallis. With our arms full of holly we started out in the station wagon, complete with sack lunches.

We had been pleased to discover that another baby would arrive in mid-summer. Heila, now twenty-one months, had recently weaned.

After arriving home, we briefly visited friends and shopped. However, our excitement and happiness were cut short a few days before Christmas when I was stricken with a tremendous headache. After a brief phone conference with physicians, it was confirmed as the second occurrence of a cerebral hemorrhage. The first had happened twelve years earlier.

My parents took care of our little Heila. I briefly remember watching her as they rolled me outdoors to the ambulance. For ten days I was in the intensive care unit. Gradually awareness returned as the swelling in the brain tissue reduced. I was then moved from intensive care to a regular room to regain strength and weight. My husband was able to stay with me during the day as much as possible. Despite the discomfort and mental strain, that I endured, my unborn baby stayed protected within me.

Three more weeks found us at my parents' home, waiting for swollen tissues to return to normal, waiting for the second trimester of pregnancy, and, last but not least, waiting to make a monumental decision whether or not to undergo brain surgery. Our physician left the decision up to me. Surgery was not absolutely necessary. However, the alternative was possible death on the delivery table, when walking across the street, or at any moment in time. Brain surgery was not without its own dangers, as well as the probability of some resulting handicap—minor to extreme—after surgery. We decided on the surgery.

Doug and a friend went after our belongings in Oregon, since his studies had to be interrupted indefinitely. We then prepared to enter the hospital once more.

The brain surgery was successful and I could lead a normal life, with no fear of another hemorrhage. But I could neither read nor write; I could not walk, or do any of the things that one takes so very much for granted. A favorite picture book of Heila's meant nothing to me; the words appeared to me as they would to a three-year-old. I could not recognize objects, limbs, directions or use the telephone. Most important, I could not take care of my daughter or the new baby to come. In short I had severe aphasia: the inability to call to the surface the functional details of existence.

After two weeks in the hospital, where I learned to walk again, and one week at my parents' home, we began to realize the magnitude of what had happened. I felt extreme fright before starting therapy. And so began the long journey back. The mountain is steep, the trail rough, and some days it seems to skirt the edge of a cliff because of the fog. I had to learn to write, to read, to add and subtract, to sew, to clean, and even to walk to a friend's home. Every area of the mind had to concentrate on relearning all these skills. The urgency of learning left little time to plan or dream of a new baby.

The great day finally came, and with surprising calmness we went to the hospital to give birth to another child. Amazingly, we had a beautiful and perfect new baby girl even though I couldn't even name a diaper pin! But the most beautiful thing I could do.
. . . I could scoop up a tiny bundle, put her to my breast, and nurse her close to my heart. I could satisfy at least one of the desperate needs I had when usurped of all my capabilities. At my request our daughter was brought to me when she cried, since rooming-in was not a hospital policy.

The care of our baby was wonderfully simple, thanks to nursing, which supplied all the baby's needs, to disposable diapers, which didn't require diaper pins, and to a helpful three-year-old who ran errands. Not so simple was the struggle to maintain a household after we returned to our home in Colorado. There I continued my therapy, and we gradually put our life back together. We say with grateful hearts that now, almost exactly two years after the surgery, almost all is back in order with the exception of reading, music, and typing which are coming along too with the patient help of my current therapist.

At twenty months our youngest daughter nurses once daily now, and our older girl is "joy in the morning" to us as she learns her colors, letters, shapes, and begins to pick out words. Soon will be the day I hope and wait for, that I will be able to read to her. The meadows of our mountain are green, and each bend in the road no longer reveals a craggy peak or impassable bog. We rejoice at the bond we feel as a family and at all the outstretched hands that steadied us over rushing streams.

What He Was Fighting For

Marge Beldue
New York
1982

Last year my husband, Gary, had some blood work done that showed he would require chemotherapy treatments. He had two operations the previous year, but it was obvious from the tests that all the cancer had not been removed. The treatments would mean daily trips back and forth to the hospital. Our daughter Rachel was five months old at the time and I gave some thought to weaning her since I knew I would be needed at his side. Gary was quick to disagree, knowing that breastfeeding was best for her.

We checked with the hospital and they agreed to let Rachel enter the treatment room with us. They were just wonderful. They gave us our own little corner with curtains so we could have our privacy. The weeks ahead were very difficult for our family, including Shawn, our four-year-old son. But having Rachel there with us seemed to make those treatments less painful. She brought a spark to the center and all the cancer patients. Through all the difficult moments that Gary experienced he had a constant reminder right there of what he was fighting for.

Rachel is now nine months old, she has just started on solids, and we are still a happy breastfeeding family. Gary seems to have a special spark for her that I don't remember seeing when Shawn was an infant. I truly believe that her constant presence during those painful days had a lot of bearing on his feelings.

We have just received blood test results that show the chemotherapy treatments were successful. Gary is beginning to regain the substantial weight loss that he experienced and he is growing stronger everyday. I am so thankful now that Rachel was not weaned.

Part Eight

As a Child Grows

Keeping the Bond Strong

Vincent Turns Two

Norma Jane Bumgarner
Oklahoma
1976

It's not a long poetic yesterday,
But yesterday—perhaps a day, a week
Since you clung infant-soft against my cheek
And let my grown-up life direct your play.

Now you decide if you will go or stay,
Confront each dictum with a "Hear-ME!" shriek,
Teach me to read your face before I speak,
To honor all the growth you do each day.

I'm wistful, thinking back to baby days
When quiet times filled my arms with joy and you.
I'm wearied by your daily changing ways
As bit by bit the growing youth shows through.
I'm tingling-keen to learn in this new phase
Still more about the child that will be you.

28

The Unpredictable Toddler

"Babies are such enjoyable creatures, and as they grow parents take great pride and interest in all of their accomplishments. Soon we find that the achievements we were so proud of—that crawl across the floor, that hesitant toddle, followed quickly by a swift run—bring new challenges to parents. When baby was in arms and controlled, all was pretty peaceful. Now baby has taken off and is showing a mind of his own."

Betty Wagner, LLL Founder, 1980

Good Intentions

Lucy Sterrett
Pennsylvania
1978

"Every household ought to have a two-year-old," says my older sister. As my second little one approaches two, I appreciate that statement more and more. My almost two-year-old serves to maintain my motherly equilibrium although he often seems to be a mixed blessing.

I awoke today with the earnest conviction "Today I WILL get something done." And I actually did get things underway. The washer was washing, breakfast was served, the beds were even made . . . and in comes Trevor with a grin a mile wide.

He's going to help. He labors to push his highchair up to the sink. Sniff-sniff. He has messed his pants but is too busy to let me change him now. Soon the dishwater is cascading down the front of the sink and his highchair. Well, it's just water and the highchair needed a good scrubbing anyway.

Why am I beginning to get tense? There goes daddy's left-over coffee on the carpeting; there goes my good tea cup crashing into the other side of the sink.

"Oh, Trevor! How can you be so naughty?" My voice rises, "I've just had it! Now get out of here!"

He stands in the doorway, a pathetic sight. His nose is running, his soaked pajamas are spotted with hot chocolate and egg yolk, and his diaper now stinks. "Mommy," he wails. "Nee, neeeee." What does that mean? I haven't figured it out yet but it's his all-purpose word.

What happened to my intentions? I pick him up tenderly, instantly full of remorse. We struggle up to the bathroom and pull off the sticky clothes. His wriggling body is bathed and dried. Double diapers, warm clothes, and a soft fluffy blanket are wrapped around his sweet-smelling cuddly body.

Ah-h-h-h, here we are in our favorite rocking chair. He snuggles in my arms and nurses so contentedly. Mothering is beautiful. I love it! I never want to do anything else.

All too soon it's time to lay him gently on our bed to sleep quietly for an hour or so until he calls me to hold him for the rest of his nap. Now where was I? Wasn't I in the midst of doing something vital? Oh well, it will come to me in a minute.

Life with a Persevering Toddler

Sally Schiller
Arizona
1984

Toddlers come in many varieties. Some effortlessly learn the family rules; some will leave forbidden objects alone if they are allowed to examine them just once; some must touch often but are content to use one finger only; and then there's the persevering toddler who is determined to do what he wants and who cannot be dissuaded. It's about as easy to distract him as it is to distract a Yosemite bear from a full picnic basket. Now you notice I didn't call this type of toddler "stubborn," "bullheaded," "naughty," or "bad." I referred to him as "persevering." Doesn't that sound a lot more positive? The first key to living with a persevering child is in our attitude. If we think of him as "bad," he'll be "bad," and he'll soon see himself as "bad." If we see him as "persevering," he'll be that and see himself as that. Perseverance is, after all, a virtue.

Now I realize it can be difficult to see this tot in a positive light when you find him swinging from your hanging plants, but first try to look ahead. For this child, nothing is impossible. His motto is "the difficult I do immediately, the impossible takes a little longer." When he grows up he'll probably discover the cure for cancer or the common cold.

The second thing we need to cultivate is a sense of humor. Sure there's a mess when he tries to chug-a-lug a gallon jug of milk, but it makes a priceless snapshot, and the cat will love to help you clean it up.

Our next goal in keeping our relationship with this little one on a positive note is to remove as many areas of conflict as possible. Resolve to teach only a few things at a time, stressing important safety rules first. Make it difficult for him to get into mischief. Use babyproof latches, safety plugs, gates to keep him out of some rooms, even put things away for a while so both of you can have happy days.

Finally, be creative. This busy, active, persevering child needs interesting things to do and explore even more than most youngsters do. He'll love his own cupboard in the kitchen, big boxes to build with, and anything with which he can use his imagination. It's up to you to channel his energy and curiosity into constructive pursuits. Enlist his help. He'll love to dust, wash walls, put dishes on the table, put bits of trash in the garbage, unload the dryer, play a music box for the baby, and fetch diapers. He'll delight in using your rolling pin on a bit of bread dough. (So what if his is gray when you bake it?) You might find dish towels in your nightie drawer, but when he's helping he's not getting into mischief! What's more, he's learning to enjoy work, which will make his whole life happier.

The persevering toddler is exactly like any other toddler, only more so. He needs to be seen in a positive light, handled with a sense of humor, placed in a simplified environment, taught a little at a time, kept constructively busy, and most of all, loved for himself. He's so full of surprises, he could easily turn out to be the delight of your life. Our persevering toddler, Matthew, certainly is.

A Study in Contrasts

Gail Berke
Massachusetts
1978

As the mother of a two-year-old impish son, I have often heard that over-used term "The Terrible Twos." I have read it in Gesell and Spock; I have heard it from doctors, mothers, grandmothers, and teachers. Why do adults see toddlers as so troublesome? After thirteen years of mothering my own brood, and having experienced four "twos" of my own, I feel that it is time to take another look at the two-year-old.

True, most "twos" are busy, curious, energetic, and active. Now and then parental fatigue and impatience can result in a bad day. After all, we are human. Just remember, it is only a bad day, not a bad child or even a bad phase. If we can remember to keep our sense of humor, incidents with our busy toddlers will not get blown out of proportion.

I am sure your two-year-old, much like mine, is a study in contrasts. Our adorable Joshua is so busy; he can undo a clean room in record time. He can accomplish things that we never expected of him. His older brothers have dubbed him "Bionic Baby." He has a fantastic vocabulary and is able to put together really impressive sentences. He has also been known to pick up a naughty word or two. He is fond of nursing and cuddling in bed, yet is adventuresome enough to climb on the top of the backyard gym without blinking an eye. He can ride a Big Wheel, but is still in diapers. He is two and terrific—and really, aren't all two-year-olds?

Nipping Tantrums in the Bud

Edwina Froehlich, LLL Founder, 1973

A temper tantrum can be devastating to both mother and child. Having had to cope with two children who had tantrums, I did learn a little. I followed the usual suggestions with the first boy—a spank on the bottom made him scream harder, of course; trying to firmly take him to his room was too hard on my shins; a stern reprimand? He couldn't hear me over his screaming. Ignoring him was the best of the lot, since at least it didn't add to the child's hysteria. Still, neither did it solve anything, and it did nothing to prevent future tantrums.

As I became better informed about nutritional needs, I became aware that the timing of the tantrums often coincided with periods of hunger. They seldom occurred immediately after a meal. A tendency to low blood sugar, which happens in between meals or after sugary snacks, reduced the tolerance level of frustration. Tantrums often take place in the supermarket (it's certainly frustrating not to be able to touch) because it's lunchtime, or perhaps the child has been nibbling on crackers or cookies for several hours. Once in progress you can't stop a full-blown tantrum by offering food, but understanding that hunger could be the cause at least enables you to cope better. Better still, it can perhaps show you the way to help prevent or at least lessen future tantrums.

When our youngest was about two and a half, a friend had come for lunch, and we spent several hours afterwards talking about how to raise children. Peter was for the most part amusing himself, but late in the afternoon when I told him to cease and desist something he was doing, his tolerance level burst and he had a beaut! I went over and sat on the floor beside him and reached over to pat him gently. At first he rejected my hand and literally threw it back at me. So I just sat by him and waited, whispering "I love you, Petey." He quieted very quickly and rolled himself over to me, burying his face in my lap, and finished sobbing in comfort. When the storm was over he had forgotten what started it and we trotted immediately to the kitchen. This was Peter's first real tantrum, and while I was happy and relieved to know that I now knew how to handle one, I girded myself for repeat performances. To my surprise, he had only two or three more, and they were mild and quickly over.

From Peter I learned two things: I stopped thinking of tantrums as naughtiness or defiance and regarded this reaction for what it really is—a highly emotional state over which the child has no control and during which he needs to be calmed down by loving reassurance. Also, that because of the blood-sugar factor I had to be careful not to expect too much just before meals. To a two-year-old child a call to stop playing and come in for lunch may on certain days be too much. Try going out there ten minutes in advance with a nutritious snack you know he'll like, and when that's finished start the getting-in process. To a four-year-old a reminder to get the toys picked up a half-hour before supper may be overwhelming. Offer the snacks, then be prepared to help him pick up. Time-consuming? You bet—but so are tantrums.

Tantrums can also occur at the end of a long or especially stimulating evening. "Unwinding time" if started before everybody gets to the hundred-decible, glassy-eyed stage can nip many a bedtime tantrum in the bud.

At Their Level

Elaine Weller
Florida
1973

So many times I get calls from harried new mothers who have a demanding toddler or two and an upset baby simultaneously. What to do? Get down on the floor to sit with the whole gang— enter your toddler's little world at *his* level, rather than making him come up to yours on a chair or couch. It really works wonders, especially when nerves are super-jangled. That's when I've found this sitting-on-the-floor position invaluable. Toddlers are happy, you relax some, baby quiets down, you can nurse peacefully, and sweet happiness reigns once again! You'll find it becomes a delightful habit, and one day you'll wake up to the realization you haven't had "one of those days" in a long time. Very effective as a treatment *and* a cure.

Notes from Grandma

Betty Wagner, LLL Founder, 1978

Did you ever wonder why grandmothers are so good at keeping your toddler quiet, happy, and interested? Why your toddler cries when it's time to leave Grandma's house? Some of the reasons are easy to spot.

We all know that Grandma, and Grandpa too, have some things parents are generally short of. First, and I think most important, is TIME. Toddlers need time and grandparents generally have it to give in abundance. They can turn their full attention to a toddler any time he visits. They have time to read, listen to interesting happenings in your toddler's life, tell and retell the same story again and again, let the toddler help with most anything they are doing and really enjoy the exchange with your toddler. Grandparents can put their work aside while the toddler visits and concentrate on him. Toddlers love and thrive on this attention.

Next, grandparents have experience. They have raised their own children and have learned that toddlers really aren't capable of understanding much in the way of discipline. They have learned how to work around and avoid most of the things that frustrate a toddler. They know that toddlers live for the moment and enjoy life to its fullest. Their attitude is more relaxed for they know how quickly time passes and how quickly these toddlers grow. They want to enjoy them while they are so little and cute. Grandparents have patience. Patience is learned, and most of the time requires years to achieve. By the time we are grandparents we've lived long enough to understand ourselves and others a bit better, and understanding helps to bring patience. Grandparents understand that toddlers quickly go from one thing to another, can create a great mess, and get into things they shouldn't. They also understand that the toddler is learning in the process and they feel good that they can help with this education.

Grandmother's house holds lots of surprises. Her refrigerator and cupboard are full of foods that are different than those available at home. She has knickknacks that she is willing to show and tell about each time the toddler visits. The toys and books are always ready for the toddler to enjoy. Life at Grandma's is relaxed, interesting, and fun. Why would any toddler want to leave?

Time Is the Answer

Rocky Smith
Indiana
1981

Not too long ago a League Leader in our area taught me a wonderful lesson and didn't even realize she had done so.

After many weeks of fighting with my two-year-old, I felt the need to escape. But after a visit one morning with this mother of seven, my thinking changed. I watched how she really enjoyed her children, how she relaxed and took the time to see the silly things they did or how their imaginations ran and how fascinated they were with things that seem so meaningless to us.

That night I was awake half the night thinking about the day and my "problem" with Jamie. The next day I spent the whole time with her doing the things she wanted to do. She loves to have someone sit in her room and show them her toys or to fix them "dinner" at the play table or even to go for walks. So we did all those things and our "problem" disappeared, and I found myself enjoying it! It wasn't getting away that helped, but getting closer. I'm convinced now that escape would have only made it worse. The answer was time. And now whenever I find myself having trouble coping, I stop and take *time*.

All of us have our bad days, even the children. Stop what you're doing, look around, and listen to your children. Take the phone off the hook, forget housework, and enjoy a day of one-on-one with your children. The rewards are endless, and you'll find out that you really didn't need to escape after all.

Catching Spiders

Sherry Bloomer
California
1983

My sixteen-month-old son, Zack, was giving me a lot of trouble. He had spent one whole week throwing tantrums. We went to a League meeting the day before yesterday, and although we discussed my problem, I didn't feel I had found the answer to Zack's trouble. We left the meeting, and several hours later, I had to go back to Jenny's house where the meeting had been held because I had forgotten something. As I tapped on her sliding glass door, I could see that dinner preparations had been dropped in what seemed to be a hurry. Then I noticed Jenny and her son, Jason, absorbed in something at the back of the house a few feet away from the door. Jenny popped up and said, "Oh, hi! Jason and I were just catching spiders."

All of a sudden the pieces fell into place and I could see the reason for all of the problems we had been having. I had been so wrapped up in other things that I forgot to "catch spiders" with Zack! You can probably guess the rest of the story. Yesterday we spent the whole day "catching spiders." And, what do you know! The tantrums have stopped abruptly.

29

Discipline à la Loving Guidance

"As a baby grows, he learns most by observation, by watching how his parents treat one another, how they talk to one another, how they treat him and others in their world. Loving guidance, combined with good example, teaches our children the behavior patterns we want for them"

Betty Wagner, LLL Founder, 1980

Emphasize the Positive

Jo-Ann Satin
New York
1973

The word "discipline" has gradually come to mean "punishment." In light of this, it is difficult for many of us to think of our ways of dealing with our children as "discipline."

Perhaps it might be of some help if we keep in mind the origins of the word. Webster says: *"discipline (Latin, disciplina— teaching, instruction; from discipulus, pupil).* Training or experience that corrects, molds, strengthens, or perfects. . . ."

Maybe if we emphasize to ourselves the positive, teaching aspect of discipline, we will be better able to apply it to ourselves and our families.

Notes from Grandma

Betty Wagner, LLL Founder, 1978

Most everyone agrees that it's silly to talk about "disciplining" a very young baby. His wants and needs are identical, and we meet them as promptly and fully as we can. The mutual love and acceptance give him a good feeling about himself and us, and form the basis for his later acceptance of our values and our ways of doing things.

As the months pass, he learns more about the world and the fascinating people and things in it, and his wants begin to multiply. Gradually we become aware that we can't satisfy them all; luckily they aren't all necessarily needs to be met immediately and fully. The older baby can be put off a bit, he can be distracted, and we start to learn the ways of doing this with love and tact. It's fairly easy, because before he can walk or crawl he stays put in one place, and as long as he's happy there, we can be quite relaxed.

But at around nine months, he begins to be able to get around on his own, and from then on we have to be on guard, ready to jump every minute he is awake. He has gained an enormous fund of knowledge during those months since his birth, and he is compelled to continue his education by exploring, feeling, smelling, tasting, and banging, if possible, each and every thing he can get his hands on. He doesn't know about dangerous objects or situations, bothering us, breaking things, ruining valuable antiques, hurting people, himself, or other toddlers. One of our jobs as parents is to help him learn while also keeping him, his fellow man, and our valued possessions safe.

It's a tall order. It would be easier for us if the child immediately and uncomplainingly accepted our verbal directions—do this, don't do that—and often this is what we are trying to accomplish, labeling our efforts "discipline." But if we attempt this, we often find ourselves on a collision course with the child's inner laws of growth, which are dictated not by us but by nature. We parents have to learn a lot more about the art of parenting, rather quickly, if the child's growth is to continue happily for him and for everyone around him.

Let's see what this example tells us. An eighteen-monther is helping Mom do the dishes. Every toddler loves this job. How nice, Mom thinks, we are learning to work together. Suddenly,

Mom notices water is being splashed on the floor, down the front of Baby, and he is wet up to his armpits. Well, this has gone too far she thinks, so sweetly she says, "Thank you for helping me so much. Now it's time for you to go play with your toys." She smiles as she lifts him down and removes the chair. But Baby isn't smiling. He liked to play in that water, feeling close to Mom, and sharing this happy time together. Mom is still playing there, so why can't he? He lies on the floor, kicking and screaming, and he looks so sad. So she relents, puts the chair and baby back up to the sink, and both are happy again.

But what do we see in this example? In this instance one of the things it has shown Baby is that when he cries loud and hard enough he might get his way. It would have been far better if Mom had thought through the situation before she delivered that "no." In this case, "no" apparently wasn't necessary. The struggle might have been prevented if Mom had thought ahead as to what the effect of an abrupt ending would mean and planned how she'd handle possible protests. If she felt able to say at once, "Oh, I didn't know you wanted to do this so badly. Come on back, honey," well and good. Otherwise, this could become one of the situations in which Mom is pitted against the baby in a contest of wills. Parents have to learn how to discipline themselves to respond carefully to their child and to use patience. Often this lack of discipline know-how on the part of parents leads to more behavior problems than the fact that the baby wants things he can't have.

You may have to back down occasionally, if you see you are handling a situation wrong. No harm done. The situation to avoid like the plague is, having said "no," to reverse yourself after a long siege of whining and crying by the child. "Oh, all right, go ahead and do such and such." What he has learned from such an outcome is that if he whines and cries long enough you will back down. If parents start when their toddler is young to say "no" only when they feel it is absolutely necessary, there will be less crying in the end.

While answers on how to raise children can sound so simple when you read them, they take on a different meaning when you, as parents, have to deal with the actual situation.

Parenthood is a very demanding job, but one with the most lasting rewards. After your children are raised, you can sit back and reap those rewards. Believe me, raising children with love is worth your best efforts.

Filling Buckets

Sue Conkright
Michigan
1973

"How about a kiss, Suzie?"

"I only have one kiss left in me and I'm saving it for my daddy!" announced my three-year-old.

So I kissed her.

"Now I can kiss you, Mommy, 'cause I have an extra kiss now and it's for you!"

The preceding dialog reminds me of my husband's theory on "Buckets." Del suggests we each have a bucket to store such things as praise, kindness, concern, love, happiness, consideration . . . qualities that help us to be happy, well-functioning individuals. If our bucket has some praise in it, we can praise another person, giving a bit of ourself—a dip from our bucket. If our bucket is empty, we can't share a dip of praise or a touch of ourselves happily. The more people who praise and share and give us dips from their buckets, the more we'll have to share with others— and the happier we, and others, can be.

A child can give only as he's taught. He can't have self-respect if he's only criticized. He must have praise—to know he's a good person, a cared-about person, a loved person.

The nursing couple has a deeply emotional give-and-take relationship—a sharing between mother and child. They keep each other's buckets overflowing.

Yesterday I awoke to a strep throat and a flooded basement from a broken sump pump, and already feeling truly lousy, proceeded to wedge a drinking glass into our garbage disposal! I sat down in frustration with tears near the surface when my little ones ran up and both gave me a big hug and a kiss and proceeded to pat me on the back. My three-year-old said soothingly, "Now you'll be a happy mommy and you'll feel better!" while my one-and-a-half year old announced, "O.K.!" Then my sixteen-year-old appeared and suggested, "I'll get the mop!" It didn't pay the plumber, but I sure felt better.

We can each help others—no matter how small or what age— by sharing ourselves, by filling each other's buckets with caring and love.

The Making of a Mother

Ronaele Berry
Nebraska
1982

It was six years ago that I became a mother. It did not happen at the birth of my first child. It began when my third child, Margaret, was a baby. My second child, Anne, was two and a half and my firstborn, Katherine, was four. I had nursed each child, and really believed that I loved each baby more because I had nursed her. I also believed breastfeeding contributed to better, happier children. Then why was I having so much trouble with my Anne? I did not know what to do with this child who was feisty, jealous, selfish, whiny, defiant, rebellious, exasperating, time-consuming, and naughty. I was in desperate need of help.

Katherine had gone through the "Terrible Twos" and I could handle that. In fact, I hadn't thought it terrible at all. I had learned with her to pack away books and breakables so we wouldn't have to hassle over them. Now I had a child who drove me to the end of my patience. She would cling to me and whine—almost continually. She had terrible tantrums that left us both feeling like zombies. She insisted on being carried *all the time.* How was I to do that with a baby who needed to be carried, too? She would hurt the baby and I would spank her. There was no reasoning with her; she defied every direction no matter how I put together the words. In frustration, I would punctuate my "no's" with swats. Others told me she was naughty and needed a "heavier hand." In desperation we tried it, but in my heart I was not happy about it. After each day that built up to a crescendo of spanking and weeping, I would lie awake with the biggest ache in my heart and dreadful fear of what ever was going to happen to us. If we couldn't have a good relationship now, what would it turn out to be when she grew older?

Then one awful day when Anne really hurt the baby, I spanked her with all my might and anger; I scared myself with my terrible anger. I had never been angry like that before. As we both sat sobbing in the rocking chair, I vowed I would never hit her again. But I knew the vow would be empty unless I had some help. But what? Where? Who? We sat long into the dark waiting for Daddy to come home and help us put ourselves together again. While I sat there I thought harder than I ever had in my life. One by one I discarded all my preconceived ideas of discipline.

Several days before I had read a one-paragraph description of a child similar to Anne in an old baby book that had belonged to my mother. The book said, "This child does not receive enough love." That hurt and I denied it vehemently. I loved Anne so much. She was pretty and darling and cute and sweet and cuddly—sometimes. But she also had this naughty side that was all wrong.

When my husband came home, he took over the care of the other children. Anne and I sat together all that night and by morning I had decided on a plan of action. I was going to remove all pressures from Anne and let her do everything she wanted unless it would hurt someone or her own body. I was going to hold her every time she whined, "Hold me!" I was going to comfort and love her every time she had a tantrum. And I was going to go looking for books to help me.

In the days that I waited for the books I had ordered (listed in the back of THE WOMANLY ART OF BREASTFEEDING), I sat and rocked and caressed, read storybooks and sang, and truly cherished Anne. I still had my other two children, too, so my husband agreed to keep them with him as much as possible and he made sandwiches so I wouldn't be pressured with cooking. For ten days Anne and I lived in the rocking chair. The first day she spent screaming and throwing herself out of my arms and then screaming for me to pick her up again. The second day there was only half as much screaming but she still went through the cycle of clinging and then fighting to pull away. The third day she would allow periods of singing and talking. By day five she allowed me to read books to her. By this time she also would allow me to nurse Margaret without having a screaming spell; she seemed willing to share me. By day eight she would climb off my lap and pull me along with her to see what her sisters were doing. By day ten she would climb off my lap and say "bye" to let me know she was off on her own. But as soon as she would discover me working and not waiting in the chair, she would come running back. Each day after that was better. It was just like a miracle to see how sweet and happy she was. I felt as though we had discovered LOVE together. All the holding, caressing, and cherishing had accomplished what no amount of spanking or harsh words could have.

When we saw the great effect this gentle mothering/discipline had on Anne we also became more loving and gentle with our other two. It was a second revelation to see these two placid, docile children become more outgoing, more individualistic, happier. We knew then it was a blessing in disguise that we had had a child like Anne. She still helps us in our parenting. Whenever she gets to be "hard to stand" we know pressures are getting too great, she's feeling unloved, and we need to ease off on our expectations and step up on one-to-one time. We know when our "love sponge" (Anne) is getting dry that probably everyone else is too, even if they aren't showing it. She's our family barometer.

When people question my feelings about spanking today I'm sure they feel I am unrealistic in saying I don't spank. But how can I, when I saw how close I came to destroying a beautiful little person who was just too sensitive to handle even my disapproval, let alone swats that inflated into hard spankings? Why should I, when we found love, gentleness, patience, and understanding of each child's feelings and abilities to be very effective discipline?

The books I read helped my confidence in my mothering feelings immensely. I could have personally hugged each author for understanding my need. One book led to another until I had quite a library of books. The reading also led me to LLL because I finally understood how the relationship of nursing really could be carried on after weaning. I understood how it formed the pattern of love and understanding of each individual relationship and it could influence and enhance our relationships for all our lives.

That was my beginning. Today Anne is nine. We lead gentle, happy lives. Not because we are all so good but because we all know the basic rules: whenever someone acts unacceptably they are really shouting "Love Me"—and we do.

The Biter

Joan Hitzges
New York
1974

How I laughed when I read in LLL NEWS the thoughts and feelings expressed by the mother whose child was bitten and then her changed feelings when one of her children did the biting!

When we had five children I felt that only poor neglected children bit. How I pitied them and glared at their "bad" mothers. Then number six arrived and shortly our "excellent" home with our "perfectly" raised children reverberated with screams of "He bit me again."

Patrick bit often, unexpectedly, and hard. At first, I thought he was reacting to the frustration of being the little one, but I watched very carefully and saw something I didn't expect. When his sister showed him a picture book, he bit her. When his brother, playing a gentle game of ball with him, bent over to get the ball from under the bookcase, he bit him on the large area thus exposed. When I rocked him, he bit me. When his dad hugged and played with him, he bit him.

Suddenly, a picture of young animals at play passed through my mind. Puppies, kittens, colts, and chimps all biting in play and perhaps in affection. Was this what Patrick really had in mind when he bit?

When next he bit, we stopped what I'm ashamed to say we had found ourselves doing—yelling and sometimes even hitting. Instead, I would kneel before him and say, "We don't bite, it hurts. Hug [I hugged him], kiss [I kissed him], don't bite."

Patrick hugs and kisses and rubs noses often now and rarely bites. At two and a half, he has almost stopped causing the windows to rattle with that cry of rage and pain, "He bit me again!" Perhaps all biters aren't frustrated, only expressing, in a primitive way, affection.

What's in a Name?

Bethel Larsen
Michigan
1982

In a casual conversation a friend recently asked me what my middle name was. As I told her, I sensed again the distaste with which I have always thought of my full name: "Bethel Lee." In childhood it was usually used in reproof, in a tone of exasperation.

I thought of my own children's names. I recalled the birth of our second daughter when it was my turn to give the name that I have considered the most beautiful of all girls' names since my own early childhood. "Maria Dawn" I read on the hospital birth certificate, and felt a lump rise in my throat to know that the name I had waited so long to give was now associated with a chubby, dark-haired, very real little human being.

Yet I, too, have found myself falling into the trap of using that name, given as an expression of love, mainly in moments of anger. Quite understandably, my daughter does not hear in her name the same beauty that I hear.

Perhaps those of us who have fallen into this habit should make a conscious effort to reverse the trend—to use our children's full given names more frequently to express our love and joy in them and less frequently to express disapproval. We might then see them in later years happier with their names and with themselves.

Along the Path of Mothering

Sharon Foster
California
1974

It is interesting to me that I could breastfeed and yet cling so strongly to my belief of rather harsh discipline. It took me a long time to see the light. Our first child, Jodi, bore the worst of this belief. She was "well" disciplined not to touch, to go to bed (at nine months), not to play in food or mouth toys. Can you believe it? Eighteen months later Niki came along and my discipline was much more relaxed, thanks to constant mothering from LLL, but often other things came before the baby. Things such as housework and having my hair perfectly combed seemed so important. Here again LLL encouraged me to let baby come first.

Things sink in slowly with me—very slowly. Our third child, Joshua, now fifteen months, was born when Niki was three. And do you know—the gears finally meshed. I've grown in mothering almost as much as he has physically. Harsh discipline and housework perfection are no longer my way, but cuddling, singing, horsey rides, mud cakes—that's the order of our days now. Funny, too, how Jodi and Niki are so loving and giving with Josh and everyone (because this is rubbing off on them).

My very perceptive husband has all along been more aware of "how to love" than I was. Thanks to his loving support, I really am someone's "Mommy" now.

Built-in Timetable

Colleen Walsh
New Zealand
1974

If a child is to grow in spirit and in skill, what he needs most of all is time, freedom to progress at his own rate, and the assurance that he is loved and accepted for himself. Every child longs for his parents' approval, and he tries hard most times to behave as they wish.

But he cannot outstrip his own built-in timetable—he must act his age, and we must be careful not to urge him to act a year or two older than he is.

A Quiet Lesson

Christine Hilston
Ohio
1984

Countless times I've made the resolution that I won't raise my voice to my children. Unfortunately, all too soon my determination vanishes and I find myself yelling again. I rationalize that they don't listen unless I yell. Of course, that's not true. A recent bout of laryngitis demonstrated once again that yelling is not necessary or even desirable. It renewed my determination not to raise my voice unnecessarily.

Speaking in no more than a whisper, I had to be within close range to talk to the boys. There was no yelling from one room to another, and this fostered lots of eye contact and touching. After all, communication is best accomplished face to face. And the boys listened! Most of the time they responded the first time I said something. They understood I was having a difficult time and, for the most part, did their best to help.

Now that I'm back in full voice, I'm sure I'll raise it again, but I am going to do my best not to. I don't plan on soon forgetting the gentle lesson of my day of silence.

There's No "Last Word" for All

Dolores Cuthbertson
Colorado
1973

There is a world of difference between a three-year-old and a five-year-old. There is also a world of difference between any dozen three-year-olds (or four- or five-year-olds). Care should be taken in writing on discipline lest some mothers misinterpret the suggestions as being "the last word" for ALL children. There is no last word for any child, let alone all children. It seems to me that many of the so-called discipline problems occur when the adult's expectations are not realistic for the particular child.

Mostly what I think discipline for the toddler and preschooler boils down to is the mother thinking far enough ahead that she can avoid situations where her child is pushed beyond his capabilities or past his point of frustration. Children should not be allowed to hurt other people or pets, destroy property, or harm themselves. That is, in my opinion, the mother and father's responsibility. It requires a lot of thought, prompt action, and a firmly worded explanation—tone is more important than volume. Spanking as the usual response to misbehavior says to me that the parents are not willing to think ahead to avoid trouble.

Children respond to tone of voice, facial expression, honesty, love, and large doses of hugging. They also need to be told what they may and may not do in a given situation; "You may not walk on the couch with your shoes on." "You may climb to the top of the jungle gym, if you wish." "You may not hit Teresa." "It's Paul's turn with the truck. You may play with the car. Then you can trade." "We sit down when the car is moving." "Please wipe your feet before you come in the house." It seems we have to say the same things over and over again. That is how children learn. We cannot expect three-, four-, and five-year-old children to know what to do if we don't tell them—nor do we need to be overly concerned that they will not know how to make decisions when they are ten, eleven, and twelve if we don't let them begin now. We can really do both—tell them what is expected when it is major and let them make choices when it isn't.

30

The Road to Independence

Mirror

Sally Simmons
Nebraska
1977

I see my mirror down the hall
Coming toward me—three feet tall!
She talks and sings and acts like me,
Magnified, for all to see.
She comforts me when I am sad,
She yells and hits when she gets mad.
Sometimes I see my finer side—
Often it's qualities I'd rather hide!
I'm happiest, though, when I can see
My love reflected back to me.

The Key to Independence

Margee McIntyre
Virginia
1978

Most of us enter motherhood with preconceived ideas that are soon dispelled after our child is born, but one idea that was especially hard for me to abandon was the notion of the Independent Child.

Ryan was a sensitive baby right from the start, and his dependence on me was gratifying most of the time. But certainly I expected him to outgrow it, at least by his second birthday. Well, two years came and went and I was still saying things such as "If other mothers can leave their children with babysitters, why can't I?" And, "If other kids can accept bedtime without rocking and lullabies, why can't mine?"

Very gradually it dawned on me that if I could be more accepting of him as he was, he could be more accepting of himself, and as a result, more self-confident.

I found that self-confidence was the key to independence (and hadn't I read that many times before?) and this was an area where I could encourage without pushing. As soon as he was able, I let Ryan dress himself, wash his own hands, choose his own clothes, and make his own lunch—even though I could do these things more quickly.

Encouraged by his success, he branched out to more and more "do-it-myself" tasks. By the time he was four he was ready, after a very gradual introduction, to attend a preschool two mornings a week. Now that he is almost five, Ryan is still not always gracious about staying with a sitter and he may sleep with his teddy bear until he's twenty-one. But I've learned that even a four-year-old is entitled to be a baby in many ways.

Ryan will always be a sensitive person, even when he's "all grown up." And I wouldn't want to change that quality in him anyway.

Crying on the Inside

Justine Clegg
Florida
1983

Recently I took my three-year-old, Sarah, to a Bible study class where an elaborate program had been arranged for the preschoolers while their mothers studied the Bible. The little ones have a three-hour class with crafts, snacks, a lesson, free play, and more. A League friend attends this study and she assured me her three-year-old loves the children's program. I made arrangements to stay with Sarah until she would be happy for me to leave. (A few raised eyebrows and comments showed me how the other mothers and teachers felt about this plan.) She was happy as long as I was there but about halfway through the program she told me I could leave, so I joined the other mothers.

An hour and a half later, I went back to pick up Sarah. "How did she do?" I asked the teacher. "Fine! She only missed you once, asked for you, and when I told her you'd be back soon she went back to playing." I gave Sarah the usual encouraging words, but when we were in the car she asked me not to leave her there again. "Why?" I asked her, "the teacher said you were having fun playing." "I was playing outside, Mommy," she answered me, "but inside I was crying for you." Of course I never left her there again, but I got to thinking, how many times do our little ones cry on the inside for us, only they are too young to be able to verbalize their feelings, and consequently we don't really understand how much they need us.

Apron Strings?

Judy Hatcher
Missouri
1983

Our two girls, Carey, three and a half, and Carissa, four months, are bright, healthy, loving children. It is gratifying to watch them grow and learn.

Carey has always been hesitant to "Let go of the apron strings." A year ago, when we were asked if she would be the flower girl at her uncle's wedding, we were thrilled. We had no doubt that by the time the wedding came she would be glad to do it.

Time passed and the wedding date neared with Carey still hesitant to do such outgoing things. Hidden food allergy and the arrival of her new baby sister complicated her life and caused regression in several areas. I knew I'd be surprised if Carey were really willing to do it. Still, I couldn't help being disappointed when on rehearsal night she grabbed me on my shoulder, pleading with us not to make her do it. Of course we didn't, and I tearfully watched as her little cousin donned Carey's beautiful dress and filled the role.

Forcing Carey would only have worsened matters, making her feel she couldn't trust us and look to us in times of stress. Meeting emotional needs is every bit as important as meeting physical ones. Yes, it hurts sometimes, but we, as parents, must sometimes be willing to set aside our wants to meet our children's needs.

I Went to Preschool, Too

Betsy Carson
Washington
1982

When my daughter, Taylor, was three and a half we enrolled in a co-op preschool. I was supposed to attend one day a week, but it soon became apparent that Taylor wanted me to come every day. Well, this is easily solved, I said. We'll get lots of paints and craft materials and stay home. But no—tears!—she wanted to go to school, but not without me. So I started going every day. I could tell that a few of the mothers felt sorry for me and were glad their children weren't "maladjusted" like mine. Then I began to look around. I noticed that most children would bring something comforting from home every day—a favorite toy, a blanket, their thumb. Then I realized that Taylor was perhaps the only one who got to bring what she really wanted from home—me!

Some children are outgoing from day one. Others, like Taylor, take their time. I'm glad now that I stayed with her. By Christmas she had made a place for herself in the group and no longer needed me every day. At seven, although she still has an occasional shy moment, she's basically quite brave, and at times even a bit wild!

It's True, It Works!

Sue Huml
Illinois
1983

My second baby, Robert, was a Clinger Extraordinaire. Until he was about eighteen months old, he would have nothing to do with anyone but me. I could not leave the room without him, much less the house. Consequently, I became the source of much gossip among neighbors and acquaintances. My only haven was with my League friends and my husband, Vince, who understood Robbie's baby ways.

Well-meaning neighbors predicted dire consequences for Robbie and me. They offered much "free advice"; they said that Rob would be so dependent on me as he grew up that my life would be ruled by him. They suggested that I leave him with a sitter on a regular basis so that he would get "used" to being without me.

I often told my husband that if we met Robert's needs when he was a baby, then when he was good and ready, he would feel happy and comfortable with other people. But I must admit to days when I questioned if I would ever have any time to myself again.

Well, today I have the morning to myself. My little Robbie, now almost five, started kindergarten.

As I walked to school with him he ran two hundred yards ahead of me, skipping, hopping, and occasionally turning around to shout, "Come on, slowpokes," to his big sister and me.

When we arrived at the school, nearly every other child was clinging to his or her mother, burying their faces in their skirts and holding on tightly. Where was Robbie? He was at the head of the line introducing himself to all the other children, not giving me a second glance. When the teacher came to call them in and all the other children were clinging to their mothers, where was Robbie? He had zoomed into the classroom, zoomed back out again, given me a big kiss, and scooted off with "Bye, Mom, I love you."

I walked home with a lump in my throat realizing his baby days were behind him. I felt so good inside, knowing he had outgrown his strong dependency needs. I would encourage any mother with a new baby not to be afraid to meet her baby's needs. It may be tough going at times but the end result is a wonderful feeling of accomplishment and many less troubles in later years.

Not all dependent little ones get over this stage as quickly as Robbie did. But, it's true that when the needs of a baby are met, sooner or later this results in a well-adjusted secure, loving, and *independent* child.

Baby Knows Best

Lynn Way
Vermont
1981

Our Christa always seemed to be one of those babies who needed to be held all the time from her earliest days on and almost never went to sleep alone in her bed. The "family bed" arrangement was a necessity for her and even as she grew older she always wanted to be held when we visited a store or in any other new situation. Through it all I had a suspicion that there was a real reason behind her seemingly extraordinary needs, possibly a visual problem, but she was too small to be tested. Finally, by the time she was three my fears were confirmed as we found Christa could not see the pictures on the wall. A trip to our ophthalmologist proved that she is quite myopic—as nearsighted as I am after many years of progression. Though the doctor said she was young for glasses, we decided to go ahead and get them.

Now she can see the deer grazing on the hill behind our house and the swallows nesting in the barn. Her world no longer fades away at a distance. At four she is attending a community play school twice a week and joins the other children, a little shyly, but with growing confidence. She wipes her own little glasses carefully and puts them in their case at night.

So many times when baby's needs seem like unreasonable demands to some, they turn out to be genuine needs—undetected allergies, illness, or other discomfort. Fears deep within a child that we don't understand can be as real as hunger and thirst. Our experience has made us all the more aware of the wisdom of trusting our little ones and following their lead as best we can.

Love and Security

Pat Orr
Illinois
1976

We were watching a wood duck herding her babies down our canal. The little mother "motored" far ahead, perhaps clearing the way for her brood or possibly catching some fish.

The children all exclaimed about this. Dear little Ben, our neighbors' foster son, whom I have grown to love, was concerned— "Look at her. She's going to leave them!" he cried.

Our Mike and Mark said with complacency: "Naw, she'll be back." Such a few words, but they may as well have been a thousand for how eloquently they pictured the differences in these boys' outlooks. I ached for Ben, whose own mother had neglected him. At ten, he has known four homes and four sets of parents. What a difference love and security can make in one's life.

Money in the Bank

Bobbe Lyon
Florida
1976

Your kids are still quite young, right? Maybe you have the new-and-nursing variety, or maybe you have a few toddlers hanging around. Then again you might have one in preschool, one in school, and another new-and-nursing. Whatever. I've been there. In every imaginable situation.

Our oldest daughter is on her own off to college, and I can't imagine how it happened, but she'll be twenty-one years old soon. Now there's an artery-hardener for you. Then there's the kid who was under the apron and not under the feet when I first wrote to LLL almost sixteen years ago. He's fifteen now and a sophomore in high school. Then in orderly (?) procession come the eighth grader, the sixth grader, and the "baby," a third grader. Sounds good, hey? It must because you, love, are in the midst—up to your eyeballs in the midst—of what are euphemistically known as the "service years."

Why not think of it as a down payment on security? Money in the bank, if you will. Your interest is piling up, and the dividends come later (yes, they will) like mine.

Oh, I know all about the nights unending when you stumble out in the dark to answer the call, be it nursing time, toilet time, or just TLC time. Will you ever get an uninterrupted night's sleep? Yes, you will. Will the baby ever—I mean really ever—wean? Yes, he will. Will they ever get into school and give you just a few short hours to yourself? Yes, they will.

One day they will walk away from you with an independence and self-reliance you will literally not believe. That is, if you invest your time and love wisely now, right now.

31

Staying in Tune with the Older Child

"I would hope that as we have discovered the rewards of mothering our small children, we will go on and discover the even greater rewards of mothering our older children. You see, it isn't just our babies and toddlers who need us. Our older children need us too, in many more complex and demanding ways than the little ones."

Mary White, LLL Founder, 1981

Time Together

Cheryl Harmston
Colorado
1977

After my oldest son, Tom, age seven, started going to school all day, I felt that we were growing apart. It seemed I could never get him to talk to me. While other mothers assured me that their children would come home anxious to tell them all about their day, Tom only wanted to go out and play. When I was able to slip a question in like: "How was school today?" I got answers like "Terrible." I began thinking, "If this is the best we can do for communication now, what is going to happen when he gets to be a teenager?"

I had been putting Tom, his younger brother, David, and his toddler sister, Mary Celeste, to bed at the same time each night. I decided that if I put David and Mary Celeste in bed first and let Tom stay up later, then I would have some time to spend alone with him each night without sacrificing too much of his sleep.

I asked Tom if he would like to spend a half-hour with me each night after his brother and sister were in bed. And I told him that he could choose what we would do. He said "yes" and got the same look on his face that he gets on Christmas morning.

Sometimes we play games and sometimes we work on other projects. A lot of times we read. That is one of his favorite things to do. And we talk! I've found out things about Tom. I knew he was interested in science, but I didn't know he knew the gravity on Jupiter was so strong you couldn't stand up or that it is so cold on Pluto that you would freeze instantly.

When we first started spending this time together I was hoping to make some changes in Tom; to give him a more positive self-image and to make him more cooperative and more communicative. There have been these changes and more. But the biggest changes are in me. Within the first week I found I was more patient and felt more affectionate toward him. I love him more now because I know him better.

When Darren Ran Away

Faye Young
Missouri
1973

I aged thirty-five years last night.

It started when Amy was making some cookies and got mad at Darren, who kept snitching dough. When she attempted to evict him from the kitchen, he informed her that she was full of "green gopher guts," which resulted in a vicious fight.

Now I was unaware of all this, as I was cleaning up five pounds of aquarium gravel that Loren had just "washed and put right back into the brown bag and the whole bottom came out of the bag. I can't figure it out, Mom!" So I was running the sweeper and missed the opening round. By the time it came to my attention, Darren was erupting, and I tried to cool him off to get some sort of explanation as to what happened. All I could get was "Nobody loves me, and I'm going to run away!"

"Well," replied the psychology minor, "everyone does love you, but if you really want to leave be sure to put on your shoes and socks!"

"I will!" he replied and stalked up the stairs to find them. Well, Amy had blown out the pilot light on the oven and I was holding my numb thumb over the red button for two consecutive minutes when Darren reappeared in shoes and coat and went out the back door. As soon as the oven lit I went in hot pursuit (a gap of not more than two-and-a-half minutes), only to be too late. He was nowhere to be found!

This all started at 5:15 and it was rapidly getting dark and drizzling. After thirty minutes I decided to try the car, thinking he could be walking to Grandma's, but no luck. By then, Mel was home, and we decided, after another check of the yard, to call the police.

It is a very heart-rending experience to fill out a missing persons report on your own seven-year-old, especially when you told him to run away! The policeman shook his head back and forth and just said, "Mother, mother, mother." Which made me feel that I should turn in all my old Mother's Day cards and join the local nunnery.

About one-and-a-half hours had gone by, and true terror had gripped its cold hand squarely around my heart. It was dark and the drizzle had turned into rain. My father and brother, as well as the neighbors, had joined the search. We had completed the house and had just finished the yard and the men were going to begin going up and down the streets when Jeff said, "Maybe he's in the leaves." (We have an 180-year-old sycamore in the backyard and you wouldn't believe the leaves.) So I quickly began kicking through the piles and looked in between our garage and the neighbor's (a place we all had checked before, but not under the leaves). And there was Darren, sound asleep. He didn't wake up until we took his clothes off to give him a hot bath. (Then he pretended to be asleep because the police were still here.) Seems that he'd gone there right off, covered himself, and went promptly to sleep. Exactly thirty feet from the back door.

As for me, I still get a chill and jello knees when I remember it and have firmly vowed that if any offspring gets the leaving itch again I will firmly reply, "Cool it, buddy; you're stuck with us and we're stuck with you, and if you make one move towards the door until you're twenty-one or married (whichever comes first), I'm withholding your birth certificate, shot records (and you will have to have them all over), and your Captain Kangaroo records, and I'll send your school giant pictures of you taking a bath when you were a baby without any clothes on, with the caption that you nursed for three years!" Should that fail, I plan to knock him out with my old psychology book.

Ten Years Later

Ramah O'Gorman
Texas
1974

Happy Birthday Sean.

Ten years ago today you had your first birthday in Dallas at St. Paul's Hospital with your dad and I as your special guests. The day before we knew you would soon be born. We went for a walk that evening, looked over all the new clothes we had for you and talked about how our Sean would soon be here. We really didn't know, of course, you would be a boy, but we had already called you Sean for many months.

About midnight, we went to the hospital, and at 4:32 AM I pushed you into the world. Your dad cried out, "It's a boy, Ramah. It's a boy!" I can't tell you how excited we both were, but you can see for yourself in the pictures. And you were big and strong. You cried, and the next thing I did was to breastfeed you. You knew how to do that right away, which really pleased and thrilled me, because I had never nursed before. The next thing we did was phone your Grandma. She was so excited—you were her first grandchild.

In a few days, we proudly took you home and began to learn all about you. You taught us so many things—how to love more unselfishly, how to laugh a lot, how to be kinder. You gave us so much—laughter, love, grins, smiles, hugs, and kisses, and year after year you have kept giving us all these gifts and more. We have learned to reorganize our lives and time—to make time for really important things—like going for walks, looking at bugs through a magnifying glass, playing in piles of autumn leaves— all the things that are done together in love. Because of you we are enjoying a second life in many ways—learning all over again about numbers, words, earthquakes, volcanoes, and God, and learning for the first time many things that we missed when we were growing up—like horseback riding, oil painting, insulator collecting, and so much more.

Because of you, we do more "fun" things, like visit the radio station, the blacksmith, the newspaper office. Because of all your questions, we keep up-to-date on current events and learn more about past history.

In these ten years you can see how you have given us so much pleasure and joy just by being you. Each year you grow stronger, wiser, and more fun-loving. We are so proud of you, and we thank you for all your hard work and the love you give back to us. Every birthday of yours has been a happy time of remembering and also a time of looking forward, when we joyfully enter with you into another year of life. We love you. *Mother and Daddy.*

Nursing and Nurturing

Judy Kahrl
Ohio
1972

The new nursing mother asks: "When will my baby ever stop wanting to be nursed? Will he ever?" "Never," say I, mother of four breastfed babies. Never, if you think of "nursing" as the British do, for the word has a different meaning over there. I discovered this other meaning when our first baby was about four weeks old and I was in the flush of enthusiasm for nursing. An Englishman had come to call. I was holding Jennifer in my lap and needed to tend to something elsewhere in our home. Our male guest kindly offered to help by saying, "Oh, can I nurse the baby for you?"

It took me a while to understand what our transatlantic visitor meant—but what a lovely extension of our American word: nursing. Over there it means cuddling, holding, comforting, rocking— all the pleasant, warm aspects of nurturing a child. So now, twelve years later, I am still nursing. No, no more breastfeeding—but all my children like hugs, back rubs, and so on—the soothing physical contact they enjoyed when breastfeeding. And I am grateful that we learned the free and easy joy of the sense of touch in those early nursing days.

To the Father of the Bride

Kathy Lyons
Texas
1973

I look up and see you coming down the aisle with our beautiful Christina on your arm. I look at your faces and the memories come flooding back.

Memories of that hot summer night almost twenty years ago when she transformed us, a couple, into a family. I feel the same sense of wonder now.

I remember when she was six and we were preparing her for the tonsillectomy. How scared she looked. And I remember how her whole face changed when we explained that you would be there.

I see again the look of excitement on her face and pride on yours as the two of you went out the door on her sixteenth birthday for her dinner alone with Dad.

And now, as you stand here beside me and we listen to them repeat the vows we made twenty-one years ago tonight, I see mirrored in your face all the things I feel. Pride—she's a daughter to be proud of. Joy—that we've been a part of her life for this span of years. Happiness—because she chose well. Pain—just a little, because things will never be quite the same for us. She's no longer just our daughter but Terry's wife. And thankfulness—we still have the younger ones—for a time.

Part Nine

Learning a Loving Way of Life

Thanks to La Leche League

LA LECHE

Page Zyromski
Virginia
1973

Oh glee
I've milk for my baby
milk in ME

It used to come in bottles you know
back in the good old days
when it was pasteurized
homogenized sterilized
boiled then chilled

(then warmed again at two a.m.
when the baby kept on squalling)

But now in these enlightened times
it comes in people
people like me
for little people like my baby
specially crafted and tailored
at home not in factories

Oh these newfangled notions
whatever will they think of next

32

La Leche League:
Why Is It Needed?

"While we can all attest to the changes La Leche League has made in our lives I have always felt LLL did not introduce a new way of mothering but instead gave mothers permission to do that which in their hearts they knew was the best way all along. Tuning into their babies instead of a schedule, letting their own baby rather than an expert set the pace, they experienced a motherhood that fulfilled all their expectations."

Marian Tompson, LLL Founder, 1981

Love and Acceptance

Carol Hamm
Manitoba
1973

When I attended my first League meeting I was nine months pregnant, with the cockiness of a twenty-two-year-old. Not only was I sure I would and could breastfeed, but I returned from the meeting convinced that the only function of La Leche League was to boost the morale of a group of insecure breastfeeding mothers. Surely I was above all this, I thought. I was, however, inspired by the aura of love and acceptance and was thoroughly amazed that after three hours in the same room with approximately twenty women and twelve babies neither had driven me crazy. In fact I, who am not exactly fond of being with large groups of women, went away liking every one of them. Still I was confident that my League manual and maybe a few telephone calls to a League Leader would suffice.

When Flannery was born, I had planned to leave the hospital as soon after delivery as possible, but I had a long labor and a forceps delivery which necessitated a two-day stay. Though I had previously felt prepared for anything, I was definitely not prepared for the hospital, where it seemed that breastfeeding not only was not encouraged but was eyed with suspicion, insulted with ignorance, and slapped with a sticker on each bassinet which read. "An SMA baby is a Happy Baby." If it had not been for the support of my husband and a dear friend (who just happens to be a League Leader), I would have been in bad shape. Despite the fact that I had almost memorized my manual, those icy glares and clicking tongues were wearing down my confidence like wind on a dry field.

Now, one month and one happy breastfed baby later, my opinions have altered greatly. Through clearer and much more humble observance, I see the League as much more than a breastfeeder's pep rally. I see women who not only are interested in being able to breastfeed but are vitally concerned with all aspects of good mothering. I see children touching and being touched—children getting a head start in being sensitive, responsive adults. I see a community of women whose first concern is not themselves and who share themselves in a very real way, not only with their families, but with the other women in the League and very probably with everyone they are associated with. Finally, I see an organization whose primary concern is not dues and the minutes of the last meeting, but the nourishment, both physical and psychological, of those whom it affects. Need I have to add that I'm proud to belong?

Home Is a Haven

Judy Kahrl
Ohio
1974

On reading women's magazines several years ago, I began to wonder if home was supposed to be a prison. "Are You Feeling
Trapped?" "Do You Feel Angry About Staying Home?"—these were
typical titles of articles. I was a little puzzled about this. Sure, there
were days of colds, runny noses, dirty diapers, fatigue—oh, yes,
chronic galloping fatigue—when I wondered if I'd make it from
one end of the day to the other. Yet I couldn't understand this
"prison" idea, because even the worst of the days had its moment
when a small child laughed, starfish fingers explored a floor, or
a new word was spoken in toddler tones. Was I naive to think
of my home as a haven of warmth? It's not easy being a woman
in these modern, fast-changing times. We are torn on all sides—
pressures to do this or that, be this or that, go here or there. Some
voices tell us to be beautiful and polish our floors. Others tell us
to get out into the outside world and have a career for only that
brings satisfaction. Still others say that marriage and parenthood
offer the only real fulfillment for a woman. Through all this maze
we have to find our own way.

For me, La Leche League has been a beautiful guidepost along
the way. It has given me support through the days of runny noses
and dirty diapers. It has helped me to build with my husband
a refuge of love and warmth for our family. And at the same time,
LLL has opened my mind, exposed me to many new people who
have different lifestyles from mine. It has led me to read, to talk,
to learn about breastfeeding, child development, human relations,
group dynamics—all new worlds for me. It has helped me to cope
with the many, many pressures of a woman today and to see that
motherhood is worthwhile, yet there is a place for me to be of
service to the world outside, to venture into interests that will leave
me with room to grow when indeed my children have walked
through that open door to live their own lives as adults. I am glad
that I have the opportunity to learn to cope now with these pressures before I am left alone and at sea without my children. La
Leche League has helped me to build on the formal education
I had before marriage. LLL has helped me to grow. I can only say
"thank you" to LLL for helping me to build my home as a refuge—
and for opening its doors.

Thinking Positively

Sue Dejanovich
Massachusetts
1975

Eight years ago, when our first child was born, I tried to nurse him, but had no support from any of my doctors and was advised to stop nursing after only four days. With our second child, I didn't even try. But when our third child arrived last year, I decided to give it another try, since my close neighbor was nursing her baby. She introduced me to La Leche League, and I'll be forever grateful to her and to the League Leaders here, who helped me adjust to this new experience.

I'm amazed at how simple nursing really is, though in our society it is looked upon as a very complex matter. Perhaps it's because our lives are so programmed to tables of time and measurements, instead of being free to bear and raise children naturally. I have surprised myself at my capabilities of nursing and am really pleased about it. You see, I'm a very uptight person normally, but this new way of life has certainly changed my way of thinking and feeling about my family and my priorities.

There have been times that I have cried, regretting that I did not nurse my two older children. However, I try to think more positively. Rather than dwell on regrets, I tell myself how fortunate I am to have such a happy nursing relationship with Michelle and what a blessing nursing has been for me and for my whole family.

A Happier Mother

Thelma Catrambone
Illinois
1965

About six months ago I became acquainted with La Leche League for the first time. Our eighth baby was only a few weeks old and my attempt to breastfeed her was becoming increasingly difficult for both the baby and me; by the time she was six weeks old she was losing weight. I was thoroughly discouraged by my apparent inability to supply enough milk. Since bottles and formula seemed inevitable, I called our doctor for instructions. He assured me that breast milk was the very best formula for my baby and advised me to contact LLL.

The first time I called the League, the Leader spent nearly two hours explaining various ways of overcoming difficulties in nursing. Her understanding and patience made me feel that my baby and I were the most important people in the world to her. After that I felt more confident and optimistic about nursing. Although I looked forward to the League meeting, I was a little skeptical about getting involved with an organization at a time when I felt incompetent to organize the next meal!

We met at the home of one of the mothers and everyone was friendly and informal. I felt at home almost immediately. As the Leader talked that evening, questions that had been on my mind since my first baby were answered. Again I was impressed by the personal concern shown to everyone. The attitude of all the mothers was reflected in their happy contented babies. I was grateful that no one could read my thoughts because after eight babies of my own, I felt as though I was seeing the beautiful aspects of motherhood for the first time.

While the natural method of feeding babies remains a novel (or worse) idea in the minds of too many women, LLL has convinced me that breastfeeding is the best way a mother can nourish her baby. I owe a debt of gratitude to the wonderful mothers of the League who have helped me to become a happier mother.

LLL Has Changed My Life

David Stewart
Missouri
1980

A recent LLL Area Conference in Missouri featured a session for fathers only. There were about twenty-five of us who attended, representing a variety of occupations, cities, states, ages, and family sizes.

What do men discuss at an LLL "fathers only" meeting? Naturally, we talked about breastfeeding and its benefits to our children, to us, and to the whole family. For some of us, all of our children had been breastfed. Those who had also experienced bottle feeding were quick to relate the relative advantages of breastfeeding and breast milk. But nursing one's babies was only the beginning. We covered much more.

The discussion centered around LLL ideals of family life. All of us would have liked to have been raised in a family that was warm and close and where the father, in particular, was affectionate and approachable. Most of us did not come from such homes. We all wanted to establish secure and loving relationships with our children—relationships most of us lacked with our own fathers. Few of us had, in our own upbringing, a model we could emulate. But we now have LLL. The LLL philosophy, as expressed in its publications and its Leaders—a spirit of giving, of unselfishness, of caring, of openness, of putting baby's needs above your own, of enjoying your children, of tuning in with your family and aligning your priorities there—this is the model so many of us had lacked and needed. The art of parenting cannot be learned by books and words alone, although these can help. One also needs living examples. Words can be persuasive, but examples are irrefutable. LLL has given us both words and examples.

We also talked about mutual support. LLL is "mother-to-mother," but it also affords an opportunity for "father-to-father" relationships. As men, we find little or no support for parenting in our jobs. Our relationships there are not father-to-father—worker-to-worker, associate-to-associate, employee-to-supervisor, and even friend-to-friend, but never father-to-father. Many jobs are downright discouraging to family life—even contradictory to it. Through LLL we meet other fathers who care about their families as we do. We discover that we are not alone. We are not completely different. There are others who also place a high priority on family, other men who also feel tenderness and affection as we do. We learn that such feelings are okay. Our friendships within the League permit us to follow our hearts.

As an LLL father, not only do I enjoy an association with thoughtful, kindhearted men and women, but I also enjoy the stimulation of free-thinking people who have the strength, character, and originality to try new ideas in all aspects of life. LLL is a meeting of new ideas for living: alternatives in health care, alternatives in childbirth, alternatives in our children's education, alternatives in family life. As LLL fathers, we found that our contacts with League families not only expanded our knowledge of alternatives, but had caused us to sharpen our judgment in everything and to question every institution. LLL has helped us to be more discriminating in all that we do.

How has LLL changed my life? It has helped me be a better and happier father, a better and happier person. The League has also

A La Leche League meeting in Illinois, 1987.

given me another family—it is large, global in fact, and it grows daily. Perhaps the way to world peace is not through world brotherhood—but through world familyhood. To that end, LLL has already given birth and now so effectively nurtures. For myself, and for all we fortunate LLL fathers, "Thank you, La Leche League International." We are the fathers of the children you have blessed. And we are also blessed.

Reflections

Debbie Miller
Oklahoma
1974

While baby number four blissfully nurses himself to sleep in my arms, it's a good time for reflections . . . looking back over these years of mothering; remembering how the League has changed me and five other people . . . the members of my family.

Of course, the obvious changes are my attitude toward childbirth and breastfeeding. Being a nurse, I came a long way from that first "knock-me-out-drag-him-out" birth to my last beautiful, natural, home delivery. Then I went from observing schedules to demand feeding and from abrupt weaning (because of being bitten) to baby-led weaning and a teether. For babies number one and two I started solids early, the commercial kind, and had the problem of getting them off that bland stuff onto table food. For the next two, it was late introduction of solids and then primarily table foods in a diversity of flavors and textures.

Less obvious changes in my attitude are in the areas of discipline and loving. I once had a firm rule: "No children sleeping in our bed!" Now, baby and four-year-old often sleep half the night there. Before the League, there were many "no's"; now I'm a magician and use sleight-of-hand tricks for diversion. It used to be "oh, the relief!" to get away from the kids. Now we take them everywhere with us.

I've come from feeling like a duty-bound, drudgery-burdened mother to being a loving, giving, fulfilled one.

A Circle of Love

Joanne Kropchuk
Ohio
1984

When I first became pregnant, I was very excited and wanted to learn all I could about pregnancy, childbirth, and babies. I didn't have any close friends, however, who had given birth or who were pregnant, so I didn't have any role models to follow.

My husband, Tom, asked me if I was going to breastfeed. I said I didn't know, that I'd have to think about it. Although Tom admitted he didn't know much about nursing, he said it had to be better than trusting manufacturing companies to provide the best nourishment for our precious baby. Besides, he thought it would be a good way to bond with the baby. I immediately got defensive and told him that I didn't want to be pushed into anything, but I would promise to read up on it. From what I read about breastfeeding in various books, it did seem that it was the best nourishment, protection, and comfort I could give our baby. I told Tom (rather reluctantly) that I would breastfeed, but only for six months. You see, I knew intellectually that "breast is best," but emotionally I wasn't comfortable with it. No one I knew, except for one acquaintance, had ever breastfed. Wanting to do what was truly best for my baby and knowing I wasn't strong enough emo-

The LLL founders in 1957, less than a year after La Leche League began.

tionally to just breastfeed by myself, I knew I needed some friends to support me. By this time I had read numerous books on pregnancy and childbirth, and I was amazed at how many of them suggested contacting a local LLL Group for further information. So I looked up LLL in the phone book and called the number. Well, that was the beginning of a whole new beautiful world for me.

I started attending meetings and immediately felt welcome. I then decided to nurse my baby for nine months, *maybe* even up to one year. Through La Leche League, I found a small circle of good friends that has grown and grown. I don't mean necessarily grown in numbers, I'm talking about the quality of life and how magnificently mine has improved because of LLL. You see, LLL is one place you can go where you'll find friendship, love, support, and most importantly, acceptance and respect of each individual's differences. We get so used to guarding and protecting ourselves mentally from people who value material things over people that it's a joy and a relief to be able to give someone a hug without being thought of as strange.

My LLL Leader and the Group as a whole have supported me in tremendous ways. From LLL I've learned that it is all right to follow your instincts, to cuddle, bathe, and sleep with your baby, to start solids late, and live on one income. I've learned that love does not create too much dependence, rather it gives the strength needed for independence. I've learned that it is not necessary to spank and yell at your child or have a whiny spoiled "brat." There is a happy medium, following the road of loving guidance. It's given me hope that it is possible to have a happy, creative, bright, considerate, gentle child in this day of advanced technology where a recurring message seems to be "consume more, *more*, MORE!" LLL has given me the courage to quietly stand proud, follow my heart, and nurse my daughter. Sixteen-month-old Erika is still happily nursing and will continue to do so until she weans herself. My story doesn't end here, however. Really, it's just the beginning.

I purchased LLL's excellent cookbook, WHOLE FOODS FOR THE WHOLE FAMILY, and I was invited to join a food co-op by one of my friends (an LLL member). I'd always been interested in better nutrition, but on a tight one-income budget, I couldn't afford to buy from expensive health-food stores. Since I've joined the co-op, our eating habits have changed drastically for the better.

My husband and I, without realizing it, began to re-evaluate every aspect of our lives. We started going back to church regularly, which we've really enjoyed, and I recently started taking a class once a week (now that Erika is happy staying home alone with Daddy).

Although we were never big television watchers, we would have it on about two hours every night. Well, now it's on about five hours a week. When the TV is off, we read more and discuss what we read with each other. We communicate with each other much more than we used to, and our personal relationships have improved greatly.

You see, I'm really not getting off the subject because it all has to do with you. The best thing I ever did for myself and my family was going to that first LLL meeting when I was six months pregnant. It's a circle of love that grows and grows and grows. LLL is more to me than a group of mothers with their nursing babies. It is a loving philosophy, a beautiful way of life. And I thank you for it.

La Leche League's founders in 1981, the League's twenty-fifth anniversary year. Left to right: Mary White, Viola Lennon, Edwina Froehlich, Mary Ann Cahill, Mary Ann Kerwin; seated in front, Marian Tompson and Betty Wagner. These seven mothers who started La Leche League in 1956 wanted only to offer their personal experience and words of encouragement to their friends who wanted to breastfeed. Since then, they have touched the lives of mothers and babies in every corner of the world and La Leche League has become an internationally recognized authority on breastfeeding.

A Founder Says Thank You

Mary Ann Kerwin, LLL Founder, 1981

To Our Leaders

Can you possibly ever realize how tremendously important you are to La Leche League International? Volunteers like you are the life-blood of our organization! The only way LLL keeps going and growing is with your loving and generous efforts on behalf of mothers and babies throughout the world.

While seven of us were able to get LLL started in 1956, there is no way we could have kept things going through the years without you. As we've said so often, but never too often, you are indeed the heart of La Leche League!

You can imagine how much a part of me La Leche League has become as I've now spent half of my lifetime in it. How enriched my family and I have been by the friendships and inspiration we all give each other. It's so true that whatever we give away comes back a hundred-fold! I hope that your lives will be as rich in love and friendship as mine is. What more can anyone ask?

So, thank you Leaders everywhere for carrying on for us. Your dedication, your willingness to help, your devotion to mothers and babies, your generosity with the little spare time you have, are precious gifts. We are infintely grateful to you!

Would You Like to Know More?

As you read through this book, you find that La Leche League is mentioned over and over again as a source of information, support, and encouragement. La Leche League Groups meet monthly in communities all over the world to share breastfeeding and mothering experiences.

Perhaps you'd like to be a part of this mother-to-mother network. It is easy to become an LLL Member. Just return the coupon below along with your annual membership fee. You'll receive six bimonthly issues of NEW BEGINNINGS, a magazine filled with personal stories, helpful hints, and up-to-date parenting information. Members automatically receive our LLLI Catalogues by mail and they are entitled to a 10% discount on most purchases. Term Life Insurance at special Group Rates is also available to LLL Members and their families. You don't need to attend Group meetings in order to join—though most members enjoy the interaction with other mothers that meetings provide.

Why should you join La Leche League? Because you care—about your own family and about mothers and babies all over the world!

Return this form to La Leche League International,
P. O. Box 1209, Franklin Park, IL 60131-8209 USA.

_____ I'd like to join La Leche League International. Enclosed is my annual membership fee of $25.

_____ In addition, I am enclosing a tax-deductible donation of $_____ to support the work of La Leche League.

_____ Please send me a copy of THE WOMANLY ART OF BREASTFEEDING, softcover, $8.95 plus $1.50 for shipping and handling. *(In California and Illinois, please add sales tax.)*

_____ Please send me La Leche League's FREE Catalogue.

_____ Please send me a FREE copy of the Directory of local LLL representatives. *(Please enclose a self-addressed, stamped envelope.)*

Name

Address   *City*

State/Province   *Zip/Postal Code*   *Country*

7/87

Other La Leche League Books

THE WOMANLY ART OF BREASTFEEDING

La Leche League's comprehensive guide to nursing your baby has long been a favorite of new mothers. THE WOMANLY ART OF BREASTFEEDING meets mothers' needs for breastfeeding information and support with a warm, practical, down-to-earth approach. With over 1.5 million copies in print, THE WOMANLY ART OF BREASTFEEDING is both a classic and a great source of mothering wisdom. $8.95

MOTHERING YOUR NURSING TODDLER

by Norma Jane Bumgarner

Warmth, wisdom, and wit illumine a lively discussion of breastfeeding past the age of one. Besides exploring the "why" of nursing a toddler, the book helps a mother cope with the challenges. "Incredibly thorough—this book is truly a classic," wrote one reader. "Very few books live up to my expectations; this one does." $7.95

NIGHTTIME PARENTING

by William Sears, MD

This book is for everyone; expectant parents, new parents, and parents of children with sleep problems. Dr. Sears explains how babies sleep differently than adults and how sharing sleep can help the whole family sleep better. Mary White, one of La Leche League's founders, writes in the foreword, "This book will help all new parents raise happier and more secure children." $7.95

WHOLE FOODS FOR THE WHOLE FAMILY

edited by Roberta Johnson

La Leche League's complete nutrition-conscious cookbook contains over 900 kitchen-tested recipes contributed by mothers all over the world. This treasury of family-pleasing dishes uses only whole unprocessed foods and minimal amounts of salt and sweeteners. Complete with protein and calorie counts, recipes include a wondrous variety of wholesome, delicious eating. $12.50

PLAYFUL LEARNING

by Anne Engelhardt and Cheryl Sullivan

This book offers a workable and enjoyable alternative to traditional preschools: the at-home cooperative preschool. You and other parents can provide a learning environment while you share in your children's emotional, intellectual, and social development. PLAYFUL LEARNING is designed to be a multi-purpose guide for adults who work with young children. $14.95

BECOMING A FATHER

by William Sears, MD

BECOMING A FATHER addresses the joys and problems of parenthood from the male perspective—everything from how to hold a tiny baby to sibling rivalry and organized sports. Bill Sears, a pediatrician and father of six, writes from personal experience and promises that becoming a father will bring rich rewards. $7.95

(Please include $1.50 shipping and handling per book.

In California and Illinois, add sales tax. Prices are subject to change and may vary outside the United States.)

La Leche League International
9616 Minneapolis Avenue
P. O. Box 1209
Franklin Park, IL 60131-8209 U.S.A.

In Canada, send orders to LLLI Canadian Office, 493 Main Street, Winchester Ontario KOC 2KO